I0309047

C-4890 CAREER EXAMINATION SERIES

This is your PASSBOOK for...

Safety & Health Program Manager

Test Preparation Study Guide
Questions & Answers

NLC®
NATIONAL LEARNING CORPORATION®

COPYRIGHT NOTICE

National Learning Corporation

212 Michael Drive, Syosset, NY 11791
(516) 921-8888 • www.passbooks.com
E-mail: info@passbooks.com

PASSBOOK® SERIES

THE *PASSBOOK® SERIES* has been created to prepare applicants and candidates for the ultimate academic battlefield – the examination room.

At some time in our lives, each and every one of us may be required to take an examination – for validation, matriculation, admission, qualification, registration, certification, or licensure.

Based on the assumption that every applicant or candidate has met the basic formal educational standards, has taken the required number of courses, and read the necessary texts, the *PASSBOOK® SERIES* furnishes the one special preparation which may assure passing with confidence, instead of failing with insecurity. Examination questions – together with answers – are furnished as the basic vehicle for study so that the mysteries of the examination and its compounding difficulties may be eliminated or diminished by a sure method.

This book is meant to help you pass your examination provided that you qualify and are serious in your objective.

The entire field is reviewed through the huge store of content information which is succinctly presented through a provocative and challenging approach – the question-and-answer method.

A climate of success is established by furnishing the correct answers at the end of each test.

You soon learn to recognize types of questions, forms of questions, and patterns of questioning. You may even begin to anticipate expected outcomes.

You perceive that many questions are repeated or adapted so that you can gain acute insights, which may enable you to score many sure points.

You learn how to confront new questions, or types of questions, and to attack them confidently and work out the correct answers.

You note objectives and emphases, and recognize pitfalls and dangers, so that you may make positive educational adjustments.

Moreover, you are kept fully informed in relation to new concepts, methods, practices, and directions in the field.

You discover that you are actually taking the examination all the time: you are preparing for the examination by "taking" an examination, not by reading extraneous and/or supererogatory textbooks.

In short, this PASSBOOK®, used directedly, should be an important factor in helping you to pass your test.

SAFETY AND HEALTH PROGRAM MANAGER

DUTIES:

As a **Safety and Health Program Manager I**, you would provide assistance and guidance in the operation of a program under the general direction of a Safety and Health Program Manager II. This includes coordinating staff development and training, preparing interpretations of rules and regulations, supporting the strategic plan through review and coordination of activities, and performing case file audits to improve inspection consistency across the State and ensure adequate case file documentation.

As a **Safety and Health Program Manager II**, you would plan, direct, administer and supervise the Statewide activities of a program under the general direction of the Director of Safety and Health. This includes coordinating work assignments; administering fee collections; preparing reports; monitoring program activities; investigating complaints; recommending policy and procedure based on program review; setting standards; and representing the Commissioner of Labor or the Division Director at meetings.

SCOPE OF THE EXAMINATION:

The written test is designed to test for knowledge, skills, and/or abilities in such areas as:

1. **Working and interacting with others** - These questions test for knowledge of how to effectively approach work and maintain professional relationships with others in the workplace. Each question presents a situation and a number of possible approaches for handling it. Question topics may include working with supervisors and coworkers, interacting with members of the public, handling conflict, and managing workplace demands and priorities. The questions are not specific to any job title or place of work.
2. **Understanding and interpreting written material** - These questions test how well you comprehend written material. You will be provided with brief reading selections and will be asked questions about the selections. All the information required to answer the questions will be presented in the selections; you will not be required to have any special knowledge relating to the subject areas of the selections.
3. **Preparing reports and official documents** - These questions test for the ability to prepare reports and other official documents for use within and among governmental agencies, in legal or regulatory settings, or for dissemination to the public. Some questions test for a knowledge of grammar, usage, punctuation, and sentence structure. Others test for the ability to present information clearly and accurately, to use the proper tone, and to organize paragraphs logically and comprehensibly.
4. **Administrative supervision** - These questions test for knowledge of the principles and practices involved in directing the activities of a large subordinate staff, including subordinate supervisors. Questions relate to the personal interactions between an upper level supervisor and his/her subordinate supervisors in the accomplishment of objectives. These questions cover such areas as assigning work to and coordinating the activities of several units, establishing and guiding staff development programs, evaluating the performance of subordinate supervisors, and maintaining relationships with other organizational sections.
5. **Evaluating conclusions based on factual information** - These questions test your ability to evaluate and draw conclusions from factual information presented. Each question consists of a set of factual statements and a conclusion. You will be asked to determine whether the conclusion can be proven to be true by the facts, proven to be false by the facts, or if the facts are inadequate to prove the conclusion.

6. **Understanding and applying administrative principles** - These questions test for knowledge of how to effectively manage and direct an organization or an organizational segment. These questions cover such areas as developing objectives, formulating policies, making decisions, forecasting and planning, developing personnel, organizing and coordinating work, communicating information, providing leadership, and delegating authority and responsibility.
7. **Analyzing and evaluating information** - These questions test for the ability to analyze, interpret, and draw reasonable conclusions from information presented in text, data, images or symbols. This may involve identifying a significant problem or issue; focusing on relevant data and text; identifying trends, relationships, and significant features; assessing relevant alternatives; suggesting or evaluating possible conclusions; and applying logical principles to information provided.

HOW TO TAKE A TEST

I. YOU MUST PASS AN EXAMINATION

A. WHAT EVERY CANDIDATE SHOULD KNOW

Examination applicants often ask us for help in preparing for the written test. What can I study in advance? What kinds of questions will be asked? How will the test be given? How will the papers be graded?

As an applicant for a civil service examination, you may be wondering about some of these things. Our purpose here is to suggest effective methods of advance study and to describe civil service examinations.

Your chances for success on this examination can be increased if you know how to prepare. Those "pre-examination jitters" can be reduced if you know what to expect. You can even experience an adventure in good citizenship if you know why civil service exams are given.

B. WHY ARE CIVIL SERVICE EXAMINATIONS GIVEN?

Civil service examinations are important to you in two ways. As a citizen, you want public jobs filled by employees who know how to do their work. As a job seeker, you want a fair chance to compete for that job on an equal footing with other candidates. The best-known means of accomplishing this two-fold goal is the competitive examination.

Exams are widely publicized throughout the nation. They may be administered for jobs in federal, state, city, municipal, town or village governments or agencies.

Any citizen may apply, with some limitations, such as the age or residence of applicants. Your experience and education may be reviewed to see whether you meet the requirements for the particular examination. When these requirements exist, they are reasonable and applied consistently to all applicants. Thus, a competitive examination may cause you some uneasiness now, but it is your privilege and safeguard.

C. HOW ARE CIVIL SERVICE EXAMS DEVELOPED?

Examinations are carefully written by trained technicians who are specialists in the field known as "psychological measurement," in consultation with recognized authorities in the field of work that the test will cover. These experts recommend the subject matter areas or skills to be tested; only those knowledges or skills important to your success on the job are included. The most reliable books and source materials available are used as references. Together, the experts and technicians judge the difficulty level of the questions.

Test technicians know how to phrase questions so that the problem is clearly stated. Their ethics do not permit "trick" or "catch" questions. Questions may have been tried out on sample groups, or subjected to statistical analysis, to determine their usefulness.

Written tests are often used in combination with performance tests, ratings of training and experience, and oral interviews. All of these measures combine to form the best-known means of finding the right person for the right job.

II. HOW TO PASS THE WRITTEN TEST

A. NATURE OF THE EXAMINATION

To prepare intelligently for civil service examinations, you should know how they differ from school examinations you have taken. In school you were assigned certain definite pages to read or subjects to cover. The examination questions were quite detailed and usually emphasized memory. Civil service exams, on the other hand, try to discover your present ability to perform the duties of a position, plus your potentiality to learn these duties. In other words, a civil service exam attempts to predict how successful you will be. Questions cover such a broad area that they cannot be as minute and detailed as school exam questions.

In the public service similar kinds of work, or positions, are grouped together in one "class." This process is known as *position-classification*. All the positions in a class are paid according to the salary range for that class. One class title covers all of these positions, and they are all tested by the same examination.

B. FOUR BASIC STEPS

1) Study the announcement

How, then, can you know what subjects to study? Our best answer is: "Learn as much as possible about the class of positions for which you've applied." The exam will test the knowledge, skills and abilities needed to do the work.

Your most valuable source of information about the position you want is the official exam announcement. This announcement lists the training and experience qualifications. Check these standards and apply only if you come reasonably close to meeting them.

The brief description of the position in the examination announcement offers some clues to the subjects which will be tested. Think about the job itself. Review the duties in your mind. Can you perform them, or are there some in which you are rusty? Fill in the blank spots in your preparation.

Many jurisdictions preview the written test in the exam announcement by including a section called "Knowledge and Abilities Required," "Scope of the Examination," or some similar heading. Here you will find out specifically what fields will be tested.

2) Review your own background

Once you learn in general what the position is all about, and what you need to know to do the work, ask yourself which subjects you already know fairly well and which need improvement. You may wonder whether to concentrate on improving your strong areas or on building some background in your fields of weakness. When the announcement has specified "some knowledge" or "considerable knowledge," or has used adjectives like "beginning principles of..." or "advanced ... methods," you can get a clue as to the number and difficulty of questions to be asked in any given field. More questions, and hence broader coverage, would be included for those subjects which are more important in the work. Now weigh your strengths and weaknesses against the job requirements and prepare accordingly.

3) Determine the level of the position

Another way to tell how intensively you should prepare is to understand the level of the job for which you are applying. Is it the entering level? In other words, is this the position in which beginners in a field of work are hired? Or is it an intermediate or advanced level? Sometimes this is indicated by such words as "Junior" or "Senior" in the class title. Other jurisdictions use Roman numerals to designate the level – Clerk I, Clerk II, for example. The word "Supervisor" sometimes appears in the title. If the level is not indicated by the title, check the description of duties. Will you be working under very close supervision, or will you have responsibility for independent decisions in this work?

4) Choose appropriate study materials

Now that you know the subjects to be examined and the relative amount of each subject to be covered, you can choose suitable study materials. For beginning level jobs, or even advanced ones, if you have a pronounced weakness in some aspect of your training, read a modern, standard textbook in that field. Be sure it is up to date and has general coverage. Such books are normally available at your library, and the librarian will be glad to help you locate one. For entry-level positions, questions of appropriate difficulty are chosen – neither highly advanced questions, nor those too simple. Such questions require careful thought but not advanced training.

If the position for which you are applying is technical or advanced, you will read more advanced, specialized material. If you are already familiar with the basic principles of your field, elementary textbooks would waste your time. Concentrate on advanced textbooks and technical periodicals. Think through the concepts and review difficult problems in your field.

These are all general sources. You can get more ideas on your own initiative, following these leads. For example, training manuals and publications of the government agency which employs workers in your field can be useful, particularly for technical and professional positions. A letter or visit to the government department involved may result in more specific study suggestions, and certainly will provide you with a more definite idea of the exact nature of the position you are seeking.

III. KINDS OF TESTS

Tests are used for purposes other than measuring knowledge and ability to perform specified duties. For some positions, it is equally important to test ability to make adjustments to new situations or to profit from training. In others, basic mental abilities not dependent on information are essential. Questions which test these things may not appear as pertinent to the duties of the position as those which test for knowledge and information. Yet they are often highly important parts of a fair examination. For very general questions, it is almost impossible to help you direct your study efforts. What we can do is to point out some of the more common of these general abilities needed in public service positions and describe some typical questions.

1) General information

Broad, general information has been found useful for predicting job success in some kinds of work. This is tested in a variety of ways, from vocabulary lists to questions about current events. Basic background in some field of work, such as sociology or economics, may be sampled in a group of questions. Often these are principles which have become familiar to most persons through exposure rather than through formal training. It is difficult to advise you how to study for these questions; being alert to the world around you is our best suggestion.

2) Verbal ability

An example of an ability needed in many positions is verbal or language ability. Verbal ability is, in brief, the ability to use and understand words. Vocabulary and grammar tests are typical measures of this ability. Reading comprehension or paragraph interpretation questions are common in many kinds of civil service tests. You are given a paragraph of written material and asked to find its central meaning.

3) Numerical ability

Number skills can be tested by the familiar arithmetic problem, by checking paired lists of numbers to see which are alike and which are different, or by interpreting charts and graphs. In the latter test, a graph may be printed in the test booklet which you are asked to use as the basis for answering questions.

4) Observation

A popular test for law-enforcement positions is the observation test. A picture is shown to you for several minutes, then taken away. Questions about the picture test your ability to observe both details and larger elements.

5) Following directions

In many positions in the public service, the employee must be able to carry out written instructions dependably and accurately. You may be given a chart with several columns, each column listing a variety of information. The questions require you to carry out directions involving the information given in the chart.

6) Skills and aptitudes

Performance tests effectively measure some manual skills and aptitudes. When the skill is one in which you are trained, such as typing or shorthand, you can practice. These tests are often very much like those given in business school or high school courses. For many of the other skills and aptitudes, however, no short-time preparation can be made. Skills and abilities natural to you or that you have developed throughout your lifetime are being tested.

Many of the general questions just described provide all the data needed to answer the questions and ask you to use your reasoning ability to find the answers. Your best preparation for these tests, as well as for tests of facts and ideas, is to be at your physical and mental best. You, no doubt, have your own methods of getting into an exam-taking mood and keeping "in shape." The next section lists some ideas on this subject.

IV. KINDS OF QUESTIONS

Only rarely is the "essay" question, which you answer in narrative form, used in civil service tests. Civil service tests are usually of the short-answer type. Full instructions for answering these questions will be given to you at the examination. But in case this is your first experience with short-answer questions and separate answer sheets, here is what you need to know:

1) Multiple-choice Questions

Most popular of the short-answer questions is the "multiple choice" or "best answer" question. It can be used, for example, to test for factual knowledge, ability to solve problems or judgment in meeting situations found at work.

A multiple-choice question is normally one of three types—

- It can begin with an incomplete statement followed by several possible endings. You are to find the one ending which *best* completes the statement, although some of the others may not be entirely wrong.
- It can also be a complete statement in the form of a question which is answered by choosing one of the statements listed.

- It can be in the form of a problem – again you select the best answer.

Here is an example of a multiple-choice question with a discussion which should give you some clues as to the method for choosing the right answer:

When an employee has a complaint about his assignment, the action which will *best* help him overcome his difficulty is to

A. discuss his difficulty with his coworkers
B. take the problem to the head of the organization
C. take the problem to the person who gave him the assignment
D. say nothing to anyone about his complaint

In answering this question, you should study each of the choices to find which is best. Consider choice "A" – Certainly an employee may discuss his complaint with fellow employees, but no change or improvement can result, and the complaint remains unresolved. Choice "B" is a poor choice since the head of the organization probably does not know what assignment you have been given, and taking your problem to him is known as "going over the head" of the supervisor. The supervisor, or person who made the assignment, is the person who can clarify it or correct any injustice. Choice "C" is, therefore, correct. To say nothing, as in choice "D," is unwise. Supervisors have and interest in knowing the problems employees are facing, and the employee is seeking a solution to his problem.

2) True/False Questions

The "true/false" or "right/wrong" form of question is sometimes used. Here a complete statement is given. Your job is to decide whether the statement is right or wrong.

SAMPLE: A roaming cell-phone call to a nearby city costs less than a non-roaming call to a distant city.

This statement is wrong, or false, since roaming calls are more expensive.

This is not a complete list of all possible question forms, although most of the others are variations of these common types. You will always get complete directions for answering questions. Be sure you understand *how* to mark your answers – ask questions until you do.

V. RECORDING YOUR ANSWERS

Computer terminals are used more and more today for many different kinds of exams.

For an examination with very few applicants, you may be told to record your answers in the test booklet itself. Separate answer sheets are much more common. If this separate answer sheet is to be scored by machine – and this is often the case – it is highly important that you mark your answers correctly in order to get credit.

An electronic scoring machine is often used in civil service offices because of the speed with which papers can be scored. Machine-scored answer sheets must be marked with a pencil, which will be given to you. This pencil has a high graphite content which responds to the electronic scoring machine. As a matter of fact, stray dots may register as answers, so do not let your pencil rest on the answer sheet while you are pondering the correct answer. Also, if your pencil lead breaks or is otherwise defective, ask for another.

Since the answer sheet will be dropped in a slot in the scoring machine, be careful not to bend the corners or get the paper crumpled.

The answer sheet normally has five vertical columns of numbers, with 30 numbers to a column. These numbers correspond to the question numbers in your test booklet. After each number, going across the page are four or five pairs of dotted lines. These short dotted lines have small letters or numbers above them. The first two pairs may also have a "T" or "F" above the letters. This indicates that the first two pairs only are to be used if the questions are of the true-false type. If the questions are multiple choice, disregard the "T" and "F" and pay attention only to the small letters or numbers.

Answer your questions in the manner of the sample that follows:

32. The largest city in the United States is
    A. Washington, D.C.
    B. New York City
    C. Chicago
    D. Detroit
    E. San Francisco

1) Choose the answer you think is best. (New York City is the largest, so "B" is correct.)
2) Find the row of dotted lines numbered the same as the question you are answering. (Find row number 32)
3) Find the pair of dotted lines corresponding to the answer. (Find the pair of lines under the mark "B.")
4) Make a solid black mark between the dotted lines.

VI. BEFORE THE TEST

Common sense will help you find procedures to follow to get ready for an examination. Too many of us, however, overlook these sensible measures. Indeed, nervousness and fatigue have been found to be the most serious reasons why applicants fail to do their best on civil service tests. Here is a list of reminders:

- Begin your preparation early – Don't wait until the last minute to go scurrying around for books and materials or to find out what the position is all about.
- Prepare continuously – An hour a night for a week is better than an all-night cram session. This has been definitely established. What is more, a night a week for a month will return better dividends than crowding your study into a shorter period of time.
- Locate the place of the exam – You have been sent a notice telling you when and where to report for the examination. If the location is in a different town or otherwise unfamiliar to you, it would be well to inquire the best route and learn something about the building.
- Relax the night before the test – Allow your mind to rest. Do not study at all that night. Plan some mild recreation or diversion; then go to bed early and get a good night's sleep.
- Get up early enough to make a leisurely trip to the place for the test – This way unforeseen events, traffic snarls, unfamiliar buildings, etc. will not upset you.
- Dress comfortably – A written test is not a fashion show. You will be known by number and not by name, so wear something comfortable.

- Leave excess paraphernalia at home – Shopping bags and odd bundles will get in your way. You need bring only the items mentioned in the official notice you received; usually everything you need is provided. Do not bring reference books to the exam. They will only confuse those last minutes and be taken away from you when in the test room.
- Arrive somewhat ahead of time – If because of transportation schedules you must get there very early, bring a newspaper or magazine to take your mind off yourself while waiting.
- Locate the examination room – When you have found the proper room, you will be directed to the seat or part of the room where you will sit. Sometimes you are given a sheet of instructions to read while you are waiting. Do not fill out any forms until you are told to do so; just read them and be prepared.
- Relax and prepare to listen to the instructions
- If you have any physical problem that may keep you from doing your best, be sure to tell the test administrator. If you are sick or in poor health, you really cannot do your best on the exam. You can come back and take the test some other time.

VII. AT THE TEST

The day of the test is here and you have the test booklet in your hand. The temptation to get going is very strong. Caution! There is more to success than knowing the right answers. You must know how to identify your papers and understand variations in the type of short-answer question used in this particular examination. Follow these suggestions for maximum results from your efforts:

1) Cooperate with the monitor

The test administrator has a duty to create a situation in which you can be as much at ease as possible. He will give instructions, tell you when to begin, check to see that you are marking your answer sheet correctly, and so on. He is not there to guard you, although he will see that your competitors do not take unfair advantage. He wants to help you do your best.

2) Listen to all instructions

Don't jump the gun! Wait until you understand all directions. In most civil service tests you get more time than you need to answer the questions. So don't be in a hurry. Read each word of instructions until you clearly understand the meaning. Study the examples, listen to all announcements and follow directions. Ask questions if you do not understand what to do.

3) Identify your papers

Civil service exams are usually identified by number only. You will be assigned a number; you must not put your name on your test papers. Be sure to copy your number correctly. Since more than one exam may be given, copy your exact examination title.

4) Plan your time

Unless you are told that a test is a "speed" or "rate of work" test, speed itself is usually not important. Time enough to answer all the questions will be provided, but this does not mean that you have all day. An overall time limit has been set. Divide the total time (in minutes) by the number of questions to determine the approximate time you have for each question.

5) Do not linger over difficult questions

If you come across a difficult question, mark it with a paper clip (useful to have along) and come back to it when you have been through the booklet. One caution if you do this – be sure to skip a number on your answer sheet as well. Check often to be sure that you have not lost your place and that you are marking in the row numbered the same as the question you are answering.

6) Read the questions

Be sure you know what the question asks! Many capable people are unsuccessful because they failed to *read* the questions correctly.

7) Answer all questions

Unless you have been instructed that a penalty will be deducted for incorrect answers, it is better to guess than to omit a question.

8) Speed tests

It is often better NOT to guess on speed tests. It has been found that on timed tests people are tempted to spend the last few seconds before time is called in marking answers at random – without even reading them – in the hope of picking up a few extra points. To discourage this practice, the instructions may warn you that your score will be "corrected" for guessing. That is, a penalty will be applied. The incorrect answers will be deducted from the correct ones, or some other penalty formula will be used.

9) Review your answers

If you finish before time is called, go back to the questions you guessed or omitted to give them further thought. Review other answers if you have time.

10) Return your test materials

If you are ready to leave before others have finished or time is called, take ALL your materials to the monitor and leave quietly. Never take any test material with you. The monitor can discover whose papers are not complete, and taking a test booklet may be grounds for disqualification.

VIII. EXAMINATION TECHNIQUES

1) Read the general instructions carefully. These are usually printed on the first page of the exam booklet. As a rule, these instructions refer to the timing of the examination; the fact that you should not start work until the signal and must stop work at a signal, etc. If there are any *special* instructions, such as a choice of questions to be answered, make sure that you note this instruction carefully.

2) When you are ready to start work on the examination, that is as soon as the signal has been given, read the instructions to each question booklet, underline any key words or phrases, such as *least, best, outline, describe* and the like. In this way you will tend to answer as requested rather than discover on reviewing your paper that you *listed without describing*, that you selected the *worst* choice rather than the *best* choice, etc.

3) If the examination is of the objective or multiple-choice type – that is, each question will also give a series of possible answers: A, B, C or D, and you are called upon to select the best answer and write the letter next to that answer on your answer paper – it is advisable to start answering each question in turn. There may be anywhere from 50 to 100 such questions in the three or four hours allotted and you can see how much time would be taken if you read through all the questions before beginning to answer any. Furthermore, if you come across a question or group of questions which you know would be difficult to answer, it would undoubtedly affect your handling of all the other questions.

4) If the examination is of the essay type and contains but a few questions, it is a moot point as to whether you should read all the questions before starting to answer any one. Of course, if you are given a choice – say five out of seven and the like – then it is essential to read all the questions so you can eliminate the two that are most difficult. If, however, you are asked to answer all the questions, there may be danger in trying to answer the easiest one first because you may find that you will spend too much time on it. The best technique is to answer the first question, then proceed to the second, etc.

5) Time your answers. Before the exam begins, write down the time it started, then add the time allowed for the examination and write down the time it must be completed, then divide the time available somewhat as follows:
   - If 3-1/2 hours are allowed, that would be 210 minutes. If you have 80 objective-type questions, that would be an average of 2-1/2 minutes per question. Allow yourself no more than 2 minutes per question, or a total of 160 minutes, which will permit about 50 minutes to review.
   - If for the time allotment of 210 minutes there are 7 essay questions to answer, that would average about 30 minutes a question. Give yourself only 25 minutes per question so that you have about 35 minutes to review.

6) The most important instruction is to *read each question* and make sure you know what is wanted. The second most important instruction is to *time yourself properly* so that you answer every question. The third most important instruction is to *answer every question*. Guess if you have to but include something for each question. Remember that you will receive no credit for a blank and will probably receive some credit if you write something in answer to an essay question. If you guess a letter – say "B" for a multiple-choice question – you may have guessed right. If you leave a blank as an answer to a multiple-choice question, the examiners may respect your feelings but it will not add a point to your score. Some exams may penalize you for wrong answers, so in such cases *only*, you may not want to guess unless you have some basis for your answer.

7) Suggestions
   a. Objective-type questions
      1. Examine the question booklet for proper sequence of pages and questions
      2. Read all instructions carefully
      3. Skip any question which seems too difficult; return to it after all other questions have been answered
      4. Apportion your time properly; do not spend too much time on any single question or group of questions

5. Note and underline key words – *all, most, fewest, least, best, worst, same, opposite,* etc.
6. Pay particular attention to negatives
7. Note unusual option, e.g., unduly long, short, complex, different or similar in content to the body of the question
8. Observe the use of "hedging" words – *probably, may, most likely,* etc.
9. Make sure that your answer is put next to the same number as the question
10. Do not second-guess unless you have good reason to believe the second answer is definitely more correct
11. Cross out original answer if you decide another answer is more accurate; do not erase until you are ready to hand your paper in
12. Answer all questions; guess unless instructed otherwise
13. Leave time for review

b. Essay questions
1. Read each question carefully
2. Determine exactly what is wanted. Underline key words or phrases.
3. Decide on outline or paragraph answer
4. Include many different points and elements unless asked to develop any one or two points or elements
5. Show impartiality by giving pros and cons unless directed to select one side only
6. Make and write down any assumptions you find necessary to answer the questions
7. Watch your English, grammar, punctuation and choice of words
8. Time your answers; don't crowd material

8) Answering the essay question

Most essay questions can be answered by framing the specific response around several key words or ideas. Here are a few such key words or ideas:

M's: manpower, materials, methods, money, management
P's: purpose, program, policy, plan, procedure, practice, problems, pitfalls, personnel, public relations

a. Six basic steps in handling problems:
1. Preliminary plan and background development
2. Collect information, data and facts
3. Analyze and interpret information, data and facts
4. Analyze and develop solutions as well as make recommendations
5. Prepare report and sell recommendations
6. Install recommendations and follow up effectiveness

b. Pitfalls to avoid
1. *Taking things for granted* – A statement of the situation does not necessarily imply that each of the elements is necessarily true; for example, a complaint may be invalid and biased so that all that can be taken for granted is that a complaint has been registered

2. *Considering only one side of a situation* – Wherever possible, indicate several alternatives and then point out the reasons you selected the best one
3. *Failing to indicate follow up* – Whenever your answer indicates action on your part, make certain that you will take proper follow-up action to see how successful your recommendations, procedures or actions turn out to be
4. *Taking too long in answering any single question* – Remember to time your answers properly

IX. AFTER THE TEST

Scoring procedures differ in detail among civil service jurisdictions although the general principles are the same. Whether the papers are hand-scored or graded by machine we have described, they are nearly always graded by number. That is, the person who marks the paper knows only the number – never the name – of the applicant. Not until all the papers have been graded will they be matched with names. If other tests, such as training and experience or oral interview ratings have been given, scores will be combined. Different parts of the examination usually have different weights. For example, the written test might count 60 percent of the final grade, and a rating of training and experience 40 percent. In many jurisdictions, veterans will have a certain number of points added to their grades.

After the final grade has been determined, the names are placed in grade order and an eligible list is established. There are various methods for resolving ties between those who get the same final grade – probably the most common is to place first the name of the person whose application was received first. Job offers are made from the eligible list in the order the names appear on it. You will be notified of your grade and your rank as soon as all these computations have been made. This will be done as rapidly as possible.

People who are found to meet the requirements in the announcement are called "eligibles." Their names are put on a list of eligible candidates. An eligible's chances of getting a job depend on how high he stands on this list and how fast agencies are filling jobs from the list.

When a job is to be filled from a list of eligibles, the agency asks for the names of people on the list of eligibles for that job. When the civil service commission receives this request, it sends to the agency the names of the three people highest on this list. Or, if the job to be filled has specialized requirements, the office sends the agency the names of the top three persons who meet these requirements from the general list.

The appointing officer makes a choice from among the three people whose names were sent to him. If the selected person accepts the appointment, the names of the others are put back on the list to be considered for future openings.

That is the rule in hiring from all kinds of eligible lists, whether they are for typist, carpenter, chemist, or something else. For every vacancy, the appointing officer has his choice of any one of the top three eligibles on the list. This explains why the person whose name is on top of the list sometimes does not get an appointment when some of the persons lower on the list do. If the appointing officer chooses the second or third eligible, the No. 1 eligible does not get a job at once, but stays on the list until he is appointed or the list is terminated.

X. HOW TO PASS THE INTERVIEW TEST

The examination for which you applied requires an oral interview test. You have already taken the written test and you are now being called for the interview test – the final part of the formal examination.

You may think that it is not possible to prepare for an interview test and that there are no procedures to follow during an interview. Our purpose is to point out some things you can do in advance that will help you and some good rules to follow and pitfalls to avoid while you are being interviewed.

What is an interview supposed to test?

The written examination is designed to test the technical knowledge and competence of the candidate; the oral is designed to evaluate intangible qualities, not readily measured otherwise, and to establish a list showing the relative fitness of each candidate – as measured against his competitors – for the position sought. Scoring is not on the basis of "right" and "wrong," but on a sliding scale of values ranging from "not passable" to "outstanding." As a matter of fact, it is possible to achieve a relatively low score without a single "incorrect" answer because of evident weakness in the qualities being measured.

Occasionally, an examination may consist entirely of an oral test – either an individual or a group oral. In such cases, information is sought concerning the technical knowledges and abilities of the candidate, since there has been no written examination for this purpose. More commonly, however, an oral test is used to supplement a written examination.

Who conducts interviews?

The composition of oral boards varies among different jurisdictions. In nearly all, a representative of the personnel department serves as chairman. One of the members of the board may be a representative of the department in which the candidate would work. In some cases, "outside experts" are used, and, frequently, a businessman or some other representative of the general public is asked to serve. Labor and management or other special groups may be represented. The aim is to secure the services of experts in the appropriate field.

However the board is composed, it is a good idea (and not at all improper or unethical) to ascertain in advance of the interview who the members are and what groups they represent. When you are introduced to them, you will have some idea of their backgrounds and interests, and at least you will not stutter and stammer over their names.

What should be done before the interview?

While knowledge about the board members is useful and takes some of the surprise element out of the interview, there is other preparation which is more substantive. It *is* possible to prepare for an oral interview – in several ways:

1) Keep a copy of your application and review it carefully before the interview

This may be the only document before the oral board, and the starting point of the interview. Know what education and experience you have listed there, and the sequence and dates of all of it. Sometimes the board will ask you to review the highlights of your experience for them; you should not have to hem and haw doing it.

2) Study the class specification and the examination announcement

Usually, the oral board has one or both of these to guide them. The qualities, characteristics or knowledges required by the position sought are stated in these documents. They offer valuable clues as to the nature of the oral interview. For example, if the job involves supervisory responsibilities, the announcement will usually indicate that knowledge of modern supervisory methods and the qualifications of the candidate as a supervisor will be tested. If so, you can expect such questions, frequently in the form of a hypothetical situation which you are expected to solve. NEVER go into an oral without knowledge of the duties and responsibilities of the job you seek.

3) Think through each qualification required

Try to visualize the kind of questions you would ask if you were a board member. How well could you answer them? Try especially to appraise your own knowledge and background in each area, *measured against the job sought*, and identify any areas in which you are weak. Be critical and realistic – do not flatter yourself.

4) Do some general reading in areas in which you feel you may be weak

For example, if the job involves supervision and your past experience has NOT, some general reading in supervisory methods and practices, particularly in the field of human relations, might be useful. Do NOT study agency procedures or detailed manuals. The oral board will be testing your understanding and capacity, not your memory.

5) Get a good night's sleep and watch your general health and mental attitude

You will want a clear head at the interview. Take care of a cold or any other minor ailment, and of course, no hangovers.

What should be done on the day of the interview?

Now comes the day of the interview itself. Give yourself plenty of time to get there. Plan to arrive somewhat ahead of the scheduled time, particularly if your appointment is in the fore part of the day. If a previous candidate fails to appear, the board might be ready for you a bit early. By early afternoon an oral board is almost invariably behind schedule if there are many candidates, and you may have to wait. Take along a book or magazine to read, or your application to review, but leave any extraneous material in the waiting room when you go in for your interview. In any event, relax and compose yourself.

The matter of dress is important. The board is forming impressions about you – from your experience, your manners, your attitude, and your appearance. Give your personal appearance careful attention. Dress your best, but not your flashiest. Choose conservative, appropriate clothing, and be sure it is immaculate. This is a business interview, and your appearance should indicate that you regard it as such. Besides, being well groomed and properly dressed will help boost your confidence.

Sooner or later, someone will call your name and escort you into the interview room. *This is it.* From here on you are on your own. It is too late for any more preparation. But remember, you asked for this opportunity to prove your fitness, and you are here because your request was granted.

What happens when you go in?

The usual sequence of events will be as follows: The clerk (who is often the board stenographer) will introduce you to the chairman of the oral board, who will introduce you to the other members of the board. Acknowledge the introductions before you sit down. Do not be surprised if you find a microphone facing you or a stenotypist sitting by. Oral interviews are usually recorded in the event of an appeal or other review.

Usually the chairman of the board will open the interview by reviewing the highlights of your education and work experience from your application – primarily for the benefit of the other members of the board, as well as to get the material into the record. Do not interrupt or comment unless there is an error or significant misinterpretation; if that is the case, do not hesitate. But do not quibble about insignificant matters. Also, he will usually ask you some question about your education, experience or your present job – partly to get you to start talking and to establish the interviewing "rapport." He may start the actual questioning, or turn it over to one of the other members. Frequently, each member undertakes the questioning on a particular area, one in which he is perhaps most competent, so you can expect each member to participate in the examination. Because time is limited, you may also expect some rather abrupt switches in the direction the questioning takes, so do not be upset by it. Normally, a board member will not pursue a single line of questioning unless he discovers a particular strength or weakness.

After each member has participated, the chairman will usually ask whether any member has any further questions, then will ask you if you have anything you wish to add. Unless you are expecting this question, it may floor you. Worse, it may start you off on an extended, extemporaneous speech. The board is not usually seeking more information. The question is principally to offer you a last opportunity to present further qualifications or to indicate that you have nothing to add. So, if you feel that a significant qualification or characteristic has been overlooked, it is proper to point it out in a sentence or so. Do not compliment the board on the thoroughness of their examination – they have been sketchy, and you know it. If you wish, merely say, "No thank you, I have nothing further to add." This is a point where you can "talk yourself out" of a good impression or fail to present an important bit of information. Remember, *you close the interview yourself.*

The chairman will then say, "That is all, Mr. ______, thank you." Do not be startled; the interview is over, and quicker than you think. Thank him, gather your belongings and take your leave. Save your sigh of relief for the other side of the door.

How to put your best foot forward

Throughout this entire process, you may feel that the board individually and collectively is trying to pierce your defenses, seek out your hidden weaknesses and embarrass and confuse you. Actually, this is not true. They are obliged to make an appraisal of your qualifications for the job you are seeking, and they want to see you in your best light. Remember, they must interview all candidates and a non-cooperative candidate may become a failure in spite of their best efforts to bring out his qualifications. Here are 15 suggestions that will help you:

1) Be natural – Keep your attitude confident, not cocky

If you are not confident that you can do the job, do not expect the board to be. Do not apologize for your weaknesses, try to bring out your strong points. The board is interested in a positive, not negative, presentation. Cockiness will antagonize any board member and make him wonder if you are covering up a weakness by a false show of strength.

2) Get comfortable, but don't lounge or sprawl

Sit erectly but not stiffly. A careless posture may lead the board to conclude that you are careless in other things, or at least that you are not impressed by the importance of the occasion. Either conclusion is natural, even if incorrect. Do not fuss with your clothing, a pencil or an ashtray. Your hands may occasionally be useful to emphasize a point; do not let them become a point of distraction.

3) Do not wisecrack or make small talk

This is a serious situation, and your attitude should show that you consider it as such. Further, the time of the board is limited – they do not want to waste it, and neither should you.

4) Do not exaggerate your experience or abilities

In the first place, from information in the application or other interviews and sources, the board may know more about you than you think. Secondly, you probably will not get away with it. An experienced board is rather adept at spotting such a situation, so do not take the chance.

5) If you know a board member, do not make a point of it, yet do not hide it

Certainly you are not fooling him, and probably not the other members of the board. Do not try to take advantage of your acquaintanceship – it will probably do you little good.

6) Do not dominate the interview

Let the board do that. They will give you the clues – do not assume that you have to do all the talking. Realize that the board has a number of questions to ask you, and do not try to take up all the interview time by showing off your extensive knowledge of the answer to the first one.

7) Be attentive

You only have 20 minutes or so, and you should keep your attention at its sharpest throughout. When a member is addressing a problem or question to you, give him your undivided attention. Address your reply principally to him, but do not exclude the other board members.

8) Do not interrupt

A board member may be stating a problem for you to analyze. He will ask you a question when the time comes. Let him state the problem, and wait for the question.

9) Make sure you understand the question

Do not try to answer until you are sure what the question is. If it is not clear, restate it in your own words or ask the board member to clarify it for you. However, do not haggle about minor elements.

10) Reply promptly but not hastily

A common entry on oral board rating sheets is "candidate responded readily," or "candidate hesitated in replies." Respond as promptly and quickly as you can, but do not jump to a hasty, ill-considered answer.

11) Do not be peremptory in your answers

A brief answer is proper – but do not fire your answer back. That is a losing game from your point of view. The board member can probably ask questions much faster than you can answer them.

12) Do not try to create the answer you think the board member wants

He is interested in what kind of mind you have and how it works – not in playing games. Furthermore, he can usually spot this practice and will actually grade you down on it.

13) Do not switch sides in your reply merely to agree with a board member

Frequently, a member will take a contrary position merely to draw you out and to see if you are willing and able to defend your point of view. Do not start a debate, yet do not surrender a good position. If a position is worth taking, it is worth defending.

14) Do not be afraid to admit an error in judgment if you are shown to be wrong

The board knows that you are forced to reply without any opportunity for careful consideration. Your answer may be demonstrably wrong. If so, admit it and get on with the interview.

15) Do not dwell at length on your present job

The opening question may relate to your present assignment. Answer the question but do not go into an extended discussion. You are being examined for a *new* job, not your present one. As a matter of fact, try to phrase ALL your answers in terms of the job for which you are being examined.

Basis of Rating

Probably you will forget most of these "do's" and "don'ts" when you walk into the oral interview room. Even remembering them all will not ensure you a passing grade. Perhaps you did not have the qualifications in the first place. But remembering them will help you to put your best foot forward, without treading on the toes of the board members.

Rumor and popular opinion to the contrary notwithstanding, an oral board wants you to make the best appearance possible. They know you are under pressure – but they also want to see how you respond to it as a guide to what your reaction would be under the pressures of the job you seek. They will be influenced by the degree of poise you display, the personal traits you show and the manner in which you respond.

ABOUT THIS BOOK

This book contains tests divided into Examination Sections. Go through each test, answering every question in the margin. We have also attached a sample answer sheet at the back of the book that can be removed and used. At the end of each test look at the answer key and check your answers. On the ones you got wrong, look at the right answer choice and learn. Do not fill in the answers first. Do not memorize the questions and answers, but understand the answer and principles involved. On your test, the questions will likely be different from the samples. Questions are changed and new ones added. If you understand these past questions you should have success with any changes that arise. Tests may consist of several types of questions. We have additional books on each subject should more study be advisable or necessary for you. Finally, the more you study, the better prepared you will be. This book is intended to be the last thing you study before you walk into the examination room. Prior study of relevant texts is also recommended. NLC publishes some of these in our Fundamental Series. Knowledge and good sense are important factors in passing your exam. Good luck also helps. So now study this Passbook, absorb the material contained within and take that knowledge into the examination. Then do your best to pass that exam.

EXAMINATION SECTION

EXAMINATION SECTION

TEST 1

DIRECTIONS: Each question or incomplete statement is followed by several suggested answers or completions. Select the one that BEST answers the question or completes the statement. *PRINT THE LETTER OF THE CORRECT ANSWER IN THE SPACE AT THE RIGHT.*

1. A group member who starts out at the same level as other group members and is able to move into a leadership position within that group would be described as what kind of a leader? 1.____
   A. Autocratic B. Democratic C. Emergent D. Informal

2. Your boss is only effective as the leader of your department when you and your coworkers are motivated experts on the topic at hand. If any of you do not really have expertise in a given field, his leadership falters somewhat. What type of leader is your boss? 2.____
   A. Laissez-faire B. Technical C. Democratic D. Autocratic

3. If a leader is in charge of an inexperienced group that does not have the appropriate information and proficiency to successfully complete a task, which of the following approaches should the leader use in order for success to follow within the group? 3.____
   A. Yelling B. Delegating C. Participating D. Selling

4. If you are a democratic leader, which of the following styles will be reflective of your leadership technique? 4.____
   A. Participating B. Telling C. Yelling D. Delegating

5. In producing equality in group member participation, which of the following should a leader NOT do? 5.____
   A. Make a statement or ask a question after each person in the group has said something
   B. Avoid taking a position during disagreements
   C. Limit comments to specific individuals within the group
   D. Control dominating speakers

6. Social capital is BEST defined as 6.____
   A. social connections that help us make more money
   B. social connections that improve our lives
   C. a type of connection that experts believe is becoming more common in Europe than the United States.
   D. none of the above

7. Communication is not simply sending a message. It is creating true 7.____
   A. connectivity B. understanding
   C. empathy D. power

8. Of the following, which is NOT a part of the speech communication process? 8.____
   A. Feedback
   B. Central idea
   C. Interference
   D. Ethics

9. You are leading a meeting and afterwards your colleagues tell you they didn't quite understand what you were communicating verbally and nonverbally to them. Which part of the communication process do you need to work on? 9.____
   A. Channel
   B. Main idea
   C. Message
   D. Specific purpose

10. If nonverbal messages contradict verbal symbols, you are sending what kind of message to your public? 10.____
   A. Clear
   B. Mixed
   C. Controversial
   D. Negative

11. Which of the following would a public speaker use to deliver verbal symbols? 11.____
   A. Words
   B. Gestures
   C. Tone
   D. Facial expression

12. You are in the process of taking a course on interacting with the public. Your instructor starts talking about "the pathway" used to transmit a message. He explains that "the pathway" is better known as a 12.____
   A. link
   B. loop
   C. transmitter
   D. channel

13. You finish an informational meeting with members of a community concerning a new park that will be built nearby. Afterwards, you are seeking feedback from them. Which of the following would NOT be a form of helpful feedback to you? 13.____
   A. Listeners raise their hands to point out a mistake
   B. Videotape the presentation
   C. Have colleagues and/or friends critique your presentation
   D. Hand out evaluation forms to listeners and have them fill it out after the presentation

14. Many public speaking experts have often repeated the famous quote, "A yawn is a silent _____," which references the quality of engagement within a presentation. 14.____
   A. rudeness
   B. insult
   C. shout
   D. protest

15. If a child is running around during your speech and making a lot of noise, what type of interference would that be? 15.____
   A. Situational
   B. External
   C. Internal
   D. Intentional

16. According to multiple recent surveys, of the five biggest mistakes that speakers make during a presentation, which one is the WORST? 16.____
   A. Being poorly prepared
   B. Trying to cover too much in one speech
   C. Failing to tailor a speech to the needs and interests of the audience
   D. Being boring

17. One of your colleagues has been asked to lead a meeting, and she confides in you that she suffers from excessive stage fright. Which of the following areas should you advise her to focus on to prevent her fear? 17.____
 A. Preparation
 B. Self-confidence
 C. Experience
 D. Sense of humor

18. When interacting with the public, which of the following elements should you NEVER imagine before engaging in public speaking? 18.____
 A. Effective delivery
 B. Nervousness
 C. Possibility of failure
 D. Success

19. A spokesperson is giving a speech to community members and you are evaluating him. You notice he tends to focus too much on himself and not enough on his audience. What is one piece of advice you can give him so he can shift his focus more to his audience? 19.____
 A. Change his amount of eye contact
 B. Work on facial expressions
 C. Alter his style of speaking
 D. All of the above

20. Most experts agree that the best way to eliminate excess energy would be to do all of the following EXCEPT 20.____
 A. using visual aids
 B. gripping the lectern
 C. walking to the right and left occasionally
 D. making gestures

21. A woman has lived in Newville her whole life. Recently, the Newville public works department made a policy change that angered her since it completely rearranged her schedule. She calls you on the phone and displays her displeasure with your department's recent policy change. What is the FIRST response you should have toward her? 21.____
 A. Interrupt her to say you cannot discuss the situation until she calms down
 B. Apologize to her that she has been negatively affected by the public works department
 C. Listen to her and demonstrate comprehension of her situation and why she was upset by your department's action
 D. Give her a detailed explanation of the reasons for the policy change

22. Which of the following is generally TRUE regarding public opinion? 22.____
 A. It is hard to move people toward a strong opinion on anything
 B. It is easy to move people toward a strong opinion on anything
 C. Most public relations are devoted to repairing negative public opinion about individuals
 D. It is easier than previously thought to move people away from an opinion they hold

23. Influencing a community member's attitude really comes down to which of the following? 23.____
 A. Journalism
 B. Public relations
 C. Social psychology
 D. Social action groups

24. If you attend a town hall meeting in which community members will bring up issues that require you to explain why your organization made the decisions it made, you will need to persuade them using evidence that is virtually indisputable. Which type of evidence should you stick to when explaining answers to the public? 24.____
    A. Facts
    B. Personal experience
    C. Emotions
    D. Using what appeals to the target public

25. In the last decade, especially after all the organizational and governmental scandals, public institutions must do which of the following in order to be successful? 25.____
    A. Work hard to earn and sustain favorable public opinion
    B. Trust the instincts expressed by the general public
    C. Be cognizant of the media's power
    D. Place the needs of the executives ahead of the needs of the public and other constituents

---

KEY (CORRECT ANSWERS)

1.	C	11.	A
2.	A	12.	D
3.	B	13.	A
4.	D	14.	C
5.	A	15.	B
6.	B	16.	C
7.	B	17.	A
8.	D	18.	B
9.	C	19.	D
10.	B	20.	B

21.	C
22.	D
23.	B
24.	A
25.	A

TEST 2

DIRECTIONS: Each question or incomplete statement is followed by several suggested answers or completions. Select the one that BEST answers the question or completes the statement. *PRINT THE LETTER OF THE CORRECT ANSWER IN THE SPACE AT THE RIGHT.*

1. Unique attributes of the Internet that people can enjoy include all of the following EXCEPT 1.____
   A. immediacy
   B. low cost
   C. pervasiveness
   D. value for building one-to-one human relationships

2. Which of the following is a reason that social media can be more effective than traditional means of advertising and communication? 2.____
   A. When someone mentions your brand in social media, there is much more potential for other people to notice
   B. It is easier to decipher tone and purpose through Twitter or Facebook than through personal communication
   C. Most of the people who would be interested in your brand or service are comfortable and familiar with using social media
   D. Almost anyone can step into a media relations role if primarily using social media, because it is easy to communicate effectively through social media platforms

3. You are tasked with building publicity for the upcoming reveal of a new art installation in the town you work in. Your boss tells you to contact journalists, reporters and bloggers to help spread the word. Which of the following would be the MOST effective way of getting the media to help build coverage? 3.____
   A. Send out a mass e-mail to any media members in the area detailing the art installation and why you need coverage for it
   B. Call each media outlet and find out who would most likely cover and build publicity for your project. Then reach out to them either face-to-face or through a phone call
   C. Using Twitter, tweet at the media members and introduce yourself and your art installation and ask them to help spread the word
   D. None of the above

4. When using written communication, which of the following is a MAJOR challenge of writing to listeners? 4.____
   A. Providing lots of statistics
   B. Grabbing the attention of the listener quickly
   C. Providing information that is easily reviewed
   D. Presenting lots of incidentals

5. In order to communicate well in writing, which of the following pieces of advice sounds good but doesn't actually help you? 5.____
   A. Write material for all audiences rather than focusing on one
   B. Think before writing
   C. Write simply and with clarity
   D. Write and rewrite until you have a polished, finished product

6. You send out a public newsletter that details a project that your team is currently working on. One week later, an employee on your team tells you she has received multiple phone calls from confused constituents claiming that the newsletter's readability was low. When you send out a corrected newsletter, you need to make sure that your communication is easy to 6.____
   A. read B. hear C. edit D. comprehend

7. You work for a biomedical company as a public outreach advocate. One day, an exciting e-mail circulates internally that states one of your scientists has discovered a cure for leukemia and your supervisor tasks you with writing the release. When writing the release, the newsworthy element inherent in the story is 7.____
   A. oddity B. conflict C. impact D. proximity

8. When communicating with the public through the Internet, news releases 8.____
   A. should not be sent via e-mail
   B. should be succinct
   C. should be sent via "snail mail"
   D. none of the above

9. What is the MAJOR advantage of organizational publications? Their ability to 9.____
   A. give sponsoring organizations a means of uncontrolled communications
   B. deliver specific, detailed information to narrowly defined target publics
   C. avoid the problems typically associated with two-way media
   D. provide a revenue source for sponsoring organizations

10. You are confronted by a question from a reporter that you do not know the answer to. What should you do? 10.____
   A. Give them other information you are certain is right
   B. Tell them that information is "off the record" and will be distributed later
   C. Say "no comment" rather than look like you're uninformed
   D. Admit that you don't know but promise to provide the information later

11. Often times, an organization will run situation analysis before they share information with the public. Which one of these "internal factors" is usually associated with a situational analysis? 11.____
   A. A communication audit
   B. Community focus groups
   C. A list of media contacts
   D. Strategy suggestions

12. When you are hired, your first task is to start a process of identifying who are involved and affected by a situation central to your organization. This process is MOST commonly referred to as a(n) 12.____
   A. situation interview
   B. communication audit
   C. exploratory survey
   D. stakeholder analysis

13. Once a public outreach plan is in the summative evaluation phase, which of the following is generally associated with it? 13.____
   A. Impact
   B. Implementation
   C. Attitude change
   D. Preparation

14. Which of the following Internet-related challenges is MOST significant in the public relations field? 14.____
   A. Finding stable, cost-effective internet provides
   B. Representing clients using new social media environments
   C. Staying abreast of changing technology
   D. Training staff to use social media

15. Which of the following BEST defines a public issue? Any 15.____
   A. problem that brings a public lawsuit
   B. concern that is of mutual distress to competitors
   C. issue that is of mutual concern to an organization and its stakeholders
   D. problem that is not a concern to an organization and/or one of its stakeholders

16. A handful of people are posting misleading and/or negative information about your organization. What is the MOST proactive approach to handling this situation? 16.____
   A. Buy up enough shares in the site where the negative posts are, and prevent those users from posting again
   B. Post anonymous comments on the sites to help combat the negativity
   C. Prepare news releases that discredit the inaccuracies
   D. Make policy changes to address complaints highlighted on the sites

17. Your supervisor has recently asked you to review present and future realities for interacting with the public. Why is it important to continually review these? 17.____
   A. It helps develop your vision statement
   B. It helps interpret trends for management
   C. It helps construe the organization's business plan
   D. To know what path the company should pursue

18. You are the community relations director for the public water utility plant that has been the focus of a group of activists who are opposed to the addition of fluoride to drinking water. These objectors are not only at the plant each day, but they are also very active on social media inciting negativity towards the practice. As the director of the plant, you have overwhelming evidence that contradicts what the protestors are arguing. You want to combat their social media with your own internet plan. Which of the following is the MOST appropriate action for you to take? 18.____

A. Use utility employees to write the blog, posing as healthcare professionals
B. Reach out to medical professionals to volunteer to tweet and message community members under their own identities, but with no reference to the utility company
C. Write a blog yourself, identifying yourself as an employee, and quote the scientific opinions of a variety of sources
D. Pay for medical professionals to respond through the internet, identifying the utility as their sponsor, but without disclosing the compensation

19. You have recently completed an advertising campaign to help assuage the anger of the community at changes in the upcoming summer program for the city. Which of the following measurements would be MOST effective for evaluating the campaign's impact on audience attitude? 19.____

A. A content analysis of media coverage
B. Studying blog postings about the issue
C. Analyzing pre- and post-numbers of people signed up for the summer programs
D. Conducting a pre- and post-analysis of public opinions

20. In order to measure how policy changes will affect the public, you recommend that your supervisors first run a focus group for research. They like the idea, but want you to be in charge of running the group. Which of the following should you keep in mind as you form the focus group? 20.____

A. Participants need to be randomly selected
B. Make sure participants are radically different from one another so you get a range of opinions
C. Include at least seven or more people in the group. Otherwise, the sample is too small to draw any conclusions.
D. Formulate a research plan and use it as a script so you can make sure the results are ones that will work for you and your supervisors

21. The public university has recently come under fire for not offering enough tuition savings options for students. You have been hired to help promote the programs they offer including new savings programs. What is the MOST appropriate first step for you to take? 21.____

A. Research pricing and development costs for the services
B. Develop a survey to discover which factors impact families' savings
C. Conduct a situation analysis to gain better understanding of the issues
D. Hold a focus group to determine which messages would be most effective for your program

22. After receiving feedback from the public on a new program, you are concerned the results have been tainted by courtesy bias. You plan on sending out a new questionnaire, but you need to make sure the bias is discouraged in it. Which of the following techniques will be MOST effective at decreasing the partiality? 22.____
   A. Make questionnaire responses confidential
   B. Employ an outside firm to run the survey
   C. Offer a larger range of responses in the survey
   D. Both "A" and "C"

23. You have just relocated from Omaha, Nebraska to a branch in Chicago, Illinois. In order to communicate well while in Chicago, you must remember that 23.____
   A. most publics have the same needs
   B. all publics are most interested only in technology you are using
   C. each audience has its own special needs and require different types of communication
   D. all audiences' needs overlap

24. Recently, the Parks and Recreation Department has come under fire because it has been accused of too much marketing and not enough public relations. Which of the following, if true, would lend credibility to these accusations? 24.____
   A. Employees are focused on signing citizens up for as many different camps and activities available over the summer as possible
   B. Management consistently tries to send appreciation gifts to members of the community when they have volunteered or attending an activity sponsored by the Park district
   C. Weekly meetings are held to determine how to best improve the Park district's image as it relates to consumers
   D. Parks and Recreation is primarily focused on making sure the public enjoys their activities and trusts them to put on educational programs for the children

25. During your speech, a community member stands up and accuses you of "spinning" a story. Which of the following BEST describes their accusation? 25.____
   A. You are relating a message through an agreed-upon ethical practice within the public relations community
   B. You are twisting a message to create performance where there is none
   C. You are trying to preserve hard-earned credibility
   D. You are providing the media with balanced and accurate information

KEY (CORRECT ANSWERS)

1. D
2. A
3. C
4. B
5. D

6. D
7. C
8. B
9. B
10. D

11. A
12. D
13. A
14. C
15. C

16. B
17. A
18. C
19. D
20. A

21. C
22. D
23. C
24. A
25. B

TEST 3

DIRECTIONS: Each question or incomplete statement is followed by several suggested answers or completions. Select the one that BEST answers the question or completes the statement. *PRINT THE LETTER OF THE CORRECT ANSWER IN THE SPACE AT THE RIGHT.*

1. In order to be successful in relating to the public, all of the following are vital EXCEPT 1.____
   A. performance
   B. relationship building
   C. formal education
   D. diversity of experience

2. Which of the following is TRUE of communicating well regarding public relations experts? 2.____
   A. It will differentiate you and your role from others with special skills in the organization you work for
   B. It should be handled delicately in order to avoid upsetting stakeholders
   C. It is not as important as looking fashionable
   D. It is less important than understanding bureaucratic peculiarities

3. You are critiquing a staffer who will lead an important meeting in two days and you note that she keeps using words that are steeped with connotation. You tell her to be careful of these words. Why? 3.____
   A. They transmit meaning too clearly, and you always want to leave wiggle room in your meaning
   B. They transmit the dictionary definition of a word that makes for a boring presentation
   C. They transmit meaning with an emotional overtone that could lead to misunderstanding in an overall message
   D. They lend themselves to stereotyping

4. If you are trying to avoid biasing your intended audience, which of the following factors could help with that? 4.____
   A. Symbols
   B. Objective reporting by media
   C. Semantics
   D. Peers

5. Of the following, which trait is MOST desirable when working with the public? 5.____
   A. Having the "gift for gab"
   B. Being an elite strategist
   C. Being able to leap organizational boundaries
   D. Performing well, especially in crises

6. Which of the following areas is likely to see continual growth in the practice of public relations? 6.____
   A. Healthcare
   B. Social media
   C. Law enforcement
   D. None of the above

7. What is the MOST commonly used public relations tactic? 7.____
   A. A news release
   B. A special event
   C. A PSA (public service announcement)
   D. A full feature news article

8. You have just been assigned to help with a new advertising campaign that will promote the new services offered by your organization. One major component of the new campaign will focus on publicity through photographs. Knowing you need to get this part of the project right, which of the following is the BEST tip to remember when taking PR photos? 8.____
   A. Don't use action shots because they usually wind up blurry
   B. Make sure there is good contrast and sharp detail
   C. Ensure that the product/services are the biggest thing(s) in the photo
   D. Photograph multiple people rather than only one

9. Which of the following situations would merit holding a press conference? 9.____
   A. When a corporation is restructured
   B. When a new public relations employee has been hired
   C. When information is of minor relevance to a specific audience
   D. When there is a new product to be released

10. On average, how long should an announcement to the public last on the radio? 10.____
   A. 2 minutes B. 20 seconds C. 1 minute D. 10 seconds

11. In educating the public, you need to develop a PR plan and analyze each situation that could arise. Which of the following should NOT be a part of the analysis? 11.____
   A. Research B. Message crafting
   C. Creating a problem statement D. Asking the 5 W's and the H

12. You are in charge of promoting an event in the near future, but social media is unavailable to you at this time. Which of the following is the BEST way to get your message out to the media and, therefore, the public? 12.____
   A. An Op-Ed piece in the local newspaper
   B. A press conference
   C. A newsletter
   D. A news release

13. In the past few months, you and your colleagues have been accused of "doublespeak". Which of the following excerpts from presentations you have used could you defend and explain why it would NOT be an example of "doublespeak"? 13.____
   A. You called combat "fighting"
   B. Fred referred to genocide as "ethnic cleansing"
   C. Your boss referred to recent layoffs as "downsizing"
   D. Susie called the janitor a "custodial engineer"

14. In relating to the public, which of the following reflects key words in defining modern day PR? 14.____
 A. Deliberate, public interest, management function
 B. Persuasive, manipulative, improvisation
 C. Management, technical, flexible
 D. Influential, creative, evaluative

15. How is educating and relating to the public different from being a journalist, marketing agent, or advertiser? 15.____
 A. It is more focused on advocacy
 B. It is about getting "free" press coverage
 C. It is about building relationships with various demographics
 D. All of the above

16. Of the following, what is the BEST tactic for learning employee attitudes? 16.____
 A. Internal communications audit B. Research
 C. Conference meeting D. Both A and B

17. When releasing news to the public, you should make sure it reads at a _____-grade reading level. 17.____
 A. 5th B. 12th C. 9th D. 7th

18. If you are using a euphemism that actually changes the meaning/impact of a concept you are trying to relay, what is that called? 18.____
 A. Insider language B. Doublespeak
 C. Stylizing D. Plagiarism

19. Which of the following should be included in a public relations campaign if you want to ensure people will hear, understand, and believe your message? 19.____
 A. Repetition B. Imagery
 C. Thoroughness D. Acceptance

20. In PR, what is it called when you track coverage and compare it over a period of time? 20.____
 A. Bookmarking B. Benchmarking
 C. Comparison analysis D. Correspondence

21. What is a baseline study PRIMARILY used for? 21.____
 A. To determine changes in audience perception and attitude
 B. To figure out how well your company is doing in the marketplace compared to your competitors
 C. To find out the cost of buying space taken up by a particular article if that article is an advertisement
 D. None of the above

22. Of the following people, who would BEST be considered a modern role model for successful public relations? 22.____
    A. Phineas T. Barnum (Barnum and Bailey)
    B. Ivy Lee
    C. Andrew Jackson
    D. Sir Walter Raleigh

23. If your organization has recently participated in a "publicity stunt," what type of PR strategy have you just used? 23.____
    A. Community
    B. Lobbying
    C. News management
    D. Crisis management

24. You tell your supervisor that you want to start using video press releases. When he presses you to explain why, you tell him that you want to take advantage of the fact that 24.____
    A. many news agencies don't review them ahead of broadcasting
    B. most reporters hired to create them have contacts within the industry
    C. they cover stories that some local news organizations cannot
    D. the production value may be better than those at local stations

25. A _____ is a type of news leak in which the source reveals large policy changes are on the table. 25.____
    A. disclosure
    B. hook
    C. exclusive
    D. trial balloon

KEY (CORRECT ANSWERS)

1. C
2. B
3. C
4. B
5. D

6. B
7. A
8. B
9. D
10. C

11. B
12. D
13. A
14. A
15. D

16. D
17. C
18. B
19. A
20. B

21. A
22. B
23. C
24. C
25. D

TEST 4

DIRECTIONS: Each question or incomplete statement is followed by several suggested answers or completions. Select the one that BEST answers the question or completes the statement. *PRINT THE LETTER OF THE CORRECT ANSWER IN THE SPACE AT THE RIGHT.*

1. The Facial Feedback Hypothesis is a popular nonverbal theory that is BEST defined as 1.____
   A. people mirroring each other's facial expressions
   B. emotions leading to certain facial expressions
   C. facial expression can lead to the experience of certain emotions
   D. looking into a mirror while making a facial expression can cause one to change their facial expression

2. Of the following, which is NOT recognized as a function of smiling? 2.____
   A. It provides feedback.
   B. It signals disinterest.
   C. It helps establish rapport.
   D. It signals attentiveness.

3. When facial expressions are limited by cultural expectations, that is referred to as 3.____
   A. display rules
   B. syntactic displays
   C. adaptors
   D. interaction intensification

4. Of the following, which is recognized as part of the six basic emotions across cultures globally? 4.____
   A. Guilt
   B. Happiness
   C. Fear
   D. Both B and C

5. Which kinds of communication scenarios are more likely to see leadership roles develop from? 5.____
   A. Small group
   B. Intrapersonal communication
   C. Face-to-face public communication
   D. Text messaging

6. Which of the following highlights the key difference between small group communication and organizational communication? 6.____
   A. Feedback is easier and more immediate in organizational.
   B. Communication is more informal in small group communication.
   C. The message is easier to adapt to the specific needs of the receiver in organizational communication.
   D. People are more spread out in small group communication.

7. Which of the following would be an example of mediated communication? 7.____
   A. A principal addresses the student body in a speech.
   B. Two friends communicate while they work together in class.
   C. An employee texts his coworkers to see if they want to hang out after work.
   D. Three friends joke with one another while attending a concert.

8. Which of the following is FALSE concerning the way interpersonal relationships can affect us physically? 8.____
   A. Without interpersonal relationships, we can become sick
   B. These interpersonal relationships are necessary for humans; according to most research, humans raised in isolation are less healthy than those raised with others
   C. Humans are not the only mammals that need relationships in order to survive and thrive
   D. Interpersonal relationships are necessary until about age 12, but not later in adulthood

9. Which of the following is a characteristic of public relationships as they compare to private relationships? 9.____
   A. Intrinsic rewards
   B. Normative rules
   C. Use of particularistic knowledge
   D. Small number of intimates

10. When someone asks how you know they were angry, it is likely they fall into which style of facial expressions? 10.____
   A. Withholder
   B. Revealer
   C. Frozen-affect expressor
   D. Unwitting expressor

11. The theory of expectancy violations is BEST defined as 11.____
   A. nonverbal behavior reciprocated based primarily on positive or negative valence and the perceived reward value of the other person
   B. the process of intimacy exchange within a dyad relationship
   C. a social rule that says we should repay in kind what another has provided us
   D. none of the above

12. If an employee has a very good idea of what is and is not socially acceptable in any given situation, which kind of linguistic competence is she strong in? 12.____
   A. Phonemic
   B. Syntactic
   C. Pragmatic
   D. Semantic

13. Which of the following would NOT be considered sexist language? 13.____
   A. Although a girl, Sonia is very brave.
   B. A gorgeous model, Johnny also likes to use his surfboard on the weekends.
   C. Jimmy's brother is a male nurse.
   D. None; all are considered to be sexist.

14. What is it called when individual experience, and NOT conventional agreement, creates meaning? 14.____
   A. Small talk communication
   B. Denotative meaning
   C. Connotative meaning
   D. Self-reflexive communication

15. Which of the following kinds of communication do students spend the MOST time engaged in? 15.____
   A. Listening
   B. Writing
   C. Reading
   D. Speaking

16. Which of the following would be evidence of active listening? 16.____
    A. Maintain eye contact
    B. Nodding and making eye contact
    C. Asking for clarification
    D. All of the above

17. When listening in an evaluative context, which of the following must be done for it to be considered successful? 17.____
    A. Precisely disseminate stimuli in a message
    B. Comprehend the intended meaning of a message
    C. Make critical assessments of the accuracy of the facts in a message
    D. All of the above

18. A friend visits one day and tells you she thinks her husband is cheating on her with his ex-wife. She tells you she doesn't know what to do because she can't imagine living without him. If you wanted to paraphrase, which of the following BEST exemplifies that? 18.____
    A. "You are feeling insecure because you don't have a very good relationship with your husband."
    B. "You're afraid your husband is seeing his ex-wife behind your back; you don't know what to do; and you can't live without him."
    C. "You're afraid that your husband may still have feelings for his ex-wife and you're afraid you'll lose him."
    D. "Don't worry; his ex-wife is not back with him. You're just being paranoid."

19. When we form impressions of others, when might the recency effect impact our assessments? If we 19.____
    A. focus on our own feelings instead of the feelings of others
    B. are motivated to be more accurate or expect to be held accountable for our own perceptions
    C. engage in self-monitoring of our behaviors
    D. employ the discounting rule

20. Which of the following BEST defines a "modal self"? 20.____
    A. The ideal person for a social order
    B. A person who does not go to extremes
    C. The kind of self valued in the 20th century but not the 21st century
    D. The person who monitors his own behavior in social situations

21. Which of the following is TRUE of today's society? 21.____
    A. People are less selfish than they have ever been.
    B. People spend most of their time trying to be a single, unitary self.
    C. People have many short-lived relationships leading to their notions of themselves changing easily.
    D. People try to be frugal, honorable, and self-sacrificing.

22. A man's childhood consisted of a dismissing attachment style. Which of the following behaviors will he MOST likely exhibit as an adult? 22.____
    A. Anxiousness and ambivalence
    B. Obsessive friendliness and dependence
    C. Autonomy and distance from others
    D. Rhetorical sensitivity

23. When practicing self-disclosure, which of the following is a good rule of thumb? 23.____
    A. Be sure to disclose more than your partner
    B. Reserve your most important disclosures for people you know well
    C. Ignore the style of disclosure; the only thing that is important is content
    D. All of the above

24. During your first meeting as project leader, you approach your group and inform them that John will serve as your assistant project leader. He will be responsible for chairing team meetings and establishing the agenda. When John is given this formal leadership position, what type of power does he have over the other members of the project? 24.____
    A. Legitimate B. Reward C. Expert D. Punishment

25. If you bring an employee to lead a project because she is knowledgeable and skilled in the area the project focuses on, what type of power does she possess? 25.____
    A. Legitimate B. Reward C. Referent D. Expert

KEY (CORRECT ANSWERS)

1.	C	11.	A
2.	B	12.	C
3.	A	13.	D
4.	D	14.	C
5.	A	15.	A
6.	B	16.	D
7.	C	17.	C
8.	D	18.	B
9.	B	19.	D
10.	D	20.	A

21.	C
22.	C
23.	B
24.	A
25.	D

EXAMINATION SECTION

TEST 1

DIRECTIONS: Each question or incomplete statement is followed by several suggested answers or completions. Select the one that BEST answers the question or completes the statement. *PRINT THE LETTER OF THE CORRECT ANSWER IN THE SPACE AT THE RIGHT.*

1. When conducting a needs assessment for the purpose of education planning, an agency's FIRST step is to identify or provide 1.____
   A. a profile of population characteristics
   B. barriers to participation
   C. existing resources
   D. profiles of competing resources

2. Research has demonstrated that of the following, the MOST effective medium for communicating with external publics is(are) 2.____
   A. video news releases
   B. television
   C. radio
   D. newspapers

3. Basic ideas behind the effort to influence the attitudes and behaviors of a constituency include each of the following EXCEPT the idea that 3.____
   A. words, rather than actions or events, are most likely to motivate
   B. demands for action are a usual response
   C. self-interest usually figures heavily into public involvement
   D. the reliability of change programs is difficult to assess

4. An agency representative is trying to craft a pithy message to constituents in order to encourage the use of agency program resources. 4.____
   Choosing an audience for such messages is easiest when the message
   A. is project- or behavior-based
   B. is combined with other messages
   C. is abstract
   D. has a broad appeal

5. Of the following factors, the MOST important to the success of an agency's external education or communication programs is the 5.____
   A. amount of resources used to implement them
   B. public's prior experiences with the agency
   C. real value of the program to the public
   D. commitment of the internal audience

6. A representative for a state agency is being interviewed by a reporter from a local news network. The representative is being asked to defend a program that is extremely unpopular in certain parts of the municipality. 6.____
   When a constituency is known to be opposed to a position, the MOST useful communication strategy is to present

A. only the arguments that are consistent with constituents' views
B. only the agency's side of the issue
C. both sides of the argument as clearly as possible
D. both sides of the argument, omitting key information about the opposing position

7. The MOST significant barriers to effective agency community relations include 7.____
I. widespread distrust of communication strategies
II. the media's "watchdog" stance
III. public apathy
IV. statutory opposition

The CORRECT answer is:
A. I only B. I and II C. II and III D. III and IV

8. In conducting an education program, many agencies use workshops and seminars in a classroom setting. 8.____
Advantages of classroom-style teaching over other means of educating the public include each of the following, EXCEPT
A. enabling an instructor to verify learning through testing and interaction with the target audience
B. enabling hands-on practice and other participatory learning techniques
C. ability to reach an unlimited number of participants in a given length of time
D. ability to convey the latest, most up-to-date information

9. The _____ model of community relations is characterized by an attempt to persuade the public to adopt the agency's point of view. 9.____
A. two-way symmetric B. two-way asymmetric
C. public information D. press agency/publicity

10. Important elements of an internal situation analysis include the 10.____
I. list of agency opponents II. communication audit
III. updated organizational almanac IV. stakeholder analysis

The CORRECT answer is:
A. I and II B. I, II, and III C. II and III D. I, II, III and IV

11. Government agency information efforts typically involve each of the following objectives, EXCEPT to 11.____
A. implement changes in the policies of government agencies to align with public opinion
B. communicate the work of agencies
C. explain agency techniques in a way that invites input from citizens
D. provide citizen feedback to government administrators

12. Factors that are likely to influence the effectiveness of an educational campaign include the 12.____
    I. level of homogeneity among intended participants
    II. number and types of media used
    III. receptivity of the intended participants
    IV. level of specificity in the message or behavior to be taught

    The CORRECT answer is:
    A. I and II B. I, II, and III C. II and III D. I, II, III, and IV

13. An agency representative is writing instructional objectives that will later help to measure the effectiveness of an educational program. 13.____
    Which of the following verbs, included in an objective, would be MOST helpful for the purpose of measuring effectiveness?
    A. Know B. Identify C. Learn D. Comprehend

14. A state education agency wants to encourage participation in a program that has just received a boost through new federal legislation. The program is intended to include participants from a wide variety of socioeconomic and other demographic characteristics. The agency wants to launch a broad-based program that will inform virtually every interested party in the state about the program's new circumstances. 14.____
    In attempting to deliver this message to such a wide-ranging constituency, the agency's BEST practice would be to
    A. broadcast the same message through as many different media channels as possible
    B. focus on one discrete segment of the public at a time
    C. craft a message whose appeal is as broad as the public itself
    D. let the program's achievements speak for themselves and rely on word-of-mouth

15. Advantages associated with using the World Wide Web as an educational tool include 15.____
    I. an appeal to younger generations of the public
    II. visually-oriented, interactive learning
    III. learning that is not confined by space, time, or institutional association
    IV. a variety of methods for verifying use and learning

    The CORRECT answer is:
    A. I only B. I and II C. I, II, and III D. I, II, II, and IV

16. In agencies involved in health care, community relations is a critical function because it 16.____
    A. serves as an intermediary between the agency and consumers
    B. generates a clear mission statement for agency goals and priorities
    C. ensures patient privacy while satisfying the media's right to information
    D. helps marketing professionals determine the wants and needs of agency constituents

17. After an extensive campaign to promote its newest program to constituents, an agency learns that most of the audience did not understand the intended message. 17._____
MOST likely, the agency has
   A. chosen words that were intended to inform, rather than persuade
   B. not accurately interpreted what the audience really needed to know
   C. overestimated the ability of the audience to receive and process the message
   D. compensated for noise that may have interrupted the message

18. The necessary elements that lead to conviction and motivation in the minds of participants in an educational or information program include each of the following, EXCEPT the _____ of the message. 18._____
   A. acceptability
   B. intensity
   C. single-channel appeal
   D. pervasiveness

19. Printed materials are often at the core of educational programs provided by public agencies. 19._____
The PRIMARY disadvantage associated with print is that it
   A. does not enable comprehensive treatment of a topic
   B. is generally unreliable in term of assessing results
   C. is often the most expensive medium available
   D. is constrained by time

20. Traditional thinking on public opinion holds that there is about _____ percent of the public who are pivotal to shifting the balance and momentum of opinion—they are concerned about an issue, but not fanatical, and interested enough to pay attention to a reasoned discussion. 20._____
   A. 2
   B. 10
   C. 33
   D. 51

21. One of the most useful guidelines for influencing attitude change among people is to 21._____
   A. invite the target audience to come to you, rather than approaching them
   B. use moral appeals as the primary approach
   C. use concrete images to enable people to see the results of behaviors or indifference
   D. offer tangible rewards to people for changes in behavior

22. An agency is attempting to evaluate the effectiveness of its educational program. For this purpose, it wants to observe several focus groups discussing the same program. 22._____
Which of the following would NOT be a guideline for the use of focus groups?
   A. Focus groups should only include those who have participated in the program.
   B. Be sure to accurately record the discussion.
   C. The same questions should be asked at each focus group meeting.
   D. It is often helpful to have a neutral, non-agency employee facilitate discussions.

23. Research consistently shows that _____ is the determinant most likely to make a newspaper editor run a news release. 23.____
    A. novelty B. prominence C. proximity D. conflict

24. Which of the following is NOT one of the major variables to take into account when considering a population-needs assessment? 24.____
    A. State of program development
    B. Resources available
    C. Demographics
    D. Community attitudes

25. The FIRST step in any communications audit is to 25.____
    A. develop a research instrument
    B. determine how the organization currently communicates
    C. hire a contractor
    D. determine which audience to assess

KEY (CORRECT ANSWERS)

1.	A	11.	A
2.	D	12.	D
3.	A	13.	B
4.	A	14.	B
5.	D	15.	C
6.	C	16.	A
7.	D	17.	B
8.	C	18.	C
9.	B	19.	B
10.	C	20.	B

21.	C
22.	A
23.	C
24.	C
25.	D

TEST 2

DIRECTIONS: Each question or incomplete statement is followed by several suggested answers or completions. Select the one that BEST answers the question or completes the statement. *PRINT THE LETTER OF THE CORRECT ANSWER IN THE SPACE AT THE RIGHT.*

1. A public relations practitioner at an agency has just composed a press release highlighting a program's recent accomplishments and success stories. In pitching such releases to print outlets, the practitioner should 1.____
   I. e-mail, mail, or send them by messenger
   II. address them to "editor" or "news director"
   III. have an assistant call all media contacts by telephone
   IV. ask reporters or editors how they prefer to receive them

   The CORRECT answer is:
   A. I and II B. I and IV C. II, III, and IV D. III only

2. The "output goals" of an educational program are MOST likely to include 2.____
   A. specified ratings of services by participants on a standardized scale
   B. observable effects on a given community or clientele
   C. the number of instructional hours provided
   D. the number of participants served

3. An agency wants to evaluate satisfaction levels among program participants, and mails out questionnaires to everyone who has been enrolled in the last year. 3.___
   The PRIMARY problem associated with this method of evaluative research is that it
   A. poses a significant inconvenience for respondents
   B. is inordinately expensive
   C. does not allow for follow-up or clarification questions
   D. usually involves a low response rate

4. A communications audit is an important tool for measuring 4.____
   A. the depth of penetration of a particular message or program
   B. the cost of the organization's information campaigns
   C. how key audiences perceive an organization
   D. the commitment of internal stakeholders

5. The "ABCs" of written learning objectives include each of the following, EXCEPT 5.____
   A. Audience B. Behavior C. Conditions D. Delineation

6. When attempting to change the behaviors of constituents, it is important to keep in mind that 6.____
   I. most people are skeptical of communications that try to get them to change their behaviors
   II. in most cases, a person selects the media to which he exposes himself
   III. people tend to react defensively to messages or programs that rely on fear as a motivating factor
   IV. programs should aim for the broadest appeal possible in order to include as many participants as possible

   The CORRECT answer is:
   A. I and II B. I, II and III C. II and III D. I, II, III, and IV

7. The "laws" of public opinion include the idea that it is 7.____
   A. useful for anticipating emergencies
   B. not sensitive to important events
   C. basically determined by self-interest
   D. sustainable through persistent appeals

8. Which of the following types of evaluations is used to measure public attitudes before and after an information/educational program? 8.____
   A. Retrieval study B. Copy test
   C. Quota sampling D. Benchmark study

9. The PRIMARY source for internal communications is(are) usually 9.____
   A. flow charts B. meetings
   C. voice mail D. printed publications

10. An agency representative is putting together informational materials—brochures and a newsletter—outlining changes in one of the state's biggest benefits programs. 10.____
   In assembling print materials as a medium for delivering information to the public, the representative should keep in mind each of the following trends:
   I. For various reasons, the reading capabilities of the public are in general decline
   II. Without tables and graphs to help illustrate the changes, it is unlikely that the message will be delivered effectively
   III. Professionals and career-oriented people are highly receptive to information written in the form of a journal article or empirical study
   IV. People tend to be put off by print materials that use itemized and bulleted (●) lists

   The CORRECT answer is:
   A. I and II B. I, II and III C. II and III D. I, II, III, and IV

11. Which of the following steps in a problem-oriented information campaign would typically be implemented FIRST? 11.____
    A. Deciding on tactics
    B. Determining a communications strategy
    C. Evaluating the problem's impact
    D. Developing an organizational strategy

12. A common pitfall in conducting an educational program is to 12.____
    A. aim it at the wrong target audience
    B. overfund it
    C. leave it in the hands of people who are in the business of education, rather than those with expertise in the business of the organization
    D. ignore the possibility that some other organization is meeting the same educational need for the target audience

13. The key factors that affect the credibility of an agency's educational program include 13.____
    A. organization
    B. scope
    C. sophistication
    D. penetration

14. Research on public opinion consistently demonstrates that it is 14.____
    A. easy to move people toward a strong opinion on anything, as long as they are approached directly through their emotions
    B. easier to move people away from an opinion they currently hold than to have them form an opinion about something they have not previously cared about
    C. easy to move people toward a strong opinion on anything, as long as the message appeals to their reason and intellect
    D. difficult to move people toward a strong opinion on anything, no matter what the approach

15. In conducting an education program, many agencies use meetings and conferences to educate an audience about the organization and its programs. Advantages associated with this approach include 15.____
    I. a captive audience that is known to be interested in the topic
    II. ample opportunities for verifying learning
    III. cost-efficient meeting space
    IV. the ability to provide information on a wider variety of subjects

    The CORRECT answer is:
    A. I and II
    B. I, III and IV
    C. II and III
    D. I, II, III and IV

16. An agency is attempting to evaluate the effectiveness of its educational programs. For this purpose, it wants to observe several focus groups discussing particular programs. 16.____
    For this purpose, a focus group should never number more than ______ participants.
    A. 5
    B. 10
    C. 15
    D. 20

17. A _____ speech is written so that several agency members can deliver it to different audiences with only minor variations. 17.____
    A. basic B. printed C. quota D. pattern

18. Which of the following statements about public opinion is generally considered to be FALSE? 18.____
    A. Opinion is primarily reactive rather than proactive.
    B. People have more opinions about goals than about the means by which to achieve them.
    C. Facts tend to shift opinion in the accepted direction when opinion is not solidly structured.
    D. Public opinion is based more on information than desire.

19. An agency is trying to promote its educational program. 19.____
    As a general rule, the agency should NOT assume that
    A. people will only participate if they perceive an individual benefit
    B. promotions need to be aimed at small, discrete groups
    C. if the program is good, the audience will find out about it
    D. a variety of methods, including advertising, special events, and direct mail, should be considered

20. In planning a successful educational program, probably the first and most important question for an agency to ask is: 20.____
    A. What will be the content of the program?
    B. Who will be served by the program?
    C. When is the best time to schedule the program?
    D. Why is the program necessary?

21. Media kits are LEAST likely to contain 21.____
    A. fact sheets B. memoranda
    C. photographs with captions D. news releases

22. The use of pamphlets and booklets as media for communication with the public often involves the disadvantage that 22.____
    A. the messages contained within them are frequently nonspecific
    B. it is difficult to measure their effectiveness in delivering the message
    C. there are few opportunities for people to refer to them
    D. color reproduction is poor

23. The MOST important prerequisite of a good educational program is an 23.____
    A. abundance of resources to implement it
    B. individual staff unit formed for the purpose of program delivery
    C. accurate needs assessment
    D. uneducated constituency

24. After an education program has been delivered, an agency conducts a program evaluation to determine whether its objectives have been met. General rules about how to conduct such an education program valuation include each of the following, EXCEPT that it 24.____
    A. must be done immediately after the program has been implemented
    B. should be simple and easy to use
    C. should be designed so that tabulation of responses can take place quickly and inexpensively
    D. should solicit mostly subjective, open-ended responses if the audience was large

25. Using electronic media such as television as means of educating the public is typically recommended ONLY for agencies that 25.____
    I. have a fairly simple message to begin with
    II. want to reach the masses, rather than a targeted audience
    III. have substantial financial resources
    IV. accept that they will not be able to measure the results of the campaign with much precision

    The CORRECT answer is:
    A. I and II B. I, II and III C. II and IV D. I, II, III and IV

KEY (CORRECT ANSWERS)

1.	B	11.	C
2.	C	12.	D
3.	D	13.	A
4.	C	14.	D
5.	D	15.	B
6.	B	16.	B
7.	C	17.	D
8.	D	18.	D
9.	D	19.	C
10.	A	20.	D

21.	B
22.	B
23.	C
24.	D
25.	D

COMMUNICATION

EXAMINATION SECTION
TEST 1

DIRECTIONS: Each question or incomplete statement is followed by several suggested answers or completions. Select the one that BEST answers the question or completes the statement. *PRINT THE LETTER OF THE CORRECT ANSWER IN THE SPACE AT THE RIGHT.*

1. In some agencies the counsel to the agency head is given the right to bypass the chain of command and issue orders directly to the staff concerning matters that involve certain specific processes and practices. 1.____
This situation MOST nearly illustrates the principle of _____ authority.
   A. the acceptance theory of
   B. multiple-linear
   C. splintered
   D. functional

2. It is commonly understood that communication is an important part of the administrative process. 2.____
Which of the following is NOT a valid principle of the communication process in administration?
   A. The channels of communication should be spontaneous.
   B. The lines of communication should be as direct and as short as possible.
   C. Communications should be authenticated.
   D. The persons serving in communications centers should be competent.

3. Of the following, the one factor which is generally considered LEAST essential to successful committee operations is 3.____
   A. stating a clear definition of the authority and scope of the committee
   B. selecting the committee chairman carefully
   C. limiting the size of the committee to four persons
   D. limiting the subject matter to that which can be handled in group discussion

4. Of the following, the failure by line managers to accept and appreciate the benefits and limitations of a new program or system VERY FREQUENTLY can be traced to the 4.____
   A. budgetary problems involved
   B. resultant need to reduce staff
   C. lack of controls it engenders
   D. failure of top management to support its implementation

5. If a manager were thinking about using a committee of subordinates to solve an operating problem, which of the following would generally NOT be an advantage of such use of the committee approach? 5.____
   A. Improved coordination
   B. Low cost
   C. Increased motivation
   D. Integrated judgment

6. Every supervisor has many occasions to lead a conference or participate in a conference of some sort. 6.____
Of the following statements that pertain to conferences and conference leadership, which is generally considered to be MOST valid?
   A. Since World War II, the trend has been toward fewer shared decisions and more conferences.
   B. The most important part of a conference leader's job is to direct discussion.
   C. In providing opportunities for group interaction, management should avoid consideration of its past management philosophy.
   D. A good administrator cannot lead a good conference if he is a poor public speaker.

7. Of the following, it is usually LEAST desirable for a conference leader to 7.____
   A. call the name of a person after asking a question
   B. summarize proceedings periodically
   C. make a practice of repeating questions
   D. ask a question without indicating who is to reply

8. Assume that, in a certain organization, a situation has developed in which there is little difference in status or authority between individuals. 8.____
Which of the following would be the MOST likely result with regard to communication in this organization?
   A. Both the accuracy and flow of communication will be improved.
   B. Both the accuracy and flow of communication will substantially decrease.
   C. Employees will seek more formal lines of communication.
   D. Neither the flow nor the accuracy of communication will be improved over the former hierarchical structure.

9. The main function of many agency administrative officers is "information management." Information that is received by an administrative officer may be classified as active or passive, depending upon whether or not it requires the recipient to take some action. 9.____
Of the following, the item received which is clearly the MOST active information is
   A. an appointment of a new staff member
   B. a payment voucher for a new desk
   C. a press release concerning a past event
   D. the minutes of a staff meeting

10. Of the following, the one LEAST considered to be a communication barrier is 10.____
   A. group feedback
   B. charged words
   C. selective perception
   D. symbolic meanings

11. Management studies support the hypothesis that, in spite of the tendency of employees to censor the information communicated to their supervisor, subordinates are more likely to communicate problem-oriented information UPWARD when they have a 11.____
   A. long period of service in the organization
   B. high degree of trust in the supervisor
   C. high educational level
   D. low status on the organizational ladder

12. Electronic data processing equipment can produce more information faster than can be generated by any other means. 12.____
In view of this, the MOST important problem faced by management at present is to
   A. keep computers fully occupied
   B. find enough computer personnel
   C. assimilate and properly evaluate the information
   D. obtain funds to establish appropriate information systems

13. A well-designed management information system essentially provides each executive and manager the information he needs for 13.____
   A. determining computer time requirements
   B. planning and measuring results
   C. drawing a new organization chart
   D. developing a new office layout

14. It is generally agreed that management policies should be periodically reappraised and restated in accordance with current conditions. 14.____
Of the following, the approach which would be MOST effective in determining whether a policy should be revised is to
   A. conduct interviews with staff members at all levels in order to ascertain the relationship between the policy and actual practice
   B. make proposed revisions in the policy and apply it to current problems
   C. make up hypothetical situations using both the old policy and a revised version in order to make comparisons
   D. call a meeting of top level staff in order to discuss ways of revising the policy

15. Your superior has asked you to notify division employees of an important change in one of the operating procedures described in the division manual. Every employee presently has a copy of this manual. 15.____
Which of the following is normally the MOST practical way to get the employees to understand such a change?
   A. Notify each employee individually of the change and answer any questions he might have
   B. Send a written notice to key personnel, directing them to inform the people under them

C. Call a general meeting, distribute a corrected page for the manual, and discuss the change
D. Send a memo to employees describing the change in general terms and asking them to make the necessary corrections in their copies of the manual

16. Assume that the work in your department involves the use of any technical terms. 16.____
In such a situation, when you are answering inquiries from the general public, it would usually be BEST to
A. use simple language and avoid the technical terms
B. employ the technical terms whenever possible
C. bandy technical terms freely, but explain each term in parentheses
D. apologize if you are forced to use a technical term

17. Suppose that you receive a telephone call from someone identifying himself as an employee in another city department who asks to be given information which your own department regards as confidential. 17.____
Which of the following is the BEST way of handling such a request?
A. Give the information requested, since your caller as official standing
B. Grant the request, provided the caller gives you a signed receipt
C. Refuse the request, because you have no way of knowing whether the caller is really who he claims to be
D. Explain that the information is confidential and inform the caller of the channels he must go through to have the information released to him

18. Studies show that office employees place high importance on the social and human aspects of the organization. What office employees like best about their jobs is the kind of people with whom they work. So strive hard to group people who are most likely to get along well together. 18.____
Based on this information, it is MOST reasonable to assume that office workers are most pleased to work in a group which
A. is congenial
B. has high productivity
C. allows individual creativity
D. is unlike other groups

19. A certain supervisor does not compliment members of his staff when they come up with good ideas. He feels that coming up with good ideas is part of the job and does not merit special attention. 19.____
This supervisor's practice is
A. *poor*, because recognition for good ideas is a good motivator
B. *poor*, because the staff will suspect that the supervisor has no good ideas of his own
C. *good*, because it is reasonable to assume that employees will tell their supervisor of ways to improve office practice
D. *good*, because the other members of the staff are not made to seem inferior by comparison

20. Some employees of a department have sent an anonymous letter containing many complaints to the department head. 20.____
Of the following, what is this MOST likely to show about the department?
   A. It is probably a good place to work.
   B. Communications are probably poor.
   C. The complaints are probably unjustified.
   D. These employees are probably untrustworthy.

21. Which of the following actions would usually be MOST appropriate for a supervisor to take after receiving an instruction sheet from his superior explaining a new procedure which is to be followed? 21.____
   A. Put the instruction sheet aside temporarily until he determines what is wrong with the old procedure.
   B. Call his superior and ask whether the procedure is one he must implement immediately.
   C. Write a memorandum to the superior asking for more details.
   D. Try the new procedure and advise the superior of any problems or possible improvements.

22. Of the following, which one is considered the PRIMARY advantage of using a committee to resolved a problem in an organization? 22.____
   A. No one person will be held accountable for the decision since a group of people was involved.
   B. People with different backgrounds give attention to the problem.
   C. The decision will take considerable time so there is unlikely to be a decision that will later be regretted.
   D. One person cannot dominate the decision-making process.

23. Employees in a certain office come to their supervisor with all their complaints about the office and the work. Almost every employee has had at least one minor complaint at some time. 23.____
The situation with respect to complaints in this office may BEST be described as probably
   A. *good*; employees who complain care about their jobs and work hard
   B. *good*; grievances brought out into the open can be corrected
   C. *bad*; only serious complaints should be discussed
   D. *bad*; it indicates the staff does not have confidence in the administration

24. The administrator who allows his staff to suggest ways to do their work will usually find that 24.____
   A. this practice contributes to high productivity
   B. the administrator's ideas produce greater output
   C. clerical employees suggest inefficient work methods
   D. subordinate employees resent performing a management function

25. The MAIN purpose for a supervisor's questioning the employees at a conference he is holding is to 25.____
   A. stress those areas of information covered but not understood by the participants
   B. encourage participants to think through the problem under discussion
   C. catch those subordinates who are not paying attention
   D. permit the more knowledgeable participants to display their grasp of the problems being discussed

---

KEY (CORRECT ANSWERS)

1.	D	11.	B
2.	A	12.	C
3.	C	13.	B
4.	D	14.	A
5.	B	15.	C
6.	B	16.	A
7.	C	17.	D
8.	D	18.	A
9.	A	19.	A
10.	A	20.	B

21.	D
22.	B
23.	B
24.	A
25.	B

TEST 2

DIRECTIONS: Each question or incomplete statement is followed by several suggested answers or completions. Select the one that BEST answers the question or completes the statement. *PRINT THE LETTER OF THE CORRECT ANSWER IN THE SPACE AT THE RIGHT.*

1. For a superior to use *consultative supervision* with his subordinates effectively, it is ESSENTIAL that he 1.____
   A. accept the fact that his formal authority will be weakened by the procedure
   B. admit that he does not know more than all his men together and that his ideas are not always best
   C. utilize a committee system so that the procedure is orderly
   D. make sure that all subordinates are consulted so that no one feels left out

2. The *grapevine* is an informal means of communication in an organization. 2.____
   The attitude of a supervisor with respect to the grapevine should be to
   A. ignore it since it deals mainly with rumors and sensational information
   B. regard it as a serious danger which should be eliminated
   C. accept it as a real line of communication which should be listened to
   D. utilize it for most purposes instead of the official line of communication

3. The supervisor of an office that must deal with the public should realize that planning in this type of work situation 3.____
   A. is useless because he does not know how many people will request service or what service they will request
   B. must be done at a higher level but that he should be ready to implement the results of such planning
   C. is useful primarily for those activities that are not concerned with public contact
   D. is useful for all the activities of the office, including those that relate to public contact

4. Assume that it is your job to receive incoming telephone calls. Those calls which you cannot handle yourself have to be transferred to the appropriate office. 4.____
   If you receive an outside call for an extension line which is busy, the one of the following which you should do FIRST is to
   A. interrupt the person speaking on the extension and tell him a call is waiting
   B. tell the caller the line is busy and let him know every thirty seconds whether or not it is free
   C. leave the caller on “hold” until the extension is free
   D. tell the caller the line is busy and ask him if he wishes to wait

5. Your superior has subscribed to several publications directly related to your division's work, and he has asked you to see to it that the publications are circulated among the supervisory personnel in the division. There are eight supervisors involved. 5.____
The BEST method of insuring that all eight see these publications is to
   A. place the publication in the division's general reference library as soon as it arrives
   B. inform each supervisor whenever a publication arrives and remind all of them that they are responsible for reading it
   C. prepare a standard slip that can be stapled to each publication, listing the eight supervisors and saying, "Please read, initial your name, and pass along"
   D. send a memo to the eight supervisors saying that they may wish to purchase individual subscriptions in their own names if they are interested in seeing each issue

6. Your superior has telephoned a number of key officials in your agency to ask whether they can meet at a certain time next month. He has found that they can all make it, and he has asked you to confirm the meeting. 6.____
Which of the following is the BEST way to confirm such a meeting?
   A. Note the meeting on your superior's calendar.
   B. Post a notice of the meeting on the agency bulletin board.
   C. Call the officials on the day of the meeting to remind them of the meeting.
   D. Write a memo to each official involved, repeating the time and place of the meeting.

7. Assume that a new city regulation requires that certain kinds of private organizations file information forms with your department. You have been asked to write the short explanatory message that will be printed on the front cover of the pamphlet containing the forms and instructions. 7.____
Which of the following would be the MOST appropriate way of beginning this message?
   A. Get the readers' attention by emphasizing immediately that there are legal penalties for organizations that fail to file before a certain date.
   B. Briefly state the nature of the enclosed forms and the types of organizations that must file.
   C. Say that your department is very sorry to have to put organizations to such an inconvenience.
   D. Quote the entire regulation adopted by the city, even if it is quite long and is expressed din complicated legal language.

8. Suppose that you have been told to make up the vacation schedule for the 18 employees in a particular unit. In order for the unit to operate effectively, only a few employees can be on vacation at the same time. 8.____
Which of the following is the MOST advisable approach in making up the schedule?
   A. Draw up a schedule assigning vacations in alphabetical order
   B. Find out when the supervisors want to take their vacations, and randomly assign whatever periods are left to the non-supervisory personnel

C. Assign the most desirable times to employees of longest standing and the least desirable times to the newest employees
D. Have all employees state their own preference, and then work out any conflicts in consultation with the people involved

9. Assume that you have been asked to prepare job descriptions for various positions in your department. 9.____
Which of the following are the basic points that should be covered in a *job description*?
A. General duties and responsibilities of the position, with examples of day-to-day tasks
B. Comments on the performances of present employees
C. Estimates of the number of openings that may be available in each category during the coming year
D. Instructions for carrying out the specific tasks assigned to your department

10. Of the following, the biggest DISADVANTAGE in allowing a free flow of communications in an agency is that such a free flow 10.____
A. decreases creativity
B. increases the use of the *grapevine*
C. lengthens the chain of command
D. reduces the executive's power to direct the flow of information

11. A downward flow of authority in an organization is one example of _____ communication. 11.____
A. horizontal B. informal C. circular D. vertical

12. Of the following, the one that would MOST likely block effective communication is 12.____
A. concentration only on the issues at hand
B. lack of interest or commitment
C. use of written reports
D. use of charts and graphs

13. An ADVANTAGE of the *lecture* as a teaching tool is that it 13.____
A. enables a person to present his ideas to a large number of people
B. allows the audience to retain a maximum of the information given
C. holds the attention of the audience for the longest time
D. enables the audience member to easily recall the main points

14. An ADVANTAGE of the *small-group* discussion as a teaching tool is that 14.____
A. it always focuses attention on one person as the leader
B. it places collective responsibility on the group as a whole
C. its members gain experience by summarizing the ideas of others
D. each member of the group acts as a member of a team

15. The one of the following that is an ADVANTAGE of a *large-group* discussion, when compared to a small-group discussion, is that the large-group discussion 15.____
    A. moves along more quickly than a small-group discussion
    B. allows its participants to feel more at ease, and speak out more freely
    C. gives the whole group a chance to exchange ideas on a certain subject at the same occasion
    D. allows its members to feel a greater sense of personal responsibility

KEY (CORRECT ANSWERS)

1.	D	6.	D	11.	D
2.	C	7.	B	12.	B
3.	D	8.	D	13.	A
4.	D	9.	A	14.	D
5.	C	10.	D	15.	C

EXAMINATION SECTION

TEST 1

DIRECTIONS: Each question or incomplete statement is followed by several suggested answers or completions. Select the one that BEST answers the question or completes the statement. *PRINT THE LETTER OF THE CORRECT ANSWER IN THE SPACE AT THE RIGHT.*

1. Managing conflict effectively by avoiding no-win situations, positively influencing the actions of others and using _____ strategies are what make a great leader. 1.____
   A. persuasive B. ambiguous C. prosecution D. performance

2. In today's business world, collaboration will bring together people from distinct backgrounds. These collaborative groups may not share common norms, morals or _____, but they can offer unique _____. 2.____
   A. vocabulary; perspectives B. salaries; vocabulary
   C. modifications; insights D. perspectives; salaries

3. E-mail is a great tool for communication; however, which of the following should you be careful of when in electronic communication with a colleague? 3.____
   A. Font size B. E-mail length
   C. Font color D. Tone of voice

4. A formal relationship can BEST be described as 4.____
   A. regulated by procedures or directives
   B. personal and relaxed
   C. emotionally distant and very uncomfortable
   D. confusing and unproductive

5. John is in a meeting with his supervisor ad coworkers. He is thinking about what he's going to have for dinner that night when his boss asks him a question. John can repeat back what his supervisor said, but he cannot retain what was said during the meeting. 5.____
   This is a classic example of failing to
   A. focus at work
   B. effectively listen
   C. leave personal plans outside the workplace
   D. care about meetings

6. A person's choice of _____ can directly affect communication. 6.____
   A. clothing B. food C. hygiene D. words

7. Why is it important to relax when communicating with team members? 7.____
   A. Relaxing always means having better ideas.
   B. People will automatically like you more if you are relaxed.

C. If you are nervous, you may talk too quickly and make it hard for others to understand your message or directive.
D. No one likes someone who is always working, so it is important to relax and not work too hard.

8. In order to show you are genuinely interested in what others have to say, you should 8.____
A. tell them how nice they are
B. repeat what they say back to them
C. nod and find something to compliment them about
D. ask questions and seek clarification from them

9. Jack and James are always arguing with one another. Their supervisor calls each one in separately to talk to them. He asks Jack to think about things from James' point of view and he asks James to do the same for Jack. What is the supervisor trying to get each person to do? 9.____
A. Get along
B. Be positive
C. Communicate effectively
D. Empathize

10. When working in groups, disagreements 10.____
A. should be avoided at all costs
B. are often a healthy way of building understanding and camaraderie
C. lead coworkers to hate one another and the company they work for
D. don't happen if the supervisor chooses the right people to work together

11. If things go wrong in a group situation, it is important to AVOID 11.____
A. the boss
B. disagreements or arguments
C. scapegoating
D. being polite and fair to one another

12. If you are a listener who likes to hear the rationale behind a message, your listening style would be described as _____ style. 12.____
A. results
B. process
C. reasons
D. eye contact

13. Which of the following BEST describes a psychological barrier in communication? 13.____
A. Molly is so stressed about her paying for her mortgage that she can't focus at work right now.
B. John doesn't understand a lot of the terms the IT specialist used in an e-mail sent out to everyone.
C. Jerry is a little older and has a hard time hearing everything so sometimes he misses parts of a conversation.
D. Linda doesn't want to be at the company for longer than a few months, so she doesn't really try too hard to fit in.

14. Body language, also known as _____, is really important when building rapport with coworkers and communicating effectively. 14.____
A. verbal language
B. kinesthetic
C. non-verbal communication
D. facial expressions

15. Which of the following might be a good example of someone who has a "closed" posture? 15.____
   A. Hands are apart on the arms of the chair.
   B. His/her arms are folded.
   C. They are directly facing you.
   D. They barely speak above a whisper.

16. Which of the following can eye contact be used for? 16.____
   A. To give and receive feedback
   B. To let someone know when it is their turn to speak
   C. To communicate how you feel about someone
   D. All of the above

17. Which of the following is NOT a form of non-verbal communication? 17.____
   A. Crossing your arms when talking to someone
   B. Using space within the room in a conversation
   C. Clearing your throat before you speak]
   D. Saying "10-4" when asked if you understand

18. Your best friend has just been hired at the company you work for. You notice he has come into work on several occasions after staying out late the night before. His work has not suffered yet, but you fear it will. 18.____
Which of the following actions should you take to help prevent future problems?
   A. Do nothing; he's your friend but it is his life
   B. Try to talk to him and help him see the importance of not creating bad habits.
   C. Talk to your supervisor and tell him your friend isn't suitable for the job
   D. Tell your friend to change his ways or to quit

19. Interacting with coworkers can be positively or negatively affected by _____ when someone's previous biases and assumptions shape their reactions in future situations. 19.____
   A. racism
   B. past experience
   C. interpersonal skills
   D. active listening

20. Which of the following scenarios BEST describes a person who is being subjective? 20.____
   A. Sally is fair and honest when she listens to coworkers. She does not take sides and wants the best solution to the problem.
   B. Mike doesn't like Steve, because he thinks Steve is only out for himself. Still, Steve offers valuable insights, so Mike tries not to let personal feelings get in the way of working together.
   C. Jamie is dating Veronica's ex and Veronica just found out. Now, Veronica immediately shoots down anything Jamie suggests during a meeting as irrational and superfluous.
   D. None of the above

21. Which important communications tem is MOST closely defined as "the quality of a sound governed by the rate of vibrations producing it; the degree of highness or lowness of a tone"? 21.____
    A. Tone
    B. Pitch
    C. Effective communication
    D. Rationalization

22. _____ is when a person tries to make an imprudent and reckless action seem reasonable. 22.____
    A. Projection
    B. Self-deception
    C. Past experience
    D. Rationalization

23. When holding conversations with coworkers, you should 23.____
    A. do most of the talking
    B. let others do most of the talking
    C. try to split time between talking and listening
    D. zone out and wait for the meeting to finish

24. A new hire just arrived and you are meeting her for the first time. Which of the following actions is MOST appropriate? 24.____
    A. Walk up and introduce yourself with a smile and a handshake
    B. Wait for her to come and introduce herself
    C. Approach her and offer a hug to make her feel welcome
    D. Ignore the new hire; she is likely your competition

25. If you are the type of listener who likes to discuss concepts or issues in detail, you would MOST likely fall under which listening style? 25.____
    A. Process
    B. Reasons
    C. Results
    D. None of the above

KEY (CORRECT ANSWERS)

1.	A	11.	C
2.	A	12.	C
3.	D	13.	A
4.	A	14.	C
5.	B	15.	B
6.	D	16.	D
7.	C	17.	D
8.	D	18.	B
9.	D	19.	B
10.	B	20.	C

21.	B
22.	D
23.	C
24.	A
25.	A

TEST 2

DIRECTIONS: Each question or incomplete statement is followed by several suggested answers or completions. Select the one that BEST answers the question or completes the statement. *PRINT THE LETTER OF THE CORRECT ANSWER IN THE SPACE AT THE RIGHT.*

1. Which of the following is an example of the BEST practice when communicating in the workplace? 1.____
   A. You are horrible with remembering names so you try to use nicknames to cover up for your poor memory.
   B. You only pay attention to the names of people who you work for or who you deem to be "important."
   C. You try to remember everyone's names and use them whenever possible.
   D. None of the above

2. Words of civility such as "please" and "thank you" should be used _____ when conversing with coworkers and business partners. 2.____
   A. always B. sometimes C. rarely D. never

3. When communicating with others, one should _____ stand as close to them as possible and make body contact in order to get an important point across. 3.____
   A. always B. sometimes C. rarely D. never

4. The MOST appropriate way to end a conversation is to 4.____
   A. seek a mutual resolution, but leave abruptly if it continues
   B. find a way to wrap up the conversation so the other person knows it is time to move on
   C. look impatient so hopefully the person will get the hint
   D. tell the other person the conversation should end

5. Another name for interpersonal communication in an office setting is 5.____
   A. peer-to-peer communication B. mass communication
   C. virtual reality D. e-mailing

6. Of the following statements, choose the one you feel is the MOST correct. 6.____
   A. Devoid of interpersonal communication, people become sick.
   B. Communication is not completely needed for humans.
   C. People are the only animals that need to have relationships in order to survive.
   D. Important communication is not really relevant until after you become an adult.

7. John is giving a presentation on ways to communicate effectively with peers. He is having trouble deciding on what to say in his speech. Which of the following statements should he AVOID using? 7.____
   A. Always try to understand another person's point of view or perspective
   B. Try to imagine what someone is going to say before they actually say it

C. Be aware of how non-verbal cues like eye contact and body language affect how your message is received
D. Both B and C

8. Which of the following would MOST affect our perception of communication with coworkers? 8.____
A. Past experiences
B. Marital problems
C. Rumors spread about coworkers
D. None of the above

9. Many people think of communication as both _____ and _____ messages. 9.____
A. formal; informal
B. hearing; listening
C. sending; receiving
D. finding; decoding

10. Why is context important in communication? 10.____
A. It's important to know which buttons to push in order to get what you want.
B. Saying something to one person may not have the same effect as saying it to someone else.
C. Context is only important if you are worried about what others think.
D. None of the above

11. If your brother is normally bright and talkative during the summer, but you notice he gets quiet and subdued in the winter, the MOST likely communication context he is dealing with would be 11.____
A. relational
B. cultural
C. inner
D. physical

12. _____ is an example of a negative nonverbal action you can take. 12.____
A. Smiling
B. Using a tone of voice that matches your message
C. Maintaining eye contact
D. Slumping your shoulders

13. Cultural context can BEST be described as 13.____
A. what people think of as it relates to the event they are participating in (i.e., wedding versus a funeral)
B. the connection between a father and his son
C. rules and patterns of Americans versus the Japanese
D. thoughts, feelings, and sensations inside a person's head

14. Which of the following BEST describes feedback? 14.____
A. Staring at the speaker while he talks
B. Nodding and smiling while listening to a speaker
C. Standing an appropriate distance away so the speaker does not get uncomfortable
D. Trying to speak while the other person is speaking because you have something more important to say

15. Being able to communicate more effectively can be improved upon by 15.____
    A. continually making an effort to be as flexible as possible when talking to others
    B. committing to one style of speaking until you master it
    C. using the same style of correspondence as the person with whom you are speaking
    D. always using the opposite style of communication from the person you are speaking to

16. John walks up to Sally and compliments her on the dress she wore to work today. In his mind, John was just being friendly, but Sally went to her manager and filed a harassment charge against John. 16.____
    This miscommunication could MOST easily be classified as an error in what?
    A. Reality B. Perception C. Friendship D. Loyalty

17. If a speaker's tone is flat and monotone, which of the following is the MOST likely reaction that listeners will have? 17.____
    They will
    A. enthused by the message
    B. enjoy the message but not be overly excited about it
    C. be polite and interested but will not seem very engaged
    D. be bored and uninterested in the message

18. When Steve speaks to his group about his ideas, he generally has a higher pitch to his voice and gesticulates frequently. 18.____
    This lead his team members to believe that Steve
    A. is enthusiastic and has great ideas for the group
    B. has had too much caffeine and needs to relax
    C. is trying to show off for the boss and make them look bad
    D. is extremely smart and great at his job

19. _____ is used when a person wants to add stress to key words in communication. It lets the audience understand the mood or feelings of particular words or phrases. 19.____
    A. Anger B. Tone C. Perception D. Inflection

20. If Barry tells Bill that his haircut looks "great" and Bill can tell Barry is being insincere, which of the following tones is Barry MOST likely using? 20.____
    A. Affectionate B. Apologetic C. Threatening D. Sarcastic

21. As a supervisor, it is important that everyone clearly comprehends everything you communicate to them. 21.____
    In order to ensure this happens, which of the following things should you avoid?
    A. Overusing jargon
    B. Explaining something more than once
    C. Speaking slowly and annunciating everything
    D. Having meetings in the morning

22. If your supervisor is looking down at the ground or has his back to you as he is speaking, it MOST clearly indicates to those who are listening to him that the supervisor 22.____
   A. is shy and doesn't like speaking in front of people
   B. is disinterested and doesn't care what he's talking about
   C. is approachable and friendly
   D. dislikes his job and wants to get out as soon as possible

23. Interpersonal communication helps you 23.____
   A. know what others are thinking
   B. turn into an inspiring speaker, especially in public
   C. learn about yourself
   D. communicate with the general public

24. In general, people who smile more are perceived as 24.____
   A. devious
   B. friendly
   C. attractive
   D. easy to manipulate

25. If your supervisor constantly takes advantage of you and expresses his or her opinion often at the expense of you or other workers, which communication style are they MOST likely using? 25.____
   A. Nonassertive B. Assertive C. Aggressive D. Peacemaking

KEY (CORRECT ANSWERS)

1.	C	11.	D
2.	A	12.	D
3.	D	13.	C
4.	B	14.	B
5.	A	15.	A
6.	A	16.	B
7.	B	17.	D
8.	A	18.	A
9.	C	19.	D
10.	B	20.	D

21.	A
22.	B
23.	D
24.	B
25.	C

EXAMINATION SECTION

TEST 1

DIRECTIONS: Each question or incomplete statement is followed by several suggested answers or completions. Select the one that BEST answers the question or completes the statement. *PRINT THE LETTER OF THE CORRECT ANSWER IN THE SPACE AT THE RIGHT.*

1. Assume that a manager is preparing a list of reasons to justify making a major change in methods and procedures in his agency. 1.____
   Which of the following reasons would be LEAST appropriate on such a list?
   A. Improve the means for satisfying needs and wants of agency personnel
   B. Increase efficiency
   C. Intensify competition and stimulate loyalty to separate work groups
   D. Contribute to the individual and group satisfaction of agency personnel

2. Many managers recognize the benefits of decentralization but are concerned about the danger of over-relaxation of control as a result of increased delegation. 2.____
   Of the following, the MOST appropriate means of establishing proper control under decentralization is for the manager to
   A. establish detailed standards for all phases of operation
   B. shift his attention from operating details to appraisal of results
   C. keep himself informed by decreasing the time span covered by reports
   D. make unilateral decisions on difficult situations that arise in decentralized locations

3. In some agencies, the counsel to the agency head is given the right to bypass the chain of command and issue orders directly to the staff concerning matters that involve certain specific processes and practices. 3.____
   This situation MOST NEARLY illustrates the principle of _____ authority.
   A. the acceptance theory of
   B. multiple-linear
   C. splintered
   D. functional

4. Assume that a manager is writing a brief report to his superior outlining the advantages of matrix organization. 4.____
   Of the following, it would be INCORRECT to state that
   A. in matrix organization, a project is emphasized by designating one individual as the focal point for all matters pertaining to it
   B. utilization of manpower can be flexible in matrix organization because a reservoir of specialists is maintained in the line operations
   C. the usual line staff arrangement is generally reversed in matrix organization
   D. in matrix organization, responsiveness to project needs is generally faster due to establishing needed communication lines and decision points

5. It is commonly understood that communication is an important part of the administrative process.
Which of the following is NOT a valid principle of the communication process in administration? 5.____
A. The channels of communication should be spontaneous.
B. The lines of communication should be as direct and as short as possible.
C. Communications should be authenticated.
D. The persons serving in communications centers should be competent.

6. The PRIMARY purpose of the quantitative approach in management is to 6.____
A. identify better alternatives for management decision-making
B. substitute data for judgment
C. match opinions to data
D. match data to opinions

7. If an executive wants to make a strong case for running his agency as a flat type of structure, he should point out that the PRIMARY advantage of doing so is to 7.____
A. provide less experience in decision-making for agency personnel
B. facilitate frequent contact between each superior and his immediate subordinates
C. improve communication and unify attitudes
D. improve communication and diversify attitudes

8. In deciding how detailed his delegation of authority to a subordinate should be, a manager should follow the general principle that 8.____
A. delegation of authority is more detailed at the top of the organizational structure
B. detailed delegation of authority is associated with detailed work assignments
C. delegation of authority should be in sufficient detail to prevent overlapping assignments
D. detailed delegation of authority is associated with broad work assignments

9. In recent years, newer and more fluid types of organizational forms have been developed. One of these is a type of free-form organization.
Another name for this type of organization is the 9.____
A. project organization
B. semimix organization
C. naturalistic structure
D. semipermanent structure

10. Which of the following is the MAJOR objective of operational or management systems audits? 10.____
A. Determining the number of personnel needed
B. Recommending opportunities for improving operating and management practices
C. Detecting fraud
D. Determining organization problems

11. Assume that a manager observes that conflict exists between his agency and another operating agency of government. 11.____
Which of the following statements is the LEAST probable cause of this conflict?
   A. Incompatibility between the agencies' goals but similarity in their resource allocations
   B. Compatibility between agencies' goals and resources
   C. Status differences between agency personnel
   D. Differences in perceptions of each other's policies

12. Of the following, a MAJOR purpose of brainstorming as a problem-solving technique is to 12.____
   A. develop the ability to concentrate
   B. encourage creative thinking
   C. evaluate employees' ideas
   D. develop critical ability

13. The one of the following requirements which is LEAST likely to accompany regular delegation of work from a manager to a subordinate is a(n) 13.____
   A. need to review the organization's workload
   B. indication of what work the subordinate is to do
   C. need to grant authority to the subordinate
   D. obligation for the subordinate who accepts the work to try to complete it

14. Of the following, the one factor which is generally considered LEAST essential to successful committee operation is 14.____
   A. stating a clear definition of the authority and scope of the committee
   B. selecting the committee chairman carefully
   C. limiting the size of the committee to four persons
   D. limiting the subject matter to that which can be handled in group discussion

15. In using the program evaluation and review technique, the *critical path* is the path that 15.____
   A. requires the shortest time
   B. requires the longest time
   C. focuses most attention on social constraints
   D. focuses most attention to repetitious jobs

16. Which one of the following is LEAST characteristic of the management-by-objectives approach? 16.____
   A. The scope within which the employee may exercise decision-making is broadened.
   B. The employee starts with a self-appraisal of his performances, abilities, and potential.
   C. Emphasis is placed on activities performed; activities orientation is maximized.
   D. Each employee participates in determining his own objectives.

17. The function of management which puts into effect the decisions, plans, and programs that have previously been worked out for achieving the goals of the group is MOST appropriately called 17.____
A. scheduling B. classifying C. budgeting D. directing

18. In the establishment of a plan to improve office productive efficiency, which of the following guidelines is LEAST helpful in setting sound work standards? 18.____
A. Employees must accept the plan's objectives.
B. Current production averages must be promulgated as work standards for a group.
C. The work flow must generally be fairly constant.
D. The operation of the plan must be expressed in terms understandable to the worker.

19. The one of the following activities which, generally speaking, is of *relatively* MAJOR importance at the lower-management level and of *somewhat* LESSER importance at higher-management levels is 19.____
A. actuating B. forecasting C. organizing D. planning

20. Three styles of leadership exist: democratic, authoritarian, and laissez-faire. Of the following work situations, the one in which a democratic approach would normally be the MOST effective is when the work is 20.____
A. routine and moderately complex B. repetitious and simple
C. complex and not routine D. simple and not routine

21. Governmental and business organizations *generally* encounter the GREATEST difficulties in developing tangible measures of which one of the following? 21.____
A. The level of expenditures B. Contributions to social welfare
C. Retention rates D. Causes of labor unrest

22. Of the following, a *management-by-objectives* program is BEST described as 22.____
A. a new comprehensive plan of organization
B. introduction of budgets and financial controls
C. introduction of long-range planning
D. development of future goals with supporting and related progress reviews

23. Research and analysis is probably the most widely used technique for selecting alternatives when major planning decisions are involved. 23.____
Of the following, a VALUABLE characteristic of research and analysis is that this technique
A. places the problem in a meaningful conceptual framework
B. involves practical application of the various alternatives
C. accurately analyzes all important tangibles
D. is much less expensive than other problem-solving methods

24. If a manager were assigned the task of using a systems approach to designing a new work unit, which of the following should he consider FIRST in carrying out his design? 24.____
   A. Networks
   B. Work flows and information processes
   C. Linkages and relationships
   D. Decision points and control loops

25. The MAIN distinction between Theory X and Theory Y approaches to organization, in accordance with Douglas McGregor's view, is that Theory Y 25.____
   A. considers that work is natural to people; Theory X assumes that people are lazy and avoid work
   B. leads to a tall, narrow organization structure, while Theory X leads to one that is flat
   C. organizations motivate people with money; Theory X organizations motivate people with good working conditions
   D. represents authoritarian management, while Theory X management is participative

KEY (CORRECT ANSWERS)

1.	C	11.	B
2.	B	12.	B
3.	D	13.	A
4.	C	14.	C
5.	A	15.	B
6.	A	16.	C
7.	C	17.	D
8.	B	18.	B
9.	A	19.	A
10.	B	20.	C

21.	B
22.	D
23.	A
24.	B
25.	A

TEST 2

DIRECTIONS: Each question or incomplete statement is followed by several suggested answers or completions. Select the one that BEST answers the question or completes the statement. *PRINT THE LETTER OF THE CORRECT ANSWER IN THE SPACE AT THE RIGHT.*

1. Of the following, the stage in decision-making which is usually MOST difficult is 1.____
   A. stating the alternatives
   B. predicting the possible outcome of each alternative
   C. evaluating the relative merits of each alternative
   D. minimizing the undesirable aspects of the alternative selected

2. In a department where a clerk is reporting both to a senior clerk in charge of the mail room and also to a supervising clerk in charge of the duplicating section, there may be a breakdown of the management principle called 2.____
   A. horizontal specialization
   B. job enrichment
   C. unity of command
   D. Graicunas' Law

3. Of the following, the failure by line managers to accept and appreciate the benefits and limitations of a new program or system VERY frequently can be traced to the 3.____
   A. budgetary problems involved
   B. resultant need to reduce staff
   C. lack of controls it engenders
   D. failure of top management to support its implementation

4. Although there is general agreement that *management-by-objectives* has made a major contribution to modern management of large organizations, criticisms of the system during the past few years have resulted in 4.____
   A. mounting pressure for relaxation of management goals
   B. renewed concern with human values and the manager's personal needs
   C. over-mechanistic application of the perceptions of the behavioral scientists
   D. disillusionment with *management-by-objectives* on the part of a majority of managers

5. Of the following, which is usually considered to be a MAJOR obstacle to the systematic analysis of potential problems by managers? 5.____
   A. Managers have a tendency to think that all the implications of some proposed step cannot be fully understood.
   B. Rewards rarely go to those managers who are most successful at resolving current problems in management.
   C. There is a common conviction of manages that their goals are difficult to achieve.
   D. Managers are far more concerned about correcting today's problems than with preventing tomorrow's.

6. Which of the following should generally have the MOST influence on the selection of supervisors? 6.____
   A. Experience within the work unit where the vacancies exist
   B. Amount of money needed to effect the promotion
   C. Personal preferences of the administration
   D. Evaluation of capacity to exercise supervisory responsibilities

7. In questioning a potential administrator for selection purposes, the one of the following practices which is MOST desirable is to 7.____
   A. encourage the job applicant to give primarily *yes* or *no* replies
   B. get the applicant to talk freely and in detail about his background
   C. let the job applicant speak most of the time
   D. probe the applicant's attitudes, motivation, and willingness to accept responsibility

8. In implementing the managerial function of training subordinates, it is USEFUL to know that a widely agreed-upon definition of human learning is that learning 8.____
   A. is a relatively permanent change in behavior that results from reinforced practice or experience
   B. involves an improvement, but not necessarily a change in behavior
   C. involves a change in behavior, but not necessarily an improvement
   D. is a temporary change in behavior which must be subject to practice or experience

9. If a manager were thinking about using a committee of subordinates to solve an operating problem, which of the following would generally NOT be an advantage of such use of the committee approach? 9.____
   A. Improved coordination
   B. Low cost
   C. Increased motivation
   D. Integrated judgment

10. Which one of the following management approaches MOST often uses model-building techniques to solve management problems? 10.____
    _____ approach.
    A. Behavioral
    B. Fiscal
    C. Quantitative
    D. Process

11. Of the following, the MOST serious risk in using budgets as a tool for management control is the 11.____
    A. probable neglect of other good management practices
    B. likelihood of guesswork because of the need to plan far in advance
    C. possibility of undue emphasis on factors that are easiest to measure
    D. danger of making qualitative rather than quantitative assessments of performance

12. In government budgeting, the problem of relating financial transactions to the fiscal year in which they are budgeted is BEST met by 12.____
    A. determining the cash balance by comparing how much money has been received and how much has been paid out
    B. applying net revenue to the fiscal year in which they are collected as offset by relevant expenses

C. adopting a system whereby appropriations are entered when they are received and expenditures are entered when they are paid out
D. entering expenditures on the books when the obligation to make the expenditure is made

13. If the agency's bookkeeping system records income when it is received and expenditures when the money is paid out this system is USUALLY known as a _____ system. 13.____
A. cash
B. flow-payment
C. deferred
D. fiscal year income

14. An audit, as the term applies to budget execution, is MOST NEARLY a 14.____
A. procedure based on the budget estimates
B. control exercised by the executive on the legislature in the establishment of program priorities
C. check on the legality of expenditures and is based on the appropriations act
D. requirement which must be met before funds can be spent

15. In government budgeting, there is a procedure known as *allotment.* 15.____
Of the following statements which relate to allotment, select the one that is MOST generally considered to be correct.
Allotment
A. increases the practice of budget units coming back to the legislature branch for supplemental appropriations
B. is simply an example of red tape
C. eliminates the requirement of timing of expenditures
D. is designed to prevent waste

16. In government budgeting, the establishment of the schedules of allotments is MOST generally the responsibility of the 16.____
A. budget unit and the legislature
B. budget unit and the executive
C. budget unit only
D. executive and the legislature

17. Of the following statements relating to preparation of an organization's budget request, which is the MOST generally valid precaution? 17.____
A. Give specific instructions on the format or budget requests and required supporting data
B. Because of the complexity of preparing a budget request, avoid argumentation to support the requests
C. Put requests in whatever format is desirable
D. Consider that final approval will be given to initial estimates

18. Of the following statements which relate to the budget process in a well-organized government, select the one that is MOST NEARLY correct. 18.____
A. The budget cycle is the step-by-step process which is repeated each and every fiscal year.
B. Securing approval of the budget does not take place within the budget cycle.

C. The development of a new budget and putting it into effect is a two-step process known as the budget cycle.
D. The fiscal period, usually a fiscal year, has no relation to the budget cycle.

19. If a manager were asked what PPBS stands for, he would be RIGHT if he said _____ budgeting system. 19.____
A. public planning
B. planning programming
C. planning projections
D. programming procedures

Questions 20-21.

DIRECTIONS: Questions 20 and 21 are to be answered on the basis of the following information.

Sample Budget

Refuse Collection	Amount
Personal Services	$30,000
Contractual Services	5,000
Supplies and Materials	5,000
Capital Outlay	10,000
	$50,000

Residential Collections	
Dwellings – 1 pickup per week	1,000
Tons of refuse collected per year	375
Cost of collections per ton	$ 8
Cost per dwelling pickup per year	$ 3
Total annual cost	$3,000

20. The sample budget shown is a simplified example of a _____ budget. 20.____
A. factorial
B. performance
C. qualitative
D. rational

21. The budget shown in the sample differs CHIEFLY from line-item and program budgets in that it includes 21.____
A. objects of expenditure but not activities or functions
B. only activities, functions, and control
C. activities and functions but not objects of expenditures
D. levels of service

Question 22.

DIRECTIONS: Question 22 is to be answered on the basis of the following information.

Sample Budget

Environmental Safety		
Air Pollution Protection		
Personal Services	$20,000,000	
Contractual Services	4,000,000	
Supplies and Materials	4,000,000	
Capital Outlay	2,000,000	
Total Air Pollution Protection		$30,000,000
Water Pollution Protection		
Personal Services	$23,000,000	
Supplies and Materials	4,500,000	
Capital Outlay	20,500,000	
Total Water Pollution Protection		$48,000,000
Total Environmental Safety		$78,000,000

22. Based on the above budget, which is the MOST valid statement? 22.____
    A. Environmental Safety, Air Pollution Protection, and Water Pollution Protection could all be considered program elements.
    B. The object listings included water pollution protection and capital outlay.
    C. Examples of the program element listings in the above are personal services and supplies and materials
    D. Contractual Services and Environmental Safety were the program element listings.

23. Which of the following is NOT an advantage of a program budget over a line-item budget? 23.____
    A program budget
    A. allows us to set up priority lists in deciding what activities we will spend our money on
    B. gives us more control over expenditures than a line-item budget
    C. is more informative in that we know the broad purposes of spending money
    D. enables us to see if one program is getting much less money than the others

24. If a manager were trying to explain the fundamental difference between traditional accounting theory and practice and the newer practice of managerial accounting, he would be MOST accurate if he said that 24.____
    A. traditional accounting practice focused on providing information for persons outside organizations, while managerial accounting focuses on providing information for people inside organizations
    B. traditional accounting practice focused on providing information for persons inside organizations while managerial accounting focuses on providing information for persons outside organizations

C. managerial accounting is exclusively concerned with historical facts while traditional accounting stresses future projections exclusively
D. traditional accounting practice is more budget-focused than managerial accounting

25. Which of the following formulas is used to determine the number of days required to process work? 25.____
_____ = Days to Process Work

A. $\frac{\text{Employees x Daily Output}}{\text{Volume}}$
B. $\frac{\text{Volume x Daily Output}}{\text{Volume}}$
C. $\frac{\text{Volume}}{\text{Employees x Daily Output}}$
D. $\frac{\text{Employees x Volume}}{\text{Daily Output}}$

KEY (CORRECT ANSWERS)

1.	C	11.	C
2.	C	12.	D
3.	D	13.	A
4.	B	14.	C
5.	D	15.	D
6.	D	16.	C
7.	D	17.	A
8.	A	18.	A
9.	B	19.	B
10.	C	20.	B

21.	D
22.	A
23.	B
24.	A
25.	C

TEST 3

DIRECTIONS: Each question or incomplete statement is followed by several suggested answers or completions. Select the one that BEST answers the question or completes the statement. *PRINT THE LETTER OF THE CORRECT ANSWER IN THE SPACE AT THE RIGHT.*

1. Electronic data processing equipment can produce more information faster than can be generated by any other means. 1.____
In view of this, the MOST important problem faced by management at present is to
   A. keep computers fully occupied
   B. find enough computer personnel
   C. assimilate and properly evaluate the information
   D. obtain funds to establish appropriate information systems

2. A well-designed management information system ESSENTIALLY provides each executive and manager the information he needs for 2.____
   A. determining computer time requirements
   B. planning and measuring results
   C. drawing a new organization chart
   D. developing a new office layout

3. It is generally agreed that management policies should be periodically reappraised and restated in accordance with current conditions. 3.____
Of the following, the approach which would be MOST effective in determining whether a policy should be revised is to
   A. conduct interviews with staff members at all levels in order to ascertain the relationship between the policy and actual practice
   B. make proposed revisions in the policy and apply it to current problems
   C. make up hypothetical situations using both the old policy and a revised version in order to make comparisons
   D. call a meeting of top level staff in order to discuss ways of revising the policy

4. Every manager has many occasions to lead a conference or participate in a conference of some sort. 4.____
Of the following statements that pertain to conferences and conference leadership, which is generally considered to be MOST valid?
   A. Since World War II, the trend has been toward fewer shared decisions and more conferences.
   B. The most important part of a conference leader's job is to direct discussion.
   C. In providing opportunities for group interaction, management should avoid consideration of its past management philosophy.
   D. A good administrator cannot lead a good conference if he is a poor public speaker.

5. Of the following, it is usually LEAST desirable for a conference leader to 5.____
   A. turn the question to the person who asked it
   B. summarize proceedings periodically
   C. make a practice of not repeating questions
   D. ask a question without indicating who is to reply

6. The behavioral school of management thought bases its beliefs on certain assumptions. 6.____
   Which of the following is NOT a belief of this school of thought?
   A. People tend to seek and accept responsibility.
   B. Most people can be creative in solving problems.
   C. People prefer security above all else.
   D. Commitment is the most important factor in motivating people.

7. The one of the following objectives which would be LEAST appropriate as a major goal of research in the field of human resources management is to 7.____
   A. predict future conditions, events, and manpower needs
   B. evaluate established policies, programs, and practices
   C. evaluate proposed policies, programs, and practices
   D. identify deficient organizational units and apply suitable penalties

8. Of the following general interviewing methods or techniques, the one that is USUALLY considered to be effective in counseling, grievances, and appraisal interviews is the _____ interview. 8.____
   A. directed B. non-directed C. panel D. patterned

9. The ESSENTIAL first phase of decision-making is 9.____
   A. finding alternative solutions
   B. making a diagnosis of the problem
   C. selecting the plan to follow
   D. analyzing and comparing alternative solutions

10. Assume that, in a certain organization, a situation has developed in which there is little difference in status or authority between individuals. 10.____
    Which of the following would be the MOST likely result with regard to communication in this organization?
    A. Both the accuracy and flow of communication will be improved.
    B. Both the accuracy and flow of communication will substantially decrease.
    C. Employees will seek more formal lines of communication.
    D. Neither the flow nor the accuracy of communication will be improved over the former hierarchical structure.

11. The main function of many agency administrative offices is *information management.* Information that is received by an administrative officer may be classified as active or passive, depending upon whether or not it requires the recipient to take some action. 11.____

Of the following, the item received which is clearly the MOST active information is
A. an appointment of a new staff member
B. a payment voucher for a new desk
C. a press release concerning a past city event
D. the minutes of a staff meeting

12. Which one of the following sets BEST describes the general order in which to teach an operation to a new employee? 12.____
A. Prepare, present, tryout, follow-up
B. Prepare, test, tryout, re-test
C. Present, test, tryout, follow-up
D. Test, present, follow-up, re-test

13. Of the following, public employees may be separated from public service 13.____
A. for the same reasons which are generally acceptable for discharging employees in private industry
B. only under the most trying circumstances
C. under procedures that are neither formalized nor subject to review
D. solely in extreme cases involving offenses of gravest character

14. Of the following, the one LEAST considered to be a communication barrier is 14.____
A. group feedback
B. charged words
C. selective perception
D. symbolic meanings

15. Of the following ways for a manager to handle his appointments, the BEST way, according to experts in administration, generally is to 15.____
A. schedule his own appointments and inform his secretary not to reserve his time without his approval
B. encourage everyone to make appointments through his secretary and tell her when he makes his own appointments
C. see no one who has not made a previous appointment
D. permit anyone to see him without an appointment

16. Assume that a manager decides to examine closely one of five units under his supervision to uncover problems common to all five. 16.____
His research technique is MOST closely related to the method called
A. experimentation
B. simulation
C. linear analysis
D. sampling

17. If one views the process of management as a dynamic process, which one of the following functions is NOT a legitimate part of that process? 17.____
A. Communication
B. Decision-making
C. Organizational slack
D. Motivation

18. Which of the following would be the BEST statement of a budget-oriented purpose for a government administrator? To 18.____
   A. provide 200 hours of instruction in basic reading for 3,500 adult illiterates at a cost of $1 million in the next fiscal year
   B. inform the public of adult educational programs
   C. facilitate the transfer to a city agency of certain functions of a federally-funded program which is being phased out
   D. improve the reading skills of the adult citizens in the city

19. Modern management philosophy and practices are changing to accommodate the expectations and motivations of organization personnel. 19.____
Which of the following terms INCORRECTLY describes these newer managerial approaches?
   A. Rational management
   B. Participative management
   C. Decentralization
   D. Democratic supervision

20. Management studies support the hypothesis that, in spite of the tendency of employees to censor the information communicated to their supervisor, subordinates are MORE likely to communicate problem-oriented information upward when they have 20.____
   A. a long period of service in the organization
   B. a high degree of trust in the supervisor
   C. a high educational level
   D. low status on the organizational ladder

KEY (CORRECT ANSWERS)

1.	C	11.	A
2.	B	12.	A
3.	A	13.	A
4.	B	14.	A
5.	A	15.	B
6.	C	16.	D
7.	D	17.	C
8.	B	18.	A
9.	B	19.	A
10.	D	20.	B

EXAMINATION SECTION

TEST 1

DIRECTIONS: Each question or incomplete statement is followed by several suggested answers or completions. Select the one that BEST answers the question or completes the statement. *PRINT THE LETTER OF THE CORRECT ANSWER IN THE SPACE AT THE RIGHT.*

1. A management approach widely used today is based on the belief that decisions should be made and actions should be taken by managers closest to the organization's problems. 1.____
This style of management is MOST appropriately called _____ management.
   A. scientific
   B. means-end
   C. decentralized
   D. internal process

2. As contrasted with tall organization structures with narrow spans of control, flat organization structures with wide spans of control MOST usually provide 2.____
   A. fast communication and information flows
   B. more levels in the organizational hierarchy
   C. fewer workers reporting to supervisors
   D. lower motivation because of tighter control standards

3. Use of the systems approach is MOST likely to lead to 3.____
   A. consideration of the impact on the whole organization of actions taken in any part of that organization
   B. the placing of restrictions on departmental activity
   C. use of mathematical models to suboptimize production
   D. consideration of the activities of each unit of an organization as a totality without regard to the remainder of the organization

4. An administrator, with overall responsibility for all administrative operations in a large operating agency, is considering organizing the agency's personnel office around either of the following two alternative concepts: 4.____
Alternative I: A corps of specialists for each branch of personnel subject matter, whose skills, counsel, or work products are coordinated only by the agency personnel officer
Alternative II: A crew of so-called *personnel generalists*, who individually work with particular segments of the organization but deal with all subspecialties of the personnel function
The one of the following which MOST tends to be a DRAWBACK of Alternative I, as compared with Alternative II, is that
   A. training and employee relations work call for education, interests, and talents that differ from those required for classification and compensation work
   B. personnel office staff may develop only superficial familiarity with the specialized areas to which they have been assigned

C. supervisors may fail to get continuing overall personnel advice on an integrated basis
D. the personnel specialists are likely to become so interested in and identified with the operating view as to particular cases that they lose their professional objectivity and become merely advocates of what some supervisor wants

5. The matrix summary or decision matrix is a useful tool for making choices. Its effectiveness is MOST dependent upon the user's ability to 5.____
A. write a computer program (Fortran or Cobol)
B. assign weights representing the relative importance of the objectives
C. solve a set of two equations with two unknowns
D. work with matrix algebra

6. An organizational form which is set up only on an *ad hoc* basis to meet specific goals is said PRIMARILY to use 6.____
A. clean break departmentation
B. matrix or task force organization
C. scalar specialization
D. geographic or area-wide decentralization

7. The concept of job enlargement would LEAST properly be implemented by 7.____
A. permitting workers to follow through on tasks or projects from start to finish
B. delegating the maximum authority possible for decision-making to lower levels in the hierarchy
C. maximizing the number of professional classes in the classification plan
D. training employees to grow beyond whatever tasks they have been performing

8. As used in the area of admission, the principle of *unity of command* MOST specifically means that 8.____
A. an individual should report to only one superior for any single activity
B. individuals make better decisions than do committees
C. in large organizations, chains of command are normally too long
D. an individual should not supervise over five subordinates

9. The method of operations research, statistical decision-making, and linear programming have been referred to as the tool kit of the manager. Utilization of these tools is LEAST useful in the performance of which of the following functions? 9.____
A. Elimination of the need for using judgment when making decisions
B. Facilitation of decision-making without the need for sub-optimization
C. Quantifying problems for management study
D. Research and analysis of management operations

10. When acting in their respective managerial capacities, the chief executive officer and the office supervisor both perform the fundamental functions of management. 10.____
Of the following differences between the two, the one which is generally considered to be the LEAST significant is the
   A. breadth of the objectives
   B. complexity of measuring actual efficiency of performance
   C. number of decisions made
   D. organizational relationships affected by actions taken

11. The ability of operations researchers to solve complicated problems rests on their use of models. 11.____
These models can BEST be described as
   A. mathematical statements of the problem
   B. physical constructs that simulate a work layout
   C. toy-like representations of employees in work environments
   D. role-playing simulations

12. Of the following, it is MOST likely to be proper for the agency head to allow the agency personnel officer to make final selection of appointees from certified eligible lists where there are 12.____
   A. *small* numbers of employees to be hired in newly-developed professional fields
   B. *large* numbers of persons to be hired for key managerial positions
   C. *large* numbers of persons to be hired in very routine occupations where the individual discretion of operating officials is not vital
   D. *small* numbers of persons to be hired in highly specialized professional occupations which are vital to the agency's operations

13. Of the following, an operating agency personnel office is LEAST likely to be able to exert strong influence or control within the operating agency by 13.____
   A. interpreting to the operating agency head what is intended by the directives and rules emanating from the central personnel agency
   B. establishing the key objectives of those line divisions of the operating agency employing large numbers of staff and operating under the management-by-objectives approach
   C. formulating and proposing to the agency head the internal policies and procedures on personnel matters required within the operating agency
   D. exercising certain discretionary authority in the application of the agency head's general personnel policies to actual specific situations

14. PERT is a recently developed system used PRIMARILY to 14.____
   A. evaluate the quality of applicants' background
   B. analyze and control the timing aspects of a major project
   C. control the total expenditure of agency funds within a monthly or quarterly time period
   D. analyze and control the differential effect on costs of purchasing different quantities

15. Assume that an operating agency has among its vacant positions two positions, each of which encompasses mixed duties. Both require appointees to have considerable education and experience, but these requirements are essential only for the more difficult duties of these positions. In the place of these positions, an administrator creates two new positions, one in which the higher duties are concentrated and the other with the lesser functions requiring only minimum preparation. 15.____
Of the following, it is generally MOST appropriate to characterize the administrator's action as a(n)
   A. *undesirable* example of deliberate downgrading of standards and requirements
   B. *undesirable* manipulation of the classification system for non-merit purposes
   C. *desirable* broadening of the definition of a class of positions
   D. *desirable* example of job redesign

16. Of the following, the LEAST important stumbling block to the development of personnel mobility among governmental jurisdictions is the 16.____
   A. limitations on lateral entry above junior levels in many jurisdictions
   B. continued collection of filing fees for civil service tests by many governmental jurisdictions
   C. absence of reciprocal exchange of retirement benefit eligibility between governments
   D. disparities in salary scales between governments

17. Of the following, the MAJOR disadvantage of a personnel system that features the *selection out* (forced retirement) of those who have been passed over a number of times for promotion is that such a system 17.____
   A. wastes manpower which is perfectly competent at one level but unable to rise above that level
   B. wastes funds by requiring review boards
   C. leads to excessive recruiting of newcomers from outside the system
   D. may not be utilized in *closed* career systems with low maximum age limits for entrance

18. Of the following, the fields in which operating agency personnel offices generally exercise the MOST stringent controls over first line supervisors in the agency are 18.____
   A. methods analysis and work simplification
   B. selection and position classification
   C. vestibule training and Gantt chart
   D. suggestion systems and staff development

19. Of the following, computers are normally MOST effective in handling 19.____
   A. large masses of data requiring simple processing
   B. small amounts of data requiring constantly changing complex processing
   C. data for which reported values are often subject to inaccuracies
   D. large amounts of data requiring continual programming and reprocessing

20. Contingency planning, which has long been used by the military and is assuming increasing importance in other organizations, may BEST be described as a process which utilizes 20.____
A. alternative plans based on varying assumptions
B. *crash programs* by organizations departmentalized along process lines
C. plans which mandate substitution of equipment for manpower at predetermined operational levels
D. plans that individually and accurately predict future events

21. In the management of inventory, two kinds of costs normally determine when to order and in what amounts. 21.____
The one of the following choices which includes BOTH of these kinds of costs is _____ costs and _____ costs.
A. carrying; storage
B. personnel; order
C. computer; order
D. personnel; computer

22. At top management levels, the one of the following which is generally the MOST important executive skill is skill in 22.____
A. budgeting procedures
B. a technical discipline
C. controlling actions in accordance with previously approved plans
D. seeing the organization as a whole

23. Of the following, the BEST way to facilitate the successful operation of a committee is to set guidelines establishing its 23.____
A. budget exclusive of personnel costs
B. location
C. schedule of meetings or conferences
D. scope of purpose

24. Executive training programs that single out particular managers and groom them for promotion create the so-called organizational *crown princes*. 24.____
Of the following, the MOST serious problem that arises in connection with this practice is that
A. the managers chosen for promotion seldom turn out to be the best managers since the future potential of persons cannot be predicted
B. not enough effort is made to remove organizational obstacles in the way of their development and achievement
C. the resentment of the managers not selected for the program has an adverse effect on the motivation of those managers not selected
D. performance appraisal and review are not carried out systematically enough

25. Of the following, the LEAST likely result of the use of the concept of job enlargement is that 25.____
A. coordination will be simplified
B. the individual's job will become less challenging
C. worker satisfaction will increase
D. fewer people will have to give attention to each piece of work

KEY (CORRECT ANSWERS)

1. C
2. A
3. A
4. C
5. B

6. B
7. C
8. A
9. A
10. C

11. A
12. C
13. B
14. B
15. D

16. B
17. A
18. B
19. A
20. A

21. A
22. D
23. D
24. C
25. B

TEST 2

DIRECTIONS: Each question or incomplete statement is followed by several suggested answers or completions. Select the one that BEST answers the question or completes the statement. *PRINT THE LETTER OF THE CORRECT ANSWER IN THE SPACE AT THE RIGHT.*

1. The one of the following which is MOST likely to be emphasized in the use of the brainstorming technique is the 1.____
   A. early consideration of cost factors of all ideas which may be suggested
   B. avoidance of impractical suggestions
   C. separation of the generation of ideas from their evaluation
   D. appraisal of suggestions concurrently with their initial presentation

2. Of the following, the BEST method for assessing managerial performance is generally to 2.____
   A. compare the manager's accomplishments against clear, specific, agreed-upon goals
   B. compare the manager's traits with those of his peers on a predetermined objective
   C. measure the manager's behavior against a listing of itemized personal traits
   D. measure the manager's success according to the enumeration of the *satisfaction* principle

3. As compared with recruitment from outside, selection from within the service must generally show GREATER concern for the 3.____
   A. prestige in which the public service as a whole is held by the public
   B. morale of the candidate group compromising the recruitment field
   C. cost of examining per candidate
   D. benefits of the use of standardized and validated tests

4. Performance budgeting focuses PRIMARY attention upon which one of the following? The 4.____
   A. things to be acquired, such as supplies and equipment
   B. general character and relative importance of the work to be done or the service to be rendered
   C. list of personnel to be employed, by specific title
   D. separation of employee performance evaluations from employee compensation

5. Of the following, the FIRST step in the installation and operation of a performance budgeting system generally should be the 5.____
   A. identification of program costs in relationship to the accounting system and operating structure
   B. identification of the specific end results of past programs in other jurisdictions

C. identification of work programs that are meaningful for management purposes
D. establishment of organizational structures each containing only one work program

6. Of the following, the MOST important purpose of a system of quarterly allotments of appropriated funds generally is to enable the 6.____
A. head of the judicial branch to determine the legality of agency requests for budget increases
B. operating agencies of government to upgrade the quality of their services without increasing costs
C. head of the executive branch to control the rate at which the operating agencies obligate and expend funds
D. operating agencies of government to avoid payment for services which have not been properly rendered by employees

7. In the preparation of the agency's budget, the agency's central budget office has two responsibilities: program review and management improvement. Which one of the following questions concerning an operating agency's program is MOST closely related to the agency budget officer's program review responsibility? 7.____
A. Can expenditures for supplies, materials, or equipment be reduced?
B. Will improved work methods contribute to a more effective program?
C. What is the relative importance of this program as compared to a higher level of program performance?
D. Will a realignment of responsibilities contribute to a higher level of program performance?

8. Of the following, the method of evaluating relative rates of return normally and generally thought to be MOST useful in evaluating government operations is _____ analysis. 8.____
A. cost-benefit
B. budget variance
C. investment capital
D. budget planning program

9. The one of the following assumptions that is LEAST likely to be made by a democratic or permissive type of leader is that 9.____
A. commitment to goals is seldom a result of monetary rewards alone
B. people can learn not only to accept, but also to seek, responsibility
C. the average person prefers security over advancement
D. creativity may be found in most segments of the population

10. In attempting to motivate subordinates, a manager should PRINCIPALLY be aware of the fact that 10.____
A. the psychological qualities of people, in general, are easily predictable
B. fear, as a traditional form of motivation, has lost much of its former power to motivate people in our modern industrial society
C. fear is still the most potent force in motivating the behavior of subordinates in the public service
D. the worker has very little control over the quality and quantity of his output

11. Assume that the following figures represent the number of work-unit that were produced during a week by each of sixteen employees in a division: 11.____

12	16	13	18
21	12	16	13
16	13	17	21
13	15	18	20

If all of the employees of the division who produced thirteen work-units during the week had instead produced fifteen work-units during that same week, then for that week the
   A. mean, median, and mode would all change
   B. mean and mode would change, but the median would remain the same
   C. mode and median would change, but the mean would remain the same
   D. mode, mean, and median would all still remain unchanged in value

12. An important law in motivation theory is called the *law of effect.* This law says that behavior which satisfies a person's needs tends to be repeated; behavior which does not satisfy a person's needs tends to be eliminated. 12.____
The one of the following which is the BEST interpretation of this law is that
   A. productivity depends on personality traits
   B. diversity of goals leads to instability and motivation
   C. the greater the satisfaction, the more likely it is that the behavior will be reinforced
   D. extrinsic satisfaction is more important than intrinsic reward

13. Of the following, the MOST acceptable reason an administrator can give for taking advice from other employees in the organization only when he asks for it is that he wants to 13.____
   A. encourage creativity and high morale
   B. keep dysfunctional pressures and inconsistent recommendations to a minimum
   C. show his superiors and peers who is in charge
   D. show his subordinates who is in charge

14. A complete picture of the communication channels in an organization can BEST be revealed by 14.____
   A. observing the planned paperwork system
   B. recording the highly intermittent patterns of communication
   C. plotting the entire flow of information over a period of time
   D. monitoring the *grapevine*

Questions 15-16.

DIRECTIONS: Questions 15 and 16 are to be answered SOLELY on the basis of the following passage.

Management by objectives (MBO) may be defined as the process by which the superior and the subordinate managers of an organization jointly define its common goals, define each individual's major areas of responsibility in terms of the results expected of him and use these measures as guides for operating the unit and assessing the contribution of each of its members.

The MBO approach requires that after organizational goals are established and communicated, targets must be set for each individual position which are congruent with organizational goals. Periodic performance reviews and a final review using the objectives set as criteria are also basic to this approach.

Recent studies have shown that MBO programs are influenced by attitudes and perceptions of the boss, the company, the reward-punishment system, and the program itself. In addition, the manner in which the MBO program is carried out can influence the success of the program. A study done in the late sixties indicates that the best results are obtained when the manager sets goals which deal with significant problem areas in the organizational unit, or with the subordinate's personal deficiencies. These goals must be clear with regard to what is expected of the subordinate. The frequency of feedback is also important in the success of a management-by-objectives program. Generally, the greater the amount of feedback, the more successful the MBO program.

15. According to the above passage, the expected output for individual employees should be determined 15.____
   A. after a number of reviews of work performance
   B. after common organizational goals are defined
   C. before common organizational goals are defined
   D. on the basis of an employee's personal qualities

16. According to the above passage, the management-by-objectives approach requires 16.____
   A. less feedback than other types of management programs
   B. little review of on-the-job performance after the initial setting of goals
   C. general conformance between individual goals and organizational goals
   D. the setting of goals which deal with minor problem area in the organization

Questions 17-19.

DIRECTIONS: Questions 17 through 19 are to be answered SOLELY on the basis of the following passage.

During the last decade, a great deal of interest has been generated around the phenomenon of organizational development, or the process of developing human resources through conscious organization effort. Organizational development (OD) stresses improving interpersonal relationships and organizational skills, such as communication, to a much greater degree than individual training ever did.

The kind of training that an organization should emphasize depends upon the present and future structure of the organization. If future organizations are to be unstable, shifting coalitions, then individual skills and abilities, particularly those emphasizing innovativeness, creativity, flexibility, and the latest technological knowledge, are crucial, and individual training is most appropriate.

But if there is to be little change in organizational structure, then the main thrust of training should be group-oriented or organizational development. This approach seems better designed for overcoming hierarchical barriers, for developing a degree of interpersonal relationships which make communication along the chain of command possible, and for retaining a modicum of innovation and/or flexibility.

17. According to the above passage, group-oriented training is MOST useful in 17.____
    A. developing a communications system that will facilitate understanding through the chain of command
    B. highly flexible and mobile organizations
    C. preventing the crossing of hierarchical barriers within an organization
    D. saving energy otherwise wasted on developing methods of dealing with rigid hierarchies

18. The one of the following conclusions which can be drawn MOST appropriately from the above passage is that 18.____
    A. behavioral research supports the use of organizational development training method rather than individualized training
    B. it is easier to provide individualized training in specific skills than to set up sensitivity training programs
    C. organizational development eliminates innovative or flexible activity
    D. the nature of an organization greatly influences which training methods will be most effective

19. According to the above passage, the one of the following which is LEAST important for large-scale organizations geared to rapid and abrupt change is 19.____
    A. current technological information
    B. development of a high degree of interpersonal relationships
    C. development of individual skills and abilities
    D. emphasis on creativity

Questions 20-25.

DIRECTIONS: Each of Questions 20 through 25 consist of a statement which contains one word that is incorrectly used because it is not in keeping with the meaning that the quotation is evidently intended to convey. Determine which word is INCORRECTLY used. Select from the choices lettered A, B, C, and D the word which, when substituted for the incorrectly used word, would BEST help to convey the meaning of the statement.

20. One of the considerations likely to affect the currency of classification, particularly in professional and managerial occupations, is the impact of the incumbent's capacities on the job. Some work is highly susceptible to change as the result of the special talents or interests of the classifier. Organization should never be so rigid as not to capitalize on the innovative or unusual proclivities of its key employees. While a machine operator may not be able, even subtly, to change the character or level of his job, the design engineer, the attorney, or the organization and methods analyst might readily do so. Reliance on his judgment and the scope of his assignments may both grow as the result of his skill, insight, and capacity. 20.____
   A. unlikely B. incumbent C. directly D. scope

21. The supply of services by the state is not governed by market price. The aim is to supply such services to all who need them and to treat all consumers equally. This objective especially compels the civil servant to maintain a role f strict impartiality, based on the principle of equality of individual citizens vis-à-vis their government. However, there is a clear difference between being neutral and impartial. If the requirement is construed to mean that all civil servants should be political eunuchs, devoid of the drive and motivation essential to dynamic administration, then the concept of impartiality is being seriously utilized. Modern governments should not be stopped from demanding that their hirelings have not only the technical but the emotional qualifications necessary for whole-hearted effort. 21.____
   A. determined B. rule C. stable D. misapplied

22. The manager was barely listening. Recently, at the divisional level, several new fronts of troubles had erupted, including a requirement to increase production yet hold down operating costs and somehow raise quality standards. Though the three objectives were basically obsolete, top departmental management was insisting on the simultaneous attainment of them, an insistence not helping the manager's ulcer, an old enemy within. Thus, the manager could not find time for interest in individuals—only in statistics which regiment of individuals, like unconsidered Army privates, added up to. 22.____
   A. quantity B. battalion C. incompatible D. quiet

23. When a large volume of data flows directly between operators and first-line supervisors, senior executives tend to be out of the mainstream of work. Summary reports can increase their remoteness. An executive needs to know the volume, quality, and cost of completed work, and exceptional problems. In addition, he may desire information on key operating conditions. Summary reports on these matters are, therefore, essential features of a communications network and make delegation without loss of control possible. 23.____
   A. unimportant B. quantity C. offset D. incomplete

24. Of major significance in management is harmony between the overall objectives of the organization and the managerial objectives within that organization. In addition, harmony among goals of managers is impossible; they should not be at cross-purposes. Each manager's goal should supplement and assist the goals of his colleagues. Likewise, the objectives of individuals or non-management members should be harmonized with those of the manager. When this is accomplished, genuine teamwork is the result, and human relations are aided materially. The integration of managers' and individuals' goals aids in achieving greater work satisfaction at all levels. 24.____
    A. competition B. dominate C. incremental D. vital

25. Change constantly challenges the manager. Some of this change is evolutionary, some revolutionary, some recognizable, some non-recognizable. Both forces within an enterprise and forces outside the enterprise cause managers to act and react in initiating changes in their immediate working environment. Change invalidates existing operations. Goals are not being accomplished in the best manner, problems develop, and frequently because of the lack of time, only patched-up solutions are followed. The result is that the mode of management is profound in nature and temporary in effectiveness. A complete overhaul of managerial operations should take place. It appears quite likely that we are just beginning to see the real effects of change in our society; the pace probably will accelerate in ways that few really understand or know how to handle. 25.____
    A. confirms B. decline C. instituting D. superficial

KEY (CORRECT ANSWERS)

1. C
2. A
3. B
4. B
5. C

6. C
7. C
8. A
9. C
10. B

11. B
12. C
13. B
14. C
15. B

16. C
17. A
18. D
19. B
20. B

21. D
22. C
23. C
24. D
25. D

EXAMINATION SECTION
TEST 1

DIRECTIONS: Each question or incomplete statement is followed by several suggested answers or completions. Select the one that BEST answers the question or completes the statement. *PRINT THE LETTER OF THE CORRECT ANSWER IN THE SPACE AT THE RIGHT.*

1. You are assigned to form a new unit to compile data which is to facilitate an executive in decision-making. 1.____
In planning the organization of this unit, the question to be answered FIRST is:

   A. What interpretations are likely to be made of the data by the executive in making a decision?
   B. At what point in the decision-making process will the data be most usefully introduced?
   C. What type of data is needed by the executive in his area of decision-making?
   D. What criteria will the executive use to evaluate the data?

2. The extent of effective decentralization within an organization is INVERSELY related to the 2.____

   A. size of the organization
   B. availability of sufficient competent personnel
   C. physical dispersion of the organization's activities
   D. effectiveness of communication within the organization

3. *The tasks of coordination, supervision, and control are likely to become more complicated as the specialization of an organization increases.* 3.____
This statement is GENERALLY

   A. *false;* better performance of these tasks is likely to follow from the detailed attention given to particular problems
   B. *false;* the proportion of specialized personnel is small in proportion to total personnel
   C. *true;* the increased interrelationships arising from increased specialization are sources of potential friction
   D. *true;* the specialist tends to resent direction from superiors who are not specialists

4. The distinctive feature between a method and a procedure may BEST be illustrated by a 4.____

   A. series of procedures comprising a method
   B. series of related methods performed usually by one person constituting a procedure
   C. procedure comprised of a series of related methods
   D. procedure encompassing a range more limited than that of a method

5. As part of your duties to analyze operating practices, you make a tour of a unit during which you talk to the employees about work methods, problems, and other pertinent topics. Such informal data gathering is often incomplete or inaccurate. At a later meeting with the unit supervisor, you question him about the information you have gathered, but he is unable to answer the questions immediately. He asks to accompany you on another tour of his unit and answer the questions on the spot. Explaining that employees will be reluctant to speak up in the presence of a supervisor, you refuse. 5.___
The situation you have created may BEST be described as a violation of the principle of organization called

A. delegation of authority
B. specialization of work
C. span of control
D. unity of command

6. A person desiring greater status and income in municipal government must, with few exceptions, move into the supervisory ranks. When he does, he will encounter certain changes in attitudes and relationships to which he must make satisfactory adjustments. His rise will create a degree of hostility and natural jealousy among his colleagues who have not tried to improve their situation or who have tried and failed. In a sense, too, he is forced upon the group he will supervise because under normal civil service practice, the group has little to say in his appointment. 6.___
A subtle change takes place also in his social situation; he must be in contact with his subordinates but he cannot be part of them, otherwise he yields a basic obligation to management, of which he is a part.
The MOST important conclusion to be made from this statement is that

A. a manager should limit his contacts with subordinates to a minimum
B. he must plan to advance himself further
C. he should isolate himself from the work of the supervised group
D. he must subordinate personnel popularity to the interest of the organization

7. A budget that itemizes expenditure estimates by detailing materials to be purchased, equipment to be maintained, salaries to be paid, etcetera, is known as a ______ budget. 7.___

A. performance
B. capital
C. line-item
D. program

8. Organizational activities for which there are no allocated funds available are financed from the ______ funds. 8.___

A. special revenue
B. sinking
C. general
D. special assessment

9. One of the real revolutions in public administration during the last half-century is the growth in importance of the budget as a planning and control instrument. Several trends account for this growing importance. Which of the following is NOT one of these trends? 9.___

A. Rapid growth of the urban population
B. The cheapening of the dollar
C. The improved standards of living
D. Full employment

10. The position classifying bureau of the personnel agency is normally NOT responsible for 10.____

A. allocating individuals to classes
B. assigning titles to classes of positions
C. establishing minimum qualifications for positions
D. determining which positions are necessary

11. Which of the following statements concerning a job analysis for position classification is FALSE? 11.____

A. It is a study of the person who is to occupy the job.
B. Time and motion studies may be used.
C. It may be used in establishing rates of compensation.
D. It is often done by staff authority.

12. Which of the following is considered to be an ESSENTIAL element of classifying a position? 12.____

A. Number of positions similar to the one being classified
B. Determination of salary to be paid for position
C. Comparison of the position with similar and related positions
D. Evaluation of the skills demanded by the position

13. The LEAST important objective of devising a service rating system is 13.____

A. validating selection procedures
B. improving quality of supervision
C. encouraging the development of employee performance
D. furnishing the basis of formulating a position classification plan

Questions 14-15.

DIRECTIONS: Questions 14 and 15 are to be answered in accordance with the following statement.

The process of validating a factual proposition is quite distinct from the process of validating a value judgment. The former is validated by its agreement with the facts, the latter by human authority.

14. According to the above statement, the one of the following methods which is MOST acceptable for determining whether or not a proposition is factually correct is to 14.____

A. prove that a related proposition is factually correct
B. derive it logically from accepted assumptions
C. show that it will lead to desired results
D. compare it with experience

15. Assuming that the above statement is correct, the theory that the correctness of all ethical propositions can be tested empirically is 15.____

A. *correct;* testing empirically is validating by agreement with facts
B. *incorrect;* ethical propositions are value judgments
C. *correct;* ethical propositions are based on rational hypotheses
D. *incorrect;* a factual proposition is validated by its agreement with facts

16. The rejection of the theory of inverse probability was, for a time, wrongly taken to imply that we cannot draw, from knowledge of a sample, inferences respecting the corresponding population. Such a view would entirely deny validity to all experimental science. According to the above statement, 16.___

A. the theory of inverse probability cannot be applied to an entire population
B. making deductions from a sample is consistent with experimental science
C. making deductions from a sample is inconsistent with experimental science
D. the theory of Inverse probability is based on the study of samples

17. May I point out that if technical employees are given assignments only in their special fields, there will be an immediate gain in conserving special skills. And, if we are to make optimum use of the abilities of the technical employees, it is necessary that these skills be conserved. 17.___
Assuming that this analysis is correct, it follows that

A. if we are not making optimum use of the abilities of technical employees, we have been giving technical employees assignments outside of their special fields
B. we are making optimum use of the abilities of technical employees if we conserve special skills
C. we are making optimum use of the abilities of technical employees if we give them assignments only in their special fields
D. we are not making optimum use of the abilities of technical employees if we give them assignments outside of their special fields

18. *It is less costly to replace old equipment than to repair it.* 18.___
Which of the following statements tends to prove this hypothesis MOST conclusively?

A. The repair of old equipment is frequently as costly as the purchase of new equipment.
B. Continuance in service of old equipment is at least as costly as its replacement by new equipment.
C. The replacement of old equipment is more desirable than its repair.
D. The cost for repairing old equipment is not a one-time cost, while the cost of new equipment is a one-time cost.

19. *An increasing birth rate will be followed by an increased school registration.* 19.___
On the basis of this statement *only,* it would be MOST accurate to state that

A. school registration does not change during a period with a level birth rate
B. an increasing school registration is preceded by a period with an increasing birth rate
C. a period with an increasing birth rate is sometimes followed by a decreasing school registration
D. a period with a decreasing birth rate is sometimes followed by a decreasing school registration

20. It is generally agreed that the *face-to-face* method of communicating is the most effective from a supervisor's standpoint. 20.____
This is true PRIMARILY because

A. the attitude of the recipient can be accurately appraised
B. it provides a two-way channel of expression which results in clarification of ideas
C. it is illustrative of the extremely desirable supervisory technique known as the *democratic approach*
D. it brings the supervisor closer to the actual level of operation

Questions 21-25.

DIRECTIONS: Questions 21 through 25 contain incorrectly used words which change the meaning of the statement. Identify the word in the statement that is incorrect and select the choice that would make the sentence correct.

21. Lack of employee input in the case of training often exists, but is frequently dealt with in evaluation of the training effort. Failure to deal with as important a factor as this can be ruinous to the training effort. 21.____

A. Seldom B. Margin C. Ancillary D. Contributory

22. It is a fallacy that policies generated at the top of the hierarchy are often not acceptable to those on the lower levels, particularly in the case of blue-collar workers among whom the rewards and sanctions of the union or members of the immediate social group are more impelling than the rewards or sanctions available to management. 22.____

A. Parologism B. Truism
C. Commands D. Undetermined

23. Basically, an organization develops when employees in it have rather free control over their behavior within the organization, when the philosophy of the organization is that maximum interpersonal interplay through a minimum number of hierarchical levels is desirable, and when a person traditionally called a *trainer* performs an integrating function. 23.____

A. Instinctively B. Total
C. Flat D. Strong

24. In gaining cooperation in human relations, the one who would influence must often foster his own ego and fertilize and feed that of the one who is to be influenced. 24.____

A. Lassitude B. Emulate C. Suppress D. Implant

25. In the United States, in general, we have been criticized for our emphasis upon physical, materialistic, and economic goals. These are still important, but the trends point toward the more complex, or appreciation of the beautiful, as for example in the architecture of our new factories and colors in the workplaces. 25.____

A. Ephemeral B. Concrete C. Prosaic D. Aesthetic

KEY (CORRECT ANSWERS)

1. C
2. D
3. C
4. C
5. D

6. D
7. C
8. C
9. D
10. D

11. A
12. C
13. D
14. D
15. B

16. B
17. D
18. B
19. B
20. B

21. A
22. B
23. D
24. C
25. D

TEST 2

DIRECTIONS: Each question or incomplete statement is followed by several suggested answers or completions. Select the one that BEST answers the question or completes the statement. *PRINT THE LETTER OF THE CORRECT ANSWER IN THE SPACE AT THE RIGHT.*

1. In the communications process, a formal communication should contain a multiplicity of ideas and several related objectives in order to provide for time-saving economy and to enhance the prospects of eventual compliance by subordinates. 1.____
   This statement is GENERALLY

   A. *true,* since it reduces to a minimum the need for issuance of frequent communications from policy-making levels
   B. *false,* since the number of ideas and objectives contained in a single communication operates in inverse ratio to the degree of compliance
   C. *true,* since continuity and cohesiveness of plans are developed by infrequent but elaborate formal communications
   D. *false,* since time-saving devices are not the concern of superiors engaged in developing an effective communications process

2. Experts in supervisory practices have been emphasizing the importance of the art of listening on the part of supervisors. A recently published text devotes over three hundred pages to a discussion on how managers and supervisors can improve their ability to listen. 2.____
   Which one of the following is NOT considered an important rule to follow in developing the skill of listening?

   A. Be attentive and concentrate on what is being said.
   B. Concentrate on the spoken word without concern for implied meanings.
   C. Ask an occasional question when appropriate to the discussion.
   D. Make sure you understand fully what is being said.

3. A supervisor who is to direct a team of senior clerks and clerks in a complex project calls them together beforehand to inform them of the tasks each employee will perform on this job. 3.____
   Of the following, the CHIEF value of this action by the supervisor is that each member of this team will be able to

   A. work independently in the absence of the supervisor
   B. understand what he will do and how this will fit into the total picture
   C. share in the process of decision-making as an equal participant
   D. judge how well the plans for this assignment have been made

4. A supervisor who has both younger and older employees under his supervision may sometimes find that employee absenteeism seriously interferes with accomplishment of goals. 4.____
   Studies of such employee absenteeism have shown that the absences of employees

   A. under 35 years of age are usually unexpected and the absences of employees over 45 years are usually unnecessary
   B. of all age groups show the same characteristics as to length of absence

C. under 35 years of age are for frequent, short periods while the absences of employees over 45 years of age are less frequent but of longer duration
D. under 35 years of age are for periods of long duration and the absences of employees over 45 years of age are for periods of short duration

5. A long-standing procedure for getting a certain job done by subordinates is apparently a good procedure. Changes in some steps of the procedure are made from time to time to handle special problems that come up. 5.____
Reviewing this procedure periodically is *desirable* MAINLY because

A. the system is working well
B. checking routines periodically is a supervisor"s chief responsibility
C. subordinates may be confused as to how the procedure operates as a result of the changes made
D. it is necessary to determine whether the procedure has become outdated or is in need of improvement

6. In conducting an interview, the BEST type of questions with which to begin the interview are those which the person interviewed is ______ to answer. 6.____

A. willing and able
B. willing but unable
C. able to, but unwilling
D. unable and unwilling

7. In order to determine accurately a child's age, it is BEST for an interviewer to rely on 7.____

A. the child's grade in school
B. what the mother says
C. birth records
D. a library card

8. In his first interview with a new employee, it would be LEAST appropriate for a unit supervisor to 8.____

A. find out the employee's preference for the several types of jobs to which he is able to assign him
B. determine whether the employee will make good promotion material
C. inform the employee of what his basic job responsibilities will be
D. inquire about the employee's education and previous employment

9. If an interviewer takes care to phrase his questions carefully and precisely, the result will MOST probably be that 9.____

A. he will be able to determine whether the person interviewed is being truthful
B. the free flow of the interview will be lost
C. he will get the information he wants
D. he will ask stereotyped questions and narrow the scope of the interview

10. During an interview, the person interviewed is LEAST likely to be cautious about what he tells the interviewer 10.____

A. shortly after the beginning when the questions normally suggest pleasant associations to the person interviewed
B. as long as the interviewer keeps the questions to the point

C. at the point where the person interviewed gains a clear insight into the area being discussed
D. when the interview appears formally ended and good-byes are being said

11. In an interview held for the purpose of getting information from the person interviewed, it is sometimes desirable for the interviewer to repeat the answer he has received to a question. 11.____
For the interviewer to rephrase such an answer in his own words is good practice MAINLY because it

A. gives the interviewer time to make up his next question
B. gives the person interviewed a chance to correct any possible misunderstanding
C. gives the person interviewed the feeling that the interviewer considers his answer important
D. prevents the person interviewed from changing his answer

12. There are several methods of formulating questions during an interview. The particular method used should be adapted to the interview problems presented by the person being questioned. 12.____
Of the following methods of formulating questions during an interview, the ACCEPTABLE one is for the interviewer to ask questions which

A. incorporate several items in order to allow a cooperative interviewee freedom to organize his statements
B. are ambiguous in order to foil a distrustful inter-viewee
C. suggest the correct answer in order to assist an interviewee who appears confused
D. would help an otherwise unresponsive interviewee to become more responsive

13. An interviewer permits the person being interviewed to read the data the interviewer writes as he records the person's responses on a routine departmental form. This practice is 13.____

A. *desirable,* because it serves to assure the person interviewed that his responses are being recorded accurately
B. *undesirable,* because it prevents the interviewer from clarifying uncertain points by asking additional questions
C. *desirable,* because it makes the time that the person interviewed must wait while the answer is written seem shorter
D. *undesirable,* because it destroys the confidentiality of the interview

14. Suppose that a stranger enters the office of which you are in charge and asks for the address and telephone number of one of your employees. 14.____
The MOST appropriate reaction would be to

A. find out why he needs the information and release it if his reason is a good one
B. explain that you are not permitted to release such information to unauthorized persons
C. give him the information but tell him it must be kept confidential
D. ask him to leave the office immediately

15. A member of the public approaches an employee who is at work at his desk. The employee cannot interrupt his work in order to take care of this person. The BEST and MOST courteous way of handling this situation is for the employee to 15.____

A. avoid looking up from his work until he is finished with what he is doing
B. tell this person that he will not be able to take care of him for quite a while
C. refer the individual to another employee who can take care of him right away
D. chat with the individual while he continues with his work

16. Some organizations, as a matter of policy, transfer their administrative staff personnel from one unit to another after stated periods of service in the unit. The MAIN advantage of such a policy is that it 16.____

A. helps keep the staff members abreast of the technical developments in their fields
B. impedes the formation of personal cliques among staff members
C. helps develop wider outlook and loyalty to the organization as a whole rather than to the unit assigned
D. permits the more effective utilization of the individual talents of staff members

17. Leaders generally are somewhat more intelligent than their followers. The CHIEF difficulty of the leader who is markedly more intelligent than his followers is that a leader has difficulty in 17.____

A. overcoming the suspicion and distrust of intellectuals on the part of the group
B. understanding the thought processes of persons who are intellectually inferior
C. accepting the irrational and emotional basis of much of human conduct
D. making himself understood by the group

18. A psychological study of leadership found that it is possible to predict the behavior of a new man in a leadership position more accurately on the basis of the behavior of his predecessor in the position than on the behavior of the man himself in his previous job. The BEST explanation of this observation is that there is a tendency 18.____

A. to select similar types of personalities to fill the same type of position
B. for a newly appointed man to avoid instituting basic changes in operational procedures
C. for a given organizational structure and set of duties to produce similar patterns of behavior
D. for increased responsibility to impose more mature patterns of behavior on an incumbent

19. An administrative official finds that the reports reaching him from his subordinates tend to exaggerate the favorable and minimize the unfavorable aspects of situations existing within the unit. The MOST valid conclusion to draw is that 19.____

A. the administrative official has been overly severe with subordinates and has instilled fear in them
B. there is a normal tendency for persons to represent themselves and their actions in the best possible light
C. members of the department tend to be optimists
D. the administrative official has not been sufficiently critical of previous reports and has not been alert to conditions in the unit

20. A special unit of a department is rife with rumors concerning plans for its future and the possibility of its abolition. As a result, morale and productivity of members assigned to it have suffered. To handle this situation, the administrative official in charge of the unit adopts a policy of promptly corroborating factual rumors and denying false ones. This method of dealing with the problem will achieve some good results, but its CHIEF weakness is that 20.____

A. it gives status to the rumors by the attention paid to them
B. the administrative official may not have the necessary information at hand to dispose promptly of all rumors
C. it *chases* the rumors rather than forestalling them by giving information concerning the unit's future
D. the administrative official may have confidential information which he should not divulge

21. An administrative official, realizing the importance of harmonious relationships within his unit, made a practice of unobtrusively intervening in any conflict situation between subordinates. Whenever friction seemed to be developing, he would attempt to soothe ruffled feelings, remove the source of difficulty by rescheduling activities or reassigning personnel,et cetera. His efforts were always behind-the-scenes and unknown to the employees involved. Although this method of operation produces some good results, its CHIEF drawback is that it 21.____

A. violates the chain of command principle
B. involves the administrative official in personal relationships which are not properly his concern
C. requires confidential sources of information about relationships within the unit, which borders on spying
D. permits subordinates to engage in unacceptable practices without correction

22. At a division conference at which a basic change in the department's procedure was to be announced, the conference leader started the discussion by asking the group for criticisms of the existing procedures. He then described the new procedures to be employed and explained the improvements in operations that were anticipated. The conference leader's method of introducing the change was 22.____

A. *good,* mainly because the conference members would be more receptive to the new procedure if they understood the inadequacies of the old
B. *bad,* mainly because the conference members would realize that the decision for change had been made before the discussion and without consideration of their comments
C. *good,* mainly because the comments and criticisms of the old procedure would provide the basis for evaluating the feasibility of the new method
D. *bad,* mainly because the focus of the discussion was on the procedure being replaced rather than on the procedure being introduced

23. A section chief in charge of a specialized unit calls a staff conference to discuss a proposed modification of some procedures. After making some introductory remarks, the chief wants the comments of the members of the staff. The staff consists of eight subordinates ranging in rank from office aide to principal administrative assistant III, each subordinate having responsibility for a different aspect of the program. Of the following, the BEST procedure for the chief to follow is to call upon each subordinate in 23.____

A. descending order of rank, mainly because the employees with the highest rank are likely to have the most experience and ability
B. ascending order of rank, mainly because the junior employees are more likely to be freer in their comments if they give their views before the senior employees speak
C. order of their specialized knowledge and competence in the subjects under discussion mainly because those with most knowledge and competence can best lead the discussion
D. order of seating around the table, mainly because informality of procedure and democrative leadership is obtained

24. As a supervisor assigned to a public relations unit in a city agency, you find a certain program under severe attack by a citizen's, group. 24.____
To be of GREATEST value to your supervisor, you should

A. present the department side of the story to all meetings or to all groups whether hostile or not
B. attempt to get another citizen's group to defend the department program
C. get greater support from the general public and the press to effectuate the program
D. ignore group opinions; rather, strive to affect individuals and let them persuade their groups

25. The commission has assigned you to present the department side to a group of citizens well-disposed to government programs. 25.____
You should present

A. *only* the department side
B. both sides of the story, but present the department side last
C. both sides of the story, but present the department side first
D. the facts and let the audience draw its own conclusion

KEY (CORRECT ANSWERS)

1. B
2. B
3. B
4. C
5. D

6. A
7. C
8. B
9. C
10. D

11. B
12. D
13. A
14. B
15. C

16. C
17. D
18. C
19. B
20. C

21. D
22. B
23. C
24. B
25. A

TEST 3

DIRECTIONS: Each question or incomplete statement is followed by several suggested answers or completions. Select the one that BEST answers the question or completes the statement. *PRINT THE LETTER OF THE CORRECT ANSWER IN THE SPACE AT THE RIGHT.*

1. Supervisor X, as a representative of the Commissioner, has been ordered to present the department arguments in reference to a new program of inspections and to emphasize such presentation by stressing the enforcement that will follow. 1.____
In this instance,

   A. a mild threat is less of a deterrent than a strong threat
   B. any form of threat should be avoided since you are seeking cooperation
   C. an overly strong threat is less of a deterrent than a mild threat
   D. the mere statement that enforcement will follow is sufficient to effect cooperation

2. If, after an investigation and further consultation with central authorities, wholesale bribe-taking has been confirmed within a certain unit, the agency involved should 2.____

   A. withhold information from the public until a more secure image can be created
   B. break the story since such agency can present the least damaging picture
   C. arrange a compromise solution and present it to the public as an accomplished fact
   D. permit the central authorities to break the story since it presents a more efficient picture

3. The characteristic of flexibility versus stability of a policy seems contradictory to subordinate A. 3.____
The difference can BEST be explained by the administrative manager if he points out that

   A. policies are decision guides and definite formulae for specific actions; therefore, stability must outweigh flexibility
   B. changing events and materials force a change in policy; therefore, flexibility refers to the ability to change policy when it becomes outmoded
   C. policy should be as stable as possible but sufficiently flexible to handle problems that vary from the normal; policy's true purpose must be understood as a guide for decisions, not an inflexible formula for action
   D. most policy at unit level is based on precedent and tradition and, therefore, subject always to the discretion of the supervisor

4. When an administrative manager devotes too much time to telling his subordinates how to handle their job problems, then he 4.____

   A. is spending too little time in formulating policies for the guidance of his subordinates
   B. is neglecting to delegate sufficient authority to his subordinates
   C. should immediately begin to plan for better use of his time
   D. should evaluate his approach to the administration of his section and establish better controls

5. Since the policies of a department are well established, an administrator does not need to formulate section policy. This statement is 5.____

   A. *true;* it is difficult for an administrator to establish a policy which will not in some way coincide or contradict established, overall policies
   B. *false;* department policies have to be broad enough to cover the whole organization; they are seldom detailed enough to guide a section in its internal organization
   C. *true;* the administrator's responsibility in this area is to formulate procedure to implement department policy
   D. *false;* uniformity of enforcement is essential, and this is impossible when the administrator does not establish his own section policy

6. Manager X, when giving a decision on a controversial item, reminds the subordinates of the policy under which such a decision was made. 6.____
   This reminder is

   A. *good;* the subordinates will be aware that he is not being arbitrary, operating by whim, or playing favorites
   B. *unnecessary;* policies have been explained over and over again to subordinates
   C. a form of buck-passing since the manager is blaming a policy for his unfavorable decision
   D. *bad;* policy commits management to specific decisions and, as such, should not be given unfavorable publicity

7. After objectives and policies have been stated, the next step should be to 7.____

   A. develop plans and procedures
   B. make forecasts
   C. examine conditions; gather data
   D. consider a budget

8. After establishing objectives and identifying problems and opportunities, the planning should be 8.____

   A. turned over to the controller. You can alter his plan if you do not agree.
   B. assigned to the division heads. Each will work out a plan for his own division
   C. a joint effort of the controller and other division heads. You and any staff experts available will cooperate and assist as planning progresses.
   D. a joint effort of all supervisors and subordinates

9. The MOST; accurate statement concerning plans and planning is: 9.____

   A. In the absence of an agency-wide plan, it is better to avoid planning in the individual work unit
   B. Every manager or supervisor must plan if he is to carry out his managerial functions
   C. Every manager should make a preliminary plan and then await the agency-wide plan
   D. The agency-wide plan should precede the preliminary plan

10. Objectives, programs, policies, budgets, and procedures are all ______ planning. 10.____

   A. elements of overall
   B. guides for
   C. alternates to
   D. methods of

11. Developing and understanding objectives, establishing policies, collecting data, developing alternative action proposals, and deciding on action are all 11.____

A. steps in planning
B. guidelines to consider in planning
C. the action motif ascribed to planning
D. alternatives to planning

12. Work measurement can be applied to operations where workload can be related to 12.____

A. available personnel for the implementation of assigned tasks
B. follow-up programs for continued progress
C. cost abatement and optimum efficiency
D. man-hour utilization on assigned tasks

13. If you ask for additional historical information on costs, caseloads, et cetera, you will be 13.____

A. refining the forecast process
B. developing the groundwork for forecasting
C. estimating the future
D. evaluating your research department's efficiency

14. Suppose that the majority of mathematical projections predicts a serious downturn in new cases, while you and your advisors believe that a mild upturn is approaching. In this situation, the BEST procedure is to 14.____

A. follow the course dictated by the mathematical projections because that is what they are there for
B. follow your own ideas and those of your advisors; management is an art, not a science
C. modify the course dictated by the mathematical projections so as to reflect both management and specialist judgment
D. consult another advisor

15. The director of a personnel bureau with 100 employees would probably operate MOST efficiently if he had under his immediate supervision approximately ______ subordinates. 15.____

A. 5 B. 25 C. 50 D. 100

16. A worker is *usually* MOST productive when he is assigned to work which 16.____

A. he is able to do best
B. involves a variety of skills
C. is under close supervision
D. requires little skill

17. It is desirable for all staff specialists to have some knowledge of line activities PRIMARILY in order that they may 17.____

A. direct line activities when necessary
B. have a proper framework for research
C. know how to deal with all types of personnel
D. take cognizance of the agency's needs and problems

18. When a supervisor delegates an assignment, he should 18.____

A. delegate his responsibility for the assignment
B. make certain that the assignment is properly performed
C. participate in the beginning and final stages of the assignment
D. retain all authority needed to complete the assignment

19. Which one of the following is LEAST important in the management of a suggestion program? 19.____

A. Giving awards which are of sufficient value to encourage competition
B. Securing full support from the department's officers and executives
C. Publicizing the program and the awards given
D. Providing suggestion boxes in numerous locations

20. The MOST certain means to *decrease* morale is to 20.____

A. insist on strict adherence to safety rules
B. make each employee responsible for the tidiness of his work area
C. overlook evidence of hostility between groups of employees
D. provide strong, aggressive leadership

KEY (CORRECT ANSWERS)

1.	C	11.	A
2.	B	12.	D
3.	C	13.	B
4.	A	14.	C
5.	B	15.	A
6.	A	16.	A
7.	C	17.	D
8.	C	18.	B
9.	B	19.	D
10.	A	20.	C

EXAMINATION SECTION

TEST 1

DIRECTIONS: Each question or incomplete statement is followed by several suggested answers or completions. Select the one that BEST answers the question or completes the statement. *PRINT THE LETTER OF THE CORRECT ANSWER IN THE SPACE AT THE RIGHT.*

1. Several employees complain informally to their supervisor regarding some new procedures which have been instituted. 1.____
The supervisor should IMMEDIATELY
   A. explain that management is responsible
   B. investigate the complaint
   C. refer the matter to the methods analyst
   D. tell the employees to submit their complaint as a formal grievance

2. The PRINCIPAL aim of an administrator is to 2.____
   A. act as liaison between employee and management
   B. get the work done
   C. keep up morale
   D. train his subordinates

3. Work measurement can be applied to operations where workload can be related to 3.____
   A. available personnel for the implementation of assigned tasks
   B. follow-up programs for continued progress
   C. cost abatement and optimum efficiency
   D. man hour utilization on assigned tasks

4. The one of the following which is NOT a primary advantage of a work measurement program is 4.____
   A. the selection of informed personnel
   B. knowledge of personnel needs
   C. support of personnel requests
   D. setting of approximate unit costs

5. A program of work measurement would be LEAST likely to 5.____
   A. point up the need for management research
   B. keep workload and personnel on an even keel
   C. measure the performance in exceptional operations
   D. evaluate the status of operations

6. Generally speaking, there are two kinds of work measurement: 6.____
(1) the traditional industrial engineering kind where performance standard are determined by time study or other engineering techniques, and (2) the statistical kind where yardsticks (so-called to distinguish them from engineered standard) are developed from a statistical analysis of past performance data. These data consist essentially of periodic reports in which work performed, expressed in identifiable work units, is related to the time required to perform it, usually expressed in man-hours.
The ESSENTIAL difference between the two kinds of work measurement is that
   A. the statistical type if based on past, current, and future determinants of a divergent nature, while engineered standards are restrictive
   B. yardsticks are less restrictive than engineered standards
   C. time study standards employ a higher ratio of man-hour data than do statistical standards
   D. engineered standards are more costly as well as more accurate than routine time study methods

7. Government has favored the use of the statistical type of work measurement over the industrial type MAINLY because 7.____
   A. government is an institution rarely hampered by money-seeking techniques
   B. as the statistical type of work measurement is broadly based, it is more capable of filling the wide expanse of government's needs
   C. employees might object vehemently against speed-ups, thereby sapping work measurement's force
   D. the former appears to be just as effective and less expensive than the latter

8. A work measurement program is a system by which a 8.____
   A. periodic account is kept of individual and group performance
   B. recurring account is kept of group performance
   C. periodic account is kept of performance by an individual
   D. periodic account is kept of performance by a group

9. Statistical standards developed during the early stages of a work measurement program are 9.____
   A. changed too rapidly and thus are of little value in the final program
   B. subject to change as the program moves forward
   C. incorporated into the final program, ultimately for research studies
   D. abandoned before the effective date of the final program

10. It is NOT an objective of a work measurement program to 10.____
   A. furnish a basis for procedural control
   B. provide a true basis for management control
   C. furnish a genuine basis for budget control
   D. provide a basis for management planning

11. The MOST valid of the following concepts of management control is that it examines 11.____
    A. the method with which work assignments have been accomplished in accordance with preconceived plans and policies
    B. preconceived plans and policies to determine their ultimate value
    C. results to determine how well work assignments have been accomplished in accordance with preconceived plans and policies
    D. the work of individual employees to get an acceptable, so as not to endanger the entire control program

12. Of the following, the LEAST likely area in which a deficiency in operations would be revealed by a work measurement program is 12.____
    A. improper personnel utilization
    B. inadequate equipment
    C. distribution of work
    D. personnel rating

13. The MOST accurate of the following statements regarding the standard as used in a work measurement program is: 13.____
    A. Standard rates of performance should not be established until the effectiveness of an operation has been determined.
    B. The measure of effectiveness should be kept separate and distinct from the application of standards to actual performance
    C. standards should not be used as guides in planning
    D. Standard rates of performance must be established before effectiveness of an operation can be determined.

14. The first and most important basic consideration in instituting a program of work measurement is the 14.____
    A. indoctrination of personnel
    B. establishment of a uniform technology
    C. selection of the time unit
    D. selection of a standard

15. A _____ is an item or a group of items, generally physical, which, when taken in the aggregate, serve to measure amounts of work. 15.____
    A. Therblig
    B. function
    C. operation
    D. work unit

16. Which of the following epitomizes the *raison d'etre* of work simplification? 16.____
    A. Waste elimination
    B. Empirical costs
    C. Time study speed-ups
    D. Charting techniques

17. A process charting analysis is likely to be of little value in the event of 17.____
    A. a major change in the department's activity
    B. a new supervisor from the outside coming in to head the unit
    C. increase in volume of work
    D. sizable personnel turnover

18. Staff or functional supervision in an organization 18.____
    A. is least justified at the operational level
    B. is contrary to the principle of Unity of Command
    C. is more effective than authoritative supervision
    D. normally does not give the right to take direct disciplinary action

19. The correlation between a flow process chart and a flow diagram is BEST described by which of the following statements? 19.____
    A. A flow process chart is supportive machinery to the flow diagram.
    B. In essence, the flow process chart exhibits time, distance, and location using standard symbols, whereas the flow diagram exhibits flow lines and uses classification symbols.
    C. Much of the information on the flow process chart is reproduced from the flow diagram.
    D. The flow diagram is complementary to the flow process chart.

20. Indicate which of the following statements is LEAST apt to clarify the underlying distinction between work simplification and other method of betterment procedures. 20.____
    Work simplification
    A. is dependent on supervisory participation
    B. is designed for employee participation
    C. emphasizes group participation
    D. emphasizes the ideas of experts

21. In describing the process of administrative management, the LEAST valid description is that it 21.____
    A. is composed of interdependent functions
    B. is comprised of related parts
    C. is cyclical
    D. consists of independent parts

22. Work activity, as to type, individual performance, and time expenditure, is BEST illustrated by a _____ chart. 22.____
    A. flow process
    B work flow
    C. work distribution
    D. operations

23. Neither the work distribution nor the flow process chart furnishes adequate intelligence as to 23.____
    A. methods
    B. activities
    C. nature of work activity
    D. unit prices

24. A graphic presentation of the steps and distribution through which each copy of a multiple copy office form travels is a(n) 24.____
    A. work distribution chart
    B. flow process chart
    C. flow diagram
    D. operations chart

25. A CHIEF target of work simplification is 25.____
    A. the achievement of greater productivity with the same effort
    B. obtaining the same work accomplishment with less effort
    C. employee participation and little resistance to change
    D. all of the above

KEY (CORRECT ANSWERS)

1.	B	11.	C
2.	B	12.	D
3.	D	13.	D
4.	A	14.	B
5.	C	15.	D
6.	B	16.	A
7.	D	17.	B
8.	B	18.	D
9.	B	19.	D
10.	A	20.	D

21.	D
22.	C
23.	D
24.	C
25.	C

TEST 2

DIRECTIONS: Each question or incomplete statement is followed by several suggested answers or completions. Select the one that BEST answers the question or completes the statement. *PRINT THE LETTER OF THE CORRECT ANSWER IN THE SPACE AT THE RIGHT.*

1. In conducting a work simplification program, which of the following office problems is the MOST likely to be solved by the use of the flow process chart? 1.____
   A. Are the employee deluged with unrelated tasks?
   B. What activities are the most costly, in terms of time consumed?
   C. Is the proper sequence of work activity employed?
   D. Is there an even distribution of work among the employees?

2. In the matter of procedural analysis, which question should be asked FIRST? 2.____
   A. When should the step be performed?
   B. Who should perform the step?
   C. What is the significance of the step?
   D. Where can this be improved upon?

3. Storage on a movement diagram is represented by 3.____
   A. ◇ B. ▽ C. □ D. all of the above

4. The use of a flow process chart is LESS desirable in indicating 4.____
   A. the time rate for each step B. distance traveled
   C. equipment-facilities layout D. sequence of activities

5. Division of work is BEST delineated by means of a _____ chart. 5.____
   A. work methods B. flow process
   C. work distribution D. flow authority

6. In seeking to conduct a work simplification analysis, the MOST appropriate first step would be to 6.____
   A. chart the procedures
   B. survey the facilities as to spatial access
   C. make problem area determination
   D. set up composition of forms analysis

7. The conception of a standard is BEST denoted as a 7.____
   A. hypothetical level B. circumscribed level of work activity
   C. level of comparing D. quintessential idea

8. With reference to office work simplification, it could be considered expedient to 8.____
   A. first simplify the procedure and then the individual methods
   B. simplify the individual methods first, then the procedure
   C. concurrently, simplify the methods and the procedure
   D. none of the above

9. The MOST valid precept relative to work analysis is 9.____
   A. the volume of work is inversely proportional to the distribution or sequence of work
   B. in meeting production standards, the sequence of work transcends its distribution
   C. work sequence and work distribution should be analyzed in relation to work volume
   D. work sequence and work distribution should be examined for work validation concepts

10. The flow process chart is PRINCIPALLY used 10.____
   A. as a useful tool to train new employees
   B. to ascertain the effectiveness of the organization's employees
   C. to pinpoint *bottlenecks* affecting an operation
   D. to determine the visibility of organizational relationships

11. The work distribution chart would generally be of little value in answering which of the following questions? 11.____
   A. In what order are the activities being carried out?
   B. Which activities consume the most time?
   C. Is a work balance maintained among the employees?
   D. Are the employees laboring under a plethora of unrelated tasks?

12. A worthwhile analytical tool in work simplification is the flow process chart. The MOST valid description is that 12.____
   A. a flow process chart is generally reliable without review for a period of a year
   B. the flow process chart should be reviewed and possibly revised at six-month intervals
   C. the flow process chart is an ad hoc instrument
   D. the value of a flow process chart is not determined by time

13. In the analysis of a method of procedure in a work simplification program, a competent analyst should FIRST focalize on the clearance or diminution of 13.____
   A. verifications B. transportations
   C. inspections D. storages

14. Which one of the following statements BEST distinguishes a method from a procedure? 14.____
   A. A method is a consistent sequence of procedures.
   B. A procedure comprises a sequence of related methods, performed in most instances by a single person.
   C. A series of related methods comprise a procedure.
   D. In breadth, a method takes precedence over a procedure.

15. The data provided by the flow process chart in a work simplification program is INADEQUATE to answer which one of the following questions? 15.____
   A. What is being performed?
   B. In what manner should the work be performed?
   C. What is the quantity of work performed?
   D. Who should perform the work?

Questions 16-17.

DIRECTIONS: Questions 16 and 17 are to be answered on the basis of the following passage.

Ideally, then, the process of budget formulation would consist of a flow of directives down the organization, and a reverse flow of recommendations in terms of alternatives among which selection would be made at every level. Ideally, also, a change in the recommendations at any level would require reconsideration and revision at all lower levels. By a process of successive approximation, everything would be taken into account and all points of view harmonized. Such a process, however, would be ideal only if the future could be foreseen clearly and time did not matter. As it is, in a complicated organization like the Federal government, the initial policy objectives established for the budget become out-of-date, before such a procedure could be carried through. While this difficulty does not in any way impugn the principle that the budget should be considered in terms of alternatives, it may call for short-cut methods of estimation rather than long drawn-out ones.

16. According to the above passage, 16.____
   A. the ideal method for estimating purposes is a short one
   B. the ideal method is not ideal for use in the Federal government
   C. directive should flow up and down via short methods
   D. the Federal government needs to speed up its reverse flow of recommendations for greater budgetary estimates

17. A suitable title for the above passage would be: 17.____
   A. Formulating the Federal Government's Budgetary Principles
   B. Directives and Recommendations: Budgetary Flow
   C. The Process of Budget Formulation
   D. The Application of the Ideal Estimate to the Federal Government

Questions 18-19.

DIRECTIONS: Questions 18 and 19 are to be answered on the basis of the following passage.

For purpose of budget formulation, the association of budgeting with accounting is less fortunate. Preparing for the future and recording the past do not necessarily require the same aptitudes or attitudes. The task of the accountant is to record past transactions in meticulous detail. Budgeting involves estimates of an uncertain future. But, because of the influence of accounts, government's budgets are prepared in a degree of detail that is quite unwarranted by the uncertain assumptions on which the estimates are based. A major source of government waste could be eliminated if estimates were prepared in no greater detail than was justified by their accuracy.

18. The author of the above paragraph 18.____
    A. is undermining the accounting profession
    B. believes accountants dwell solely in the past and cannot deal with the future efficiently
    C. wants the accountants out of government unless they become more accurate in their findings
    D. wishes to redirect the accountants' handling of budget procedures

19. The author's attitude appears to be 19.____
    A. tongue-in-cheek B morose
    C. strident D. constructive

20. The idea that classic organizational structure tends to create work situations having requirements counter to those for psychological success and self-esteem, sometimes called the *organizational dilemma*, is MOST closely associated with 20.____
    A. Argyris B. Taylor C. Gulick D. Maslow

Questions 21-25.

DIRECTIONS: Questions 21 through 25 contain incorrectly used words which change the meaning of the statement. Identify the word in the statement that is incorrect and select the choice that would make the sentence correct.

21. Standards of production performance are necessary to reveal the quantities of material, the number of hours of labor, the machine hours, and quantities of service (as, for example, power, steam, etc.) necessary to perform the various production operations. The establishment of such standards is an engineering rather than an accounting task, but it should be emphasized that such standards are needless to the development of the budgetary procedure—at least insofar as the budget is to serve as a tool of control. Such standards serve not only in the development of the budget and in measuring efficiency of production performance, but also in developing purchase requirements and in estimating costs. 21.____
    A. Manifest B. Evaluation C. Essential D. Function

22. Where standard costs are not available or their use is impracticable due to uncertainty of prices, estimates of the costs must be made on the basis of past experience and expected conditions. Ability to use standards largely eliminates the use of the budget for purposes of control of costs but its value remains for purposes of coordination of the program with purchases and finance. 22.____
    A. Failure B. Current C. Culmination D. Apparent

23. While one of the first objectives of the labor budget is to provide the highest practicable degree of regularity of employment, consideration must also be given to the estimating and perdurability of labor cost. Regularity of employment in itself effects some reduction in labor cost, but when carried beyond the point of practicality, it may increase other costs. For example, additional sales effort may be required to expand sales volume or to develop new products for slack periods; the cost of carrying inventories and the dangers of obsolescence and price declines must also be considered. A proper balance must be secured. 23.____

    A. Material B. Control C. Futures D. To

24. The essentials of budgeting perhaps can be summarized in this manner: 24.____
    I. Develop a sound business program
    II. Report on the progress in achieving that program
    III. Take necessary action as to all variances which are inevitable
    IV. Revise the program to meet the changing conditions as required

    A. Perfect B. Plans C. Controllable D. Secure

25. If a planning and control procedure is considered worthwhile, then it is a syllogism that preparation for the installation should be adequate. Time devoted to this educational aspect ordinarily will prove quite rewarding. The management to be involved with the budget, and particularly the middle management, must have a clear understanding of the budgetary procedure. 25.____

    A. Acquired B. Remedial C. Monetary D. Truism

KEY (CORRECT ANSWERS)

1. D
2. C
3. D
4. C
5. C

6. C
7. C
8. A
9. C
10. C

11. A
12. D
13. D
14. C
15. C

16. B
17. C
18. D
19. D
20. A

21. C
22. B
23. B
24. C
25. D

TEST 3

DIRECTIONS: Each question or incomplete statement is followed by several suggested answers or completions. Select the one that BEST answers the question or completes the statement. *PRINT THE LETTER OF THE CORRECT ANSWER IN THE SPACE AT THE RIGHT.*

1. The MOST important element in job satisfaction is 1.____
   A. job security
   B. responsibility or recognition
   C. salary
   D. type of supervision

2. The point of view that the average person wishes to avoid responsibility, wishes to be directed, as little ambition, and wants security above all, is described by Douglas MacGregor as Theory 2.____
   A. X
   B. Y
   C. Z
   D. X and Y combined

3. To prepare a work distribution chart, two other types of lists must generally be prepared. 3.____
   In usual order of preparation, they are a(n) _____ and a(n) _____ list.
   A. flow chart; activity
   B. skills list; task
   C. task list; activity
   D. activity list; task

4. A statistical control program in an office is valuable to direct deterioration in operations. 4.____
   It is, however, LEAST likely to reveal
   A. when preventative action is needed
   B. when a variation is due to chance
   C. when an assignable cause is present
   D. what the cause of error or deterioration is

5. Which of the following BEST defines an organization chart? 5.____
   An organizational chart
   A. depicts informal channels of communication within an organization
   B. depicts the major functions of an organization and the normal work flow between subdivisions of the organization
   C. presents graphically the arrangement and interrelationships of the subdivisions and the functions of the organization as they exist
   D. presents graphically the arrangement and relationships of all the positions authorized in an organization

6. In considering an office layout for a unit, which of the following factors should generally receive the LEAST consideration? 6.____
   A. Lighting levels in the existing area
   B. Major work flow—the processing of paper
   C. Present and projected growth rate of the unit
   D. Traffic patterns of employees and visitors

7. The BEST way to secure effective management is usually to 7.____
   A. allow staff to help solve administrative problems of line management
   B. provide a good organization structure
   C. select capable managers
   D. set up conservative spans of control

8. Which of the following is NOT an advantage of oral instruction as compared with written instructions? 8.____
   Oral
   A. instructions can be easily changed
   B. instructions are superior in transmitting complex directives
   C. instructions facilitate exchange of information between a supervisor and his subordinate(s)
   D. discussions are possible with oral instructions, making it easier to ascertain understanding

9. Which organization principle is MOST closely related to procedural analysis and improvement? 9.____
   A. Duplication, overlapping, and conflict should be eliminated.
   B. The objectives of the organization should be clearly defined.
   C. Managerial authority should be clearly defined.
   D. Top management should be freed of burdensome details.

10. Of the following control techniques, a _____ is MOST useful on large, complex projects. 10.____
    A. general work plan
    B. Gantt chart
    C. monthly progress report
    D. PERT chart

11. Work is organized so that the work is broken down into a series of jobs. Each unit of work moves progressively from position to position until completion. 11.____
    This paragraph BEST describes a
    A. parallel plan of work subdivision
    B. serial plan
    C. unit assembly plan
    D. unit process plan

12. According to the classic studies of Rensis Likert, the GREATEST factor making for good morale and increased productivity was having a 12.____
    A. good program of employee benefits and wage scales
    B. supervisor who gave his employees free rein after they were fully trained and did not interfere with them
    C. supervisor who was primarily interested in production
    D. supervisor who, while interested in production, was primarily *employee-centered*

13. The managerial grid shows two concerns and a range of interaction between them.
In this grid, the horizontal axis indicates a concern for _____ and the vertical axis indicates a concern for _____.
A. production; people
B. hierarchy; people
C. organization; people
D. people; costs

13.____

14. It has been decided to make a few important revisions in the methods and procedures of a particular work unit.
Of the following, which method of implementing these revisions would probably be the MOST desirable in terms of morale and of efficiency?
A. Give all employees in unit individual instructions in the revised procedures and make sure each employee knows them before instructing the next
B. Institute all revisions at once, followed by on-the-job training for all members of the work unit
C. Introduce the revisions one at a time and accompany each revision with an orientation for employees
D. Set up a training course for the employees which instructs them in all aspects of the revised procedures prior to their implementation

14.____

15. An operations research technique which would be employed to determine the optimum number of window clerks or interviewers to have in an agency serving the public would MOST likely be the use of
A. line of balance
B. queueing theory
C. simulation
D. work sampling

15.____

16. Douglas MacGregor's theory of human motivation classifies worker behavior into two distinct categories: Theory X and Theory Y. Theory X, the traditional view, states that the average man dislikes working and will avoid work if he can, unless coerced. Theory Y holds essentially the opposite view.
The manager can apply both of these theories to worker behavior BEST if he
A. follows an *open-door* policy only with respect to his immediate subordinates
B. recognizes his subordinates' mental and social needs as well as agency needs
C. recognizes that executive responsibility is primarily limited to fulfillment of agency productivity goals
D. directs his subordinate managers to follow a policy of close supervision

16.____

17. In interpersonal communications, it is important to ascertain whether oral directions and instruction are understood.
One of the MOST important sources of such information is known as
A. the *halo* effect
B. evaluation
C. feedback
D. quantitative analysis

17.____

18. The *grapevine* MOST often provides a useful service by 18.____
   A. correcting some of the deficiencies of the formal communication system
   B. rapidly conveying a true picture of events
   C. involving staff in current organizational changes
   D. interfering with the operation of the formal communication system

19. People who are in favor of a leadership style in which the subordinates help make decisions contend that it produces favorable effects in a work unit. According to these people, which of the following is NOT likely to be an effect of such *participative management*? 19.____
   A. Reduced turnover
   B. Accelerated learning of duties
   C. Greater acceptance of change
   D. Reduced appearance of the work unit's goals

20. Employees of a public service agency will be MOST likely to develop meaningful goals for both the agency and the employee and become committed to attaining them if supervisors 20.____
   A. allow them unilaterally to set their own goals
   B. provide them with a clear understanding of the premises underlying the agency's goals
   C. encourage them to concentrate on setting only short-range goals for themselves
   D. periodically review the agency's goals in order to suggest changes in accordance with current conditions

---

KEY (CORRECT ANSWERS)

1.	B	11.	B
2.	A	12.	D
3.	C	13.	A
4.	D	14.	D
5.	C	15.	B
6.	A	16.	B
7.	B	17.	C
8.	B	18.	A
9.	A	19.	D
10.	D	20.	B

EVALUATING CONCLUSIONS IN LIGHT OF KNOWN FACTS

EXAMINATION SECTION

TEST 1

DIRECTIONS: Each question or incomplete statement is followed by several suggested answers or completions. Select the one that BEST answers the question or completes the statement. *PRINT THE LETTER OF THE CORRECT ANSWER IN THE SPACE AT THE RIGHT.*

Questions 1-9.

DIRECTIONS: In Questions 1 through 9, you will read a set of facts and a conclusion drawn from them. The conclusion may be valid or invalid, based on the facts. It is your task to determine the validity of the conclusion.
For each question, select the letter before the statement that BEST expresses the relationship between the given facts and the conclusion that has been drawn from them. Your choices are:

A. The facts prove the conclusion.
B. The facts disprove the conclusion; or
C. The facts neither prove nor disprove the conclusion.

1. FACTS: Lauren must use Highway 29 to get to work. Lauren has a meeting today at 9:00 A.M. If she misses the meeting, Lauren will probably lose a major account. Highway 29 is closed all day today for repairs. 1.____

CONCLUSION: Lauren will not be able to get to work.

A. The facts prove the conclusion.
B. The facts disprove the conclusion.
C. The facts neither prove nor disprove the conclusion.

2. FACTS: The Tumbleweed Follies, a traveling burlesque show, is looking for a new line dancer. The position requires both singing and dancing skills. If the show cannot fill the position by Friday, it will begin to look for a magician to fill the time slot currently held by the line dancers. Willa, who wants to audition for the line dancing position, can sing, but cannot dance. 2.____

CONCLUSION: Willa is qualified to audition for the part of line dancer.

A. The facts prove the conclusion.
B. The facts disprove the conclusion.
C. The facts neither prove nor disprove the conclusion.

3. FACTS: Terry owns two dogs, Spike and Stan. One of the dogs is short-haired and has blue eyes. One dog as a pink nose. The blue-eyed dog never barks. One of the dogs has white fur on its paws. Sam has long hair. 3.____

CONCLUSION: Spike never barks.

A. The facts prove the conclusion.
B. The facts disprove the conclusion.
C. The facts neither prove nor disprove the conclusion.

4. FACTS: No science teachers are members of the PTA. Some English teachers are members of the PTA. Some English teachers in the PTA also wear glasses. Every PTA member is required to sit on the dunking stool at the student carnival except for those who wear glasses, who will be exempt. Those who are exempt, however, will have to officiate the hamster races. All of the English teachers in the PTA who do not wear glasses are married. 4.____

CONCLUSION: All the married English teachers in the PTA will set on the dunking stool at the student carnival.

A. The facts prove the conclusion.
B. The facts disprove the conclusion.
C. The facts neither prove nor disprove the conclusion.

5. FACTS: If the price of fuel is increased and sales remain constant, oil company profits will increase. The price of fuel was increased, and market experts project that sales levels are likely to be maintained. 5.____

CONCLUSION: The price of fuel will increase.

A. The facts prove the conclusion.
B. The facts disprove the conclusion.
C. The facts neither prove nor disprove the conclusion.

6. FACTS: Some members of the gymnastics team are double-jointed, and some members of the gymnastics team ae also on the lacrosse team. Some double-jointed members of the gymnastics team are also coaches. All gymnastics team members perform floor exercises, except the coaches. All the double-jointed members of the gymnastics team who are not coaches are freshmen. 6.____

CONCLUSION: Some double-jointed freshmen are coaches.

A. The facts prove the conclusion.
B. The facts disprove the conclusion.
C. The facts neither prove nor disprove the conclusion.

7. FACTS: Each member of the International Society speaks at least one foreign language, but no member speaks more than four foreign languages. Five members speak Spanish; three speak Mandarin; four speak French; four speak German; and five speak a foreign language other than Spanish, Mandarin, French, or German. 7.____

CONCLUSION: The lowest possible number of members in the International Society is eight.

A. The facts prove the conclusion.
B. The facts disprove the conclusion.
C. The facts neither prove nor disprove the conclusion.

8. FACTS: Mary keeps seven cats in her apartment. Only three of the cats will eat the same kind of food. Mary wants to keep at least one extra bag of each kind of food. 8.____

CONCLUSION: The minimum number of bags Mary will need to keep as extra is 7.

A. The facts prove the conclusion.
B. The facts disprove the conclusion.
C. The facts neither prove nor disprove the conclusion.

9. FACTS: In Ed and Marie's exercise group, everyone likes the treadmill or the stationary bicycle, or both, but Ed does not like the stationary bicycle. Marie has not expressed a preference, but spends most of her time on the stationary bicycle. 9.____

CONCLUSION: Everyone in the group who does not like the treadmill likes the stationary bicycle.

A. The facts prove the conclusion.
B. The facts disprove the conclusion.
C. The facts neither prove nor disprove the conclusion.

Questions 10-17.

DIRECTIONS: Questions 10 through 17 are based on the following reading passage. It is not your knowledge of the particular topic that is being tested, but your ability to reason based on what you have read. The passage is likely to detail several proposed courses of action and factors affecting these proposals. The reading passage is followed by a conclusion or outcome based on the facts in the passage, or a description of a decision taken regarding the situation. The conclusion is followed by a number of statements that have a possible connection to the conclusion. For each statement, you are to determine whether:

A. The statement proves the conclusion.
B. The statement supports the conclusion but does not prove it.
C. The statement disproves the conclusion.
D. The statement weakens the conclusion but does not disprove it.
E. The statement has no relevance to the conclusion.

Remember that the conclusion after the passage is to be accepted as the outcome of what actually happened, and that you are being asked to evaluate the impact each statement would have had on the conclusion.

PASSAGE

The Owyhee Mission School District's Board of Directors is hosting a public meeting to debate the merits of the proposed abolition of all bilingual education programs within the district. The group that has made the proposal believes the programs, which teach immigrant children academic subjects in their native language until they have learned English well enough to join mainstream classes, inhibit the ability of students to acquire English quickly and succeed in school and in the larger American society. Such programs, they argue, are also a wasteful drain on the district's already scant resources.

At the meeting, several teachers and parents stand to speak out against the proposal. The purpose of an education, they say, should be to build upon, rather than dismantle, a minority child's language and culture. By teaching children in academic subjects in their native tongues, while simultaneously offering English language instruction, schools can meet the goals of learning English and progressing through academic subjects along with their peers.

Hiram Nguyen, a representative of the parents whose children are currently enrolled in bilingual education, stands at the meeting to express the parents' wishes. The parents have been polled, he says, and are overwhelmingly of the opinion that while language and culture are important to them, they are not things that will disappear from the students' lives if they are no longer taught in the classroom. The most important issue for the parents is whether their children will succeed in school and be competitive in the larger American society. If bilingual education can be demonstrated to do that, then the parents are in favor of continuing it.

At the end of the meeting, a proponent of the plan, Oscar Ramos, stands to clarify some misconceptions about the proposal. It does not call for a "sink or swim" approach, he says, but allows for an interpreter to be present in mainstream classes to explain anything a student finds too complex or confusing.

The last word of the meeting is given to Delia Cruz, a bilingual teacher at one of the district's elementary schools. A student is bound to find anything complex or confusing, she says, if it is spoken in a language he has never heard before. It is more wasteful to place children in classrooms where they don't understand anything, she says, than it is to try to teach them something useful as they are learning the English language.

CONCLUSION: After the meeting, the Owyhee Mission School District's Board of Directors votes to terminate all the district's bilingual education programs at the end of the current academic year, but to maintain the current level of funding to each of the schools that have programs cut.

10. A poll conducted by the *Los Angeles Times* at approximately the same time as the Board's meeting indicated that 75% of the people were opposed to bilingual education; among Latinos, opposition was 84%. 10.____
   A. The statement proves the conclusion.
   B. The statement supports the conclusion but does not prove it.
   C. The statement disproves the conclusion.
   D. The statement weakens the conclusion but does not disprove it.
   E. The statement has no relevance to the conclusion.

11. Of all the studies connected on bilingual education programs, 64% indicate that students learned English grammar better in "sink or swim" classes without any special features than they did in bilingual education classes. 11.____
   A. The statement proves the conclusion.
   B. The statement supports the conclusion but does not prove it.
   C. The statement disproves the conclusion.
   D. The statement weakens the conclusion but does not disprove it.
   E. The statement has no relevance to the conclusion.

12. In the academic year that begins after the Board's vote, Montgomery Burns Elementary, an Owyhee Mission District school, launches a new bilingual program for the children of Somali immigrants. 12.____
   A. The statement proves the conclusion.
   B. The statement supports the conclusion but does not prove it.
   C. The statement disproves the conclusion.
   D. The statement weakens the conclusion but does not disprove it.
   E. The statement has no relevance to the conclusion.

13. In the previous academic year, under severe budget restraints, the Owyhee Mission District cut all physical education, music, and art classes, but its funding for bilingual education classes increased by 18%. 13.____
   A. The statement proves the conclusion.
   B. The statement supports the conclusion but does not prove it.
   C. The statement disproves the conclusion.
   D. The statement weakens the conclusion but does not disprove it.
   E. The statement has no relevance to the conclusion.

14. Before the Board votes, a polling consultant conducts randomly sampled assessments of immigrant students who enrolled in Owyhee District schools at a time when they did not speak any English at all. Ten years after graduating from high school, 44% of those who received bilingual education were professionals – doctors, lawyers, educators, engineers, etc. Of those who did not receive bilingual education, 38% were professionals. 14.____
   A. The statement proves the conclusion.
   B. The statement supports the conclusion but does not prove it.
   C. The statement disproves the conclusion.
   D. The statement weakens the conclusion but does not disprove it.
   E. The statement has no relevance to the conclusion.

15. Over the past several years, the scores of Owyhee District students have gradually declined, and enrollment numbers have followed as anxious parents transferred their children to other schools or applied for a state-funded voucher program. 15.____
   A. The statement proves the conclusion.
   B. The statement supports the conclusion but does not prove it.
   C. The statement disproves the conclusion.
   D. The statement weakens the conclusion but does not disprove it.
   E. The statement has no relevance to the conclusion.

16. California and Massachusetts, two of the most liberal states in the country, have each passed ballot measures banning bilingual education in public schools. 16.____
   A. The statement proves the conclusion.
   B. The statement supports the conclusion but does not prove it.
   C. The statement disproves the conclusion.
   D. The statement weakens the conclusion but does not disprove it.
   E. The statement has no relevance to the conclusion.

17. In the academic year that begins after the Board's vote, no Owyhee Mission Schools are conducting bilingual instruction. 17.____
   A. The statement proves the conclusion.
   B. The statement supports the conclusion but does not prove it.
   C. The statement disproves the conclusion.
   D. The statement weakens the conclusion but does not disprove it.
   E. The statement has no relevance to the conclusion.

Questions 18-25.

DIRECTIONS: Questions 18 through 25 each provide four factual statements and a conclusion based on these statements. After reading the entire question, you will decide whether:
   A. The conclusion is proved by Statements 1-4;
   B. The conclusion is disproved by Statements 1-4;
   C. The facts are not sufficient to prove or disprove the conclusion.

18. FACTUAL STATEMENTS: 18.____
   1) Gear X rotates in a clockwise direction if Switch C is in the OFF position.
   2) Gear X will rotate in a counter-clockwise direction if Switch C is ON.
   3) If Gear X is rotating in a clockwise direction, then Gear Y will not be rotating at all.
   4) Switch C is OFF.

   CONCLUSION: Gear Y is rotating.

   A. The conclusion is proved by Statements 1-4;
   B. The conclusion is disproved by Statements 1-4;
   C. The facts are not sufficient to prove or disprove the conclusion.

19. FACTUAL STATEMENTS: 19.____
1) Mark is older than Jim but younger than Dan.
2) Fern is older than Mark but younger than Silas.
3) Dan is younger than Silas but older than Edward.
4) Edward is older than Mark but younger than Fern.

CONCLUSION: Dan is older than Fern.

A. The conclusion is proved by Statements 1-4;
B. The conclusion is disproved by Statements 1-4;
C. The facts are not sufficient to prove or disprove the conclusion.

20. FACTUAL STATEMENTS: 20.____
1) Each of Fred's three sofa cushions lies on top of four lost coins.
2) The cushion on the right covers two pennies and two dimes.
3) The middle cushion covers two dimes and two quarters.
4) The cushion on the left covers two nickels and two quarters.

CONCLUSION: To be guaranteed of retrieving at least one coin of each denomination, and without looking at any of the coins, Frank must take three coins each from under the cushions on the right and the left.

A. The conclusion is proved by Statements 1-4;
B. The conclusion is disproved by Statements 1-4;
C. The facts are not sufficient to prove or disprove the conclusion.

21. FACTUAL STATEMENTS: 21.____
1) The door to the hammer mill chamber is locked if light 6 is red.
2) The door to the hammer mill chamber is locked only when the mill is operating.
3) If the mill is not operating, light 6 is blue.
4) The door to the hammer mill chamber is locked.

CONCLUSION: The mill is in operation.

A. The conclusion is proved by Statements 1-4;
B. The conclusion is disproved by Statements 1-4;
C. The facts are not sufficient to prove or disprove the conclusion.

22. FACTUAL STATEMENTS: 22.____
1) In a five-story office building, where each story is occupied by a single professional, Dr. Kane's office is above Dr. Assad's.
2) Dr. Johnson's office is between Dr. Kane's and Dr. Conlon's.
3) Dr. Steen's office is between Dr. Conlon's and Dr. Assad's.
4) Dr. Johnson is on the fourth story.

CONCLUSION: Dr. Steen occupies the second story.

A. The conclusion is proved by Statements 1-4;
B. The conclusion is disproved by Statements 1-4;
C. The facts are not sufficient to prove or disprove the conclusion.

23. FACTUAL STATEMENTS: 23.____
1) On Saturday, farmers Hank, Earl, Roy, and Cletus plowed a total of 520 acres.
2) Hank plowed twice as many acres as Roy.
3) Roy plowed half as much as the farmer who plowed the most.
4) Cletus plowed 160 acres.

CONCLUSION: Hank plowed 200 acres.
A. The conclusion is proved by Statements 1-4;
B. The conclusion is disproved by Statements 1-4;
C. The facts are not sufficient to prove or disprove the conclusion.

24. FACTUAL STATEMENTS: 24.____
1) Four travelers – Tina, Jodie, Alex, and Oscar – each traveled to a different island – Aruba, Jamaica, Nevis, and Barbados – but not necessarily respectively.
2) Tina did not travel as far to Jamaica as Jodie traveled to her island.
3) Oscar traveled twice as far as Alex, who traveled the same distance as the traveler who went to Aruba.
4) Oscar went to Barbados.

CONCLUSION: Oscar traveled the farthest.

A. The conclusion is proved by Statements 1-4;
B. The conclusion is disproved by Statements 1-4;
C. The facts are not sufficient to prove or disprove the conclusion.

25. FACTUAL STATEMENT: 25.____
1) In the natural history museum, every Native American display that contains pottery also contains beadwork.
2) Some of the displays containing lodge replicas also contain beadwork.
3) The display on the Choctaw, a Native American tribe, contains pottery.
4) The display on the Modoc, a Native American tribe, contains only two of these items.

CONCLUSION: If the Modoc display contains pottery, it does not contain lodge replicas.

A. The conclusion is proved by Statements 1-4;
B. The conclusion is disproved by Statements 1-4;
C. The facts are not sufficient to prove or disprove the conclusion.

KEY (CORRECT ANSWERS)

1.	A	11.	B
2.	B	12.	C
3.	A	13.	B
4.	A	14.	D
5.	C	15.	E
6.	B	16.	E
7.	B	17.	A
8.	B	18.	B
9.	A	19.	C
10.	B	20.	A

21. A
22. A
23. C
24. A
25. A

TEST 2

DIRECTIONS: Each question or incomplete statement is followed by several suggested answers or completions. Select the one that BEST answers the question or completes the statement. *PRINT THE LETTER OF THE CORRECT ANSWER IN THE SPACE AT THE RIGHT.*

Questions 1-9.

DIRECTIONS: In Questions 1 through 9, you will read a set of facts and a conclusion drawn from them. The conclusion may be valid or invalid, based on the facts. It is your task to determine the validity of the conclusion.
For each question, select the letter before the statement that BEST expresses the relationship between the given facts and the conclusion that has been drawn from them. Your choices are:

A. The facts prove the conclusion.
B. The facts disprove the conclusion; or
C. The facts neither prove nor disprove the conclusion.

1. FACTS: If the maximum allowable income for Medicaid recipients is increased, the number of Medicaid recipients will increase. If the number of Medicaid recipients increases, more funds must be allocated to the Medicaid program, which will require a tax increase. Taxes cannot be approved without the approval of the legislature. The legislature probably will not approve a tax increase. 1.____

CONCLUSION: The maximum allowable income for Medicaid recipients will increase.

A. The facts prove the conclusion.
B. The facts disprove the conclusion; or
C. The facts neither prove nor disprove the conclusion.

2. FACTS: All the dentists on the baseball team are short. Everyone in the dugout is a dentist, but not everyone in the dugout is short. The baseball team is not made up of people of any particular profession. 2.____

CONCLUSION: Some people who are not dentists are in the dugout.

A. The facts prove the conclusion.
B. The facts disprove the conclusion; or
C. The facts neither prove nor disprove the conclusion.

3. FACTS: A taxi company's fleet is divided into two fleets. Fleet One contains cabs A, B, C, and D. Fleet Two contains E, F, G, and H. Each cab is either yellow or green. Five of the cabs are yellow. Cabs A and E are not both yellow. Either Cab C or F, or both, are not yellow. Cabs B and H are either both yellow or both green. 3.____

CONCLUSION: Cab H is green.

A. The facts prove the conclusion.
B. The facts disprove the conclusion; or
C. The facts neither prove nor disprove the conclusion.

4. FACTS: Most people in the skydiving club are not afraid of heights. Everyone in the skydiving club makes three parachute jumps a month. 4.____

CONCLUSION: At least one person who is afraid of heights makes three parachute jumps a month.

A. The facts prove the conclusion.
B. The facts disprove the conclusion; or
C. The facts neither prove nor disprove the conclusion.

5. FACTS: If the Board approves the new rule, the agency will move to a new location immediately. If the agency moves, five new supervisors will be immediately appointed. The Board has approved the new proposal. 5.____

CONCLUSION: No new supervisors were appointed.

A. The facts prove the conclusion.
B. The facts disprove the conclusion; or
C. The facts neither prove nor disprove the conclusion.

6. FACTS: All the workers at the supermarket chew gum when they sack groceries. Sometimes Lance, a supermarket worker, doesn't chew gum at all when he works. Another supermarket worker, Jenny, chews gum the whole time she is at work. 6.____

CONCLUSION: Jenny always sacks groceries when she is at work.

7. FACTS: Lake Lottawatta is bigger than Lake Tacomi. Lake Tacomi and Lake Ottawa are exactly the same size. All lakes in Montana are bigger than Lake Ottawa. 7.____

CONCLUSION: Lake Lottawatta is in Montana.

A. The facts prove the conclusion.
B. The facts disprove the conclusion; or
C. The facts neither prove nor disprove the conclusion.

8. FACTS: Two men, Cox and Taylor, are playing poker at a table. Taylor has a pair of aces in his hand. One man is smoking a cigar. One of them has no pairs in his hand and is wearing an eye patch. The man wearing the eye patch is smoking a cigar. One man is bald. 8.____

CONCLUSION: Cox is smoking a cigar.

A. The facts prove the conclusion.
B. The facts disprove the conclusion; or
C. The facts neither prove nor disprove the conclusion.

9. FACTS: All Kwakiutls are Wakashan Indians. All Wakashan Indians originated on Vancouver Island. The Nootka also originated on Vancouver Island. 9.____

CONCLUSION: Kwakiutls originated on Vancouver Island.

A. The facts prove the conclusion.
B. The facts disprove the conclusion; or
C. The facts neither prove nor disprove the conclusion.

Questions 10-17.

DIRECTIONS: Questions 10 through 17 are based on the following reading passage. It is not your knowledge of the particular topic that is being tested, but your ability to reason based on what you have read. The passage is likely to detail several proposed courses of action and factors affecting these proposals. The reading passage is followed by a conclusion or outcome based on the facts in the passage, or a description of a decision taken regarding the situation. The conclusion is followed by a number of statements that have a possible connection to the conclusion. For each statement, you are to determine whether:

A. The statement proves the conclusion.
B. The statement supports the conclusion but does not prove it.
C. The statement disproves the conclusion.
D. The statement weakens the conclusion but does not disprove it.
E. The statement has no relevance to the conclusion.

Remember that the conclusion after the passage is to be accepted as the outcome of what actually happened, and that you are being asked to evaluate the impact each statement would have had on the conclusion.

PASSAGE

The World Wide Web portal and search engine, HipBot, is considering becoming a subscription-only service, locking out nonsubscribers from the content on its web site. HipBot currently relies solely on advertising revenues.

HipBot's content director says that by taking in an annual fee from each customer, the company can both increase profits and provide premium content that no other portal can match.

The marketing director disagrees, saying that there is no guarantee that anyone who now visits the web site for free will agree to pay for the privilege of visiting it again. Most will probably simply use the other major portals. Also, HipBot's advertising clients will not be happy when they learn that the site will be viewed by a more limited number of people.

CONCLUSION: In January of 2016, the CEO of HipBot decides to keep the portal open to all web users, with some limited "premium content" available to subscribers who don't mind paying a little extra to access it. The company will aim to maintain, or perhaps increase, its advertising revenue.

10. In an independent marketing survey, 62% of respondents said they "strongly agree" with the following statement: "I almost never pay attention to advertisements that appear on the World Wide Web." 10.____
    A. The statement proves the conclusion.
    B. The statement supports the conclusion but does not prove it.
    C. The statement disproves the conclusion.
    D. The statement weakens the conclusion but does not disprove it.
    E. The statement has no relevance to the conclusion.

11. When it learns about the subscription-only debate going on at HipBot, Wernham Hogg Entertainment, one of HipBot's most reliable clients, says it will withdraw its ads and place them on a free web portal if HipBot decides to limit its content to subscribers. Wernham Hogg pays HipBot about $6 million annually – about 12% of HipBot's gross revenues – to run its ads online. 11.____
    A. The statement proves the conclusion.
    B. The statement supports the conclusion but does not prove it.
    C. The statement disproves the conclusion.
    D. The statement weakens the conclusion but does not disprove it.
    E. The statement has no relevance to the conclusion.

12. At the end of the second quarter of FY 2016, after continued stagnant profits, the CEO of HipBot assembles a blue ribbon commission to gather and analyze data on the costs, benefits, and feasibility of adding a limited amount of "premium" content to the HipBot portal. 12.____
    A. The statement proves the conclusion.
    B. The statement supports the conclusion but does not prove it.
    C. The statement disproves the conclusion.
    D. The statement weakens the conclusion but does not disprove it.
    E. The statement has no relevance to the conclusion.

13. In the following fiscal year, Wernham Hogg Entertainment, satisfied with the "hit counts" on HipBot's free web site, spends another $1 million on advertisements that will appear on web pages that are available to HipBot's "premium subscribers. 13.____
    A. The statement proves the conclusion.
    B. The statement supports the conclusion but does not prove it.
    C. The statement disproves the conclusion.
    D. The statement weakens the conclusion but does not disprove it.
    E. The statement has no relevance to the conclusion.

14. HipBot's information technology director reports that the engineers in his department have come up with a feature that will search not only individual web pages, but tie into other web-based search engines, as well, and then comb through all these results to find those most relevant to the user's search. 14.____

A. The statement proves the conclusion.
B. The statement supports the conclusion but does not prove it.
C. The statement disproves the conclusion.
D. The statement weakens the conclusion but does not disprove it.
E. The statement has no relevance to the conclusion.

15. In an independent marketing survey, 79% of respondents said they "strongly agree" with the following statement: "Many web sites are so dominated by advertisements these days that it is increasingly frustrating to find the content I want to read or see." 15.____
A. The statement proves the conclusion.
B. The statement supports the conclusion but does not prove it.
C. The statement disproves the conclusion.
D. The statement weakens the conclusion but does not disprove it.
E. The statement has no relevance to the conclusion.

16. After three years of studies at the federal level, the Department of Commerce releases a report suggesting that, in general, the only private "subscriber-only" web sites that do well financially are those with a very specialized user population. 16.____
A. The statement proves the conclusion.
B. The statement supports the conclusion but does not prove it.
C. The statement disproves the conclusion.
D. The statement weakens the conclusion but does not disprove it.
E. The statement has no relevance to the conclusion.

17. HipBot's own marketing research indicates that the introduction of premium content has the potential to attract new users to the HipBot portal. 17.____
A. The statement proves the conclusion.
B. The statement supports the conclusion but does not prove it.
C. The statement disproves the conclusion.
D. The statement weakens the conclusion but does not disprove it.
E. The statement has no relevance to the conclusion.

Questions 18-25.

DIRECTIONS: Questions 18 through 25 each provide four factual statements and a conclusion based on these statements. After reading the entire question, you will decide whether:
A. The conclusion is proved by Statements 1-4;
B. The conclusion is disproved by Statements 1-4;
C. The facts are not sufficient to prove or disprove the conclusion.

18. FACTUAL STATEMENTS: 18.____
 1) If the alarm goes off, Sam will wake up.
 2) If Tandy wakes up before 4:00, Linda will leave the bedroom and sleep on the couch.
 3) If Linda leaves the bedroom, she'll check the alarm to make sure it is working.
 4) The alarm goes off.

CONCLUSION: Tandy woke up before 4:00.

 A. The conclusion is proved by Statements 1-4;
 B. The conclusion is disproved by Statements 1-4;
 C. The facts are not sufficient to prove or disprove the conclusion.

19. FACTUAL STATEMENTS: 19.____
 1) Four brothers are named Earl, John, Gary, and Pete.
 2) Earl and Pete are unmarried.
 3) John is shorter than the youngest of the four.
 4) The oldest brother is married, and is also the tallest.

CONCLUSION: Pete is the youngest brother.

 A. The conclusion is proved by Statements 1-4;
 B. The conclusion is disproved by Statements 1-4;
 C. The facts are not sufficient to prove or disprove the conclusion.

20. FACTUAL STATEMENTS: 20.____
 1) Automobile engines are cooled either by air or by liquid.
 2) If the engine is small and simple enough, air from a belt-driven fan will cool it sufficiently.
 3) Most newer automobile engines are too complicated to be air-cooled.
 4) Air-cooled engines are cheaper and easier to build then liquid-cooled engines.

CONCLUSION: Most newer automobile engines use liquid coolant.

 A. The conclusion is proved by Statements 1-4;
 B. The conclusion is disproved by Statements 1-4;
 C. The facts are not sufficient to prove or disprove the conclusion.

21. FACTUAL STATEMENTS: 21.____
 1) Erica will only file a lawsuit if she is injured while parasailing.
 2) If Rick orders Trip to run a rope test, Trip will check the rigging.
 3) If the rigging does not malfunction, Erica will not be injured.
 4) Rick orders Trip to run a rope test.

CONCLUSION: Erica does not file a lawsuit.

A. The conclusion is proved by Statements 1-4;
B. The conclusion is disproved by Statements 1-4;
C. The facts are not sufficient to prove or disprove the conclusion.

22. FACTUAL STATEMENTS: 22.____
1) On Maple Street, which is four blocks long, Bill's shop is two blocks east of Ken's shop.
2) Ken's shop is one block west of the only shop on Maple Street with an awning.
3) Erma's shop is one block west of the easternmost block.
4) Bill's shop is on the easternmost block.

CONCLUSION: Bill's shop has an awning.

A. The conclusion is proved by Statements 1-4;
B. The conclusion is disproved by Statements 1-4;
C. The facts are not sufficient to prove or disprove the conclusion.

23. FACTUAL STATEMENTS: 23.____
1) Gear X rotates in a clockwise direction if Switch C is in the OFF position.
2) Gear X will rotate in a counter-clockwise direction if Switch C is ON.
3) If Gear X is rotating in a clockwise direction, then Gear Y will not be rotating at all.
4) Gear Y is rotating.

CONCLUSION: Gear X is rotating in a counter-clockwise direction.

A. The conclusion is proved by Statements 1-4;
B. The conclusion is disproved by Statements 1-4;
C. The facts are not sufficient to prove or disprove the conclusion.

24. FACTUAL STATEMENTS: 24.____
1) The Republic of Garbanzo's currency system has four basic denominations: the pastor, the noble, the donner, and the rojo.
2) A pastor is worth 2 nobles.
3) 2 donners can be exchanged for a rojo.
4) 3 pastors are equal in value to 2 donners.

CONCLUSION: The rojo is most valuable.

A. The conclusion is proved by Statements 1-4;
B. The conclusion is disproved by Statements 1-4;
C. The facts are not sufficient to prove or disprove the conclusion.

25. FACTUAL STATEMENTS: 25.____
    1) At Prickett's Nursery, the only citrus trees left are either Meyer lemons or Valencia oranges, and every citrus tree left is either a dwarf or a semidwarf.
    2) Half of the semidwarf trees are Meyer lemons.
    3) There are more semidwarf trees left than dwarf trees.
    4) A quarter of the dwarf trees are Valencia oranges.

    CONCLUSION: There are more Valencia oranges left at Prickett's Nursery than Meyer lemons.

    A. The conclusion is proved by Statements 1-4;
    B. The conclusion is disproved by Statements 1-4;
    C. The facts are not sufficient to prove or disprove the conclusion.

KEY (CORRECT ANSWERS)

1. C
2. B
3. B
4. A
5. B

6. C
7. C
8. A
9. A
10. E

11. B
12. C
13. A
14. E
15. D

16. B
17. B
18. C
19. C
20. A

21. C
22. B
23. C
24. A
25. B

LOGICAL REASONING
EVALUATING CONCLUSIONS IN LIGHT OF KNOWN FACTS

EXAMINATION SECTION

TEST 1

COMMENTARY

This section is designed to provide practice questions in evaluating conclusions when you are given specific data to work with.

We suggest you do the questions three at a time, consulting the answer key and then the solution section for any questions you may have missed. It's a good idea to try the questions again a week before the exam.

In the validity of conclusion type of question, you are first given a reading passage which describes a particular situation. The passage may be on any topic, as it is not your knowledge of the topic that is being tested, but your reasoning abilities. The passage is likely to detail several proposed courses of action and factors affecting these proposals. The reading passage is followed by a conclusion based on the facts in the passage, or a description of a decision taken regarding the situation. The conclusion is followed by a number of statements which have a possible connection to the conclusion. For each statement, you are to determine whether:

A. The statement proves the conclusion.
B. The statement supports the conclusion but does not prove it.
C. The statement disproves the conclusion.
D. The statement weakens the conclusion but does not disprove it.
E. The statement has no relevance to the conclusion.

Remember that the conclusion after the passage is to be accepted as the outcome of what actually happened, and that you are being asked to evaluate the impact each statement would have had on the conclusion.

Questions 1-8.

DIRECTIONS: Questions 1 through 8 are based on the following paragraph.

In May of 2018, Mr. Bryan inherited a clothing store on Main Street in a small New England town. The store has specialized in selling quality men's and women's clothing since 1920. Business has been stable throughout the years, neither increasing nor decreasing. He has an opportunity to buy two adjacent stores which would enable him to add a wider range and style of clothing. In order to do this, he would have to borrow a substantial amount of money. He also risks losing the goodwill of his present clientele.

CONCLUSION: On November 7, 2018, Mr. Bryan tells the owner of the two adjacent stores that he has decided not to purchase them. He feels that it would be best to simply maintain his present marketing position, as there would not be enough new business to support an expansion.

A. The statement proves the conclusion.
B. The statement supports the conclusion but does not prove it.
C. The statement disproves the conclusion.
D. The statement weakens the conclusion.
E. The statement is irrelevant to the conclusion.

1. A large new branch of the county's community college holds its first classes in September. 1.____

2. The town's largest factory shuts down with no indication that it will reopen. 2.____

3. The United States Census showed that the number of children per household dropped from 2.4 to 2.1 since the last census. 3.____

4. Mr. Bryan's brother tells him of a new clothing boutique specializing in casual women's clothing which is opening soon. 4.____

5. Mr. Bryan's sister buys her baby several items for Christmas at Mr. Bryan's store. 5.____

6. Mrs. McIntyre, the President of the Town Council, brings Mr. Bryan a home-baked pumpkin pie in honor of his store's 100th anniversary. They discuss the changes that have taken place in the town, and she comments on how his store has maintained the same look and feel over the years. 6.____

7. In October, Mr. Bryan's aunt lends him $50,000. 7.____

8. The Town Council has just announced that the town is eligible for funding from a federal project designed to encourage the location of new businesses in the central districts of cities and towns. 8.____

Questions 9-18.

DIRECTIONS: Questions 9 through 18 are based on the following paragraph.

A proposal was put before the legislative body of a country to require air bags in all automobiles manufactured for domestic use in that country after 2019. The air bag, made of nylon or plastic, is designed to inflate automatically within a car at the impact of a collision, thus protecting front-seat occupants from being thrown forward. There has been much support of the measure from consumer groups, the insurance industry, key legislators, and the general public. The country's automobile manufacturers, who contend the new crash equipment would add up to $1,000 to car prices and provide no more protection than existing seat belts, are against the proposed legislation

CONCLUSION: On April 21, 2014, the legislation requiring air bags in all automobiles manufactured for domestic use in that country after 2019.

A. The statement proves the conclusion.
B. The statement supports the conclusion but does not prove it.
C. The statement disproves the conclusion.
D. The statement weakens the conclusion.
E. The statement is irrelevant to the conclusion.

9. A study has shown that 59% of car occupants do not use seat belts. 9.____

10. The country's Department of Transportation has estimated that the crash protection equipment would save up to 5,900 lives each year. 10.____

11. On April 27, 2013, Augusta Raneoni was named head of an advisory committee to gather and analyze data on the costs, benefits, and feasibility of the proposed legislation on air bags in automobiles. 11.____

12. Consumer groups and the insurance industry accuse the legislature of rejecting passage of the regulation for political reasons. 12.____

13. A study by the Committee on Imports and Exports projected that the sales of imported cars would rise dramatically in 2019 because imported cars do not have to include air bags, and can be sold more cheaply. 13.____

14. Research has shown that air bags, if produced on a large scale, would cost about $200 apiece, and would provide more reliable protection than any other type of seat belt. 14.____

15. Auto sales in 2011 increased 3% over the previous year. 15.____

16. A Department of Transportation report in July of 2020 credits a drop in automobile deaths of 4,100 to the use of air bags. 16.____

17. In June of 2014, the lobbyist of the largest insurance company receives a bonus for her work on the passage of the air bag legislation. 17.____

18. In 2020, the stock in crash protection equipment has risen three-fold over the previous year. 18.____

Questions 19-25.

DIRECTIONS: Questions 19 through 25 are based on the following paragraph.

On a national television talk show, Joan Rivera, a famous comedienne, has recently insulted the physical appearances of a famous actress and the dead wife of an ex-President. There has been a flurry of controversy over her comments, and much discussion of the incident has appeared in the press. Most of the comments have been negative. It appears that this tie she might have gone too far. There have been cancellations of two of her five scheduled performances in the two weeks since the show was televised, and Joan's been receiving a lot of negative mail. Because of the controversy, she has an interview with a national news magazine at the end of the week, and her press agent is strongly urging her to apologize publicly. She feels strongly that her comments were no worse than any other she has ever made, and that the whole incident will *blow over* soon. She respects her press agent's judgment, however, as his assessment of public sentiment tends to be very accurate.

CONCLUSION: Joan does not apologize publicly, and during the interview she challenges the actress to a weight-losing contest. For every pound the actress loses, Joan says she will donate $1 to the Cellulite Prevention League.

A. The statement proves the conclusion.
B. The statement supports the conclusion but does not prove it.
C. The statement disproves the conclusion.
D. The statement weakens the conclusion.
E. The statement is irrelevant to the conclusion.

19. Joan's mother, who she is very fond of, is very upset with Joan's comments. 19.____

20. Six months after the interview, Joan's income has doubled. 20.____

21. Joan's agent is pleased with the way Joan handles the interview. 21.____

22. Joan's sister has been appointed Treasurer of the Cellulite Prevention League In her report, she states that Joan's $12 contribution is the only amount that has been donated to the League in its first six months. 22.____

23. The magazine receives many letters commending Joan for the courage it took for her to apologize publicly in the interview. 23.____

24. Immediately after the interview appears, another one of Joan's performances is cancelled. 24.____

25. Due to a printers' strike, the article was not published until the following week. 25.____

Questions 26-30.

DIRECTIONS: Questions 25 through 30 are based on the following paragraph.

The law-making body of Country X must decide what to do about the issue of recording television shows for home use. There is currently no law against recording shows directly from the TV as long as the DVDs are not used for commercial purposes. The increasing popularity of pay TV and satellite systems, combined with the increasing number of homes that own recording equipment, has caused a great deal of concern in some segments of the entertainment industry. Companies that own the rights to films, popular television shows, and sporting events feel that their copyright privileges are being violated, and they are seeking compensation or the banning of TV recording. Legislation has been introduced to make it illegal to record television programs for home use. Separate proposed legislation is also pending that would continue to allow recording of TV shows for home use, but would place a tax of 10% on each DVD that is purchased for home use. The income from that tax would then be proportionately distributed as royalties to those owning the rights to programs being aired. A weighted point system coupled with the averaging of several national viewing rating systems would be used to determine the royalties. There is a great deal of lobbying being done for both bills, as the manufacturers of DVDs and recording equipment are against the passage of the bills.

CONCLUSION: The legislature of Country X rejects both bills by a wide margin.

A. The statement proves the conclusion.
B. The statement supports the conclusion but does not prove it.
C. The statement disproves the conclusion.
D. The statement weakens the conclusion.
E. The statement is irrelevant to the conclusion.

26. Country X's Department of Taxation hires 500 new employees to handle the increased paperwork created by the new tax on DVDs. 26.____

27. A study conducted by the country's most prestigious accounting firm shows that the cost of implementing the proposed new DVD tax would be greater than the income expected from it. 27.____

28. It is estimated that 80% of all those working in the entertainment industry, excluding performers, own DVD recorders. 28.____

29. The head of Country X's law enforcement agency states that legislation banning the home recording of TV shows would be unenforceable. 29.____

30. Financial experts predict that unless a tax is placed on DVDs, several large companies in the entertainment industry will have to file for bankruptcy. 30.____

Questions 31-38.

DIRECTIONS: Questions 31 through 38 are variations on the type of question you just had. It is important that you read the question very carefully to determine exactly what is required.

31. In this question, select the choice that is MOST relevant to the conclusion. 31.____
   I. The Buffalo Bills football team is in second place in its division.
   II. The New England Patriots are in first place in the same division.
   III. There are two games left to play in the season, and the Bills will not play the Patriots again.
   IV. The New England Patriots won ten games and lost four games, and the Buffalo Bills have won eight games and lost six games.

   CONCLUSION: The Buffalo Bills win their division.

   A. The conclusion is proved by sentences I-IV.
   B. The conclusion is disproved by sentences I-IV.
   C. The facts are not sufficient to prove or disprove the conclusion.

32. In this question, select the choice that is MOST relevant to the conclusion. 32.____
I. On the planet of Zeinon there are only two different eye colors and only two different hair colors.
II. Half of those beings with purple hair have golden eyes.
III. There are more inhabitants with purple hair than there are inhabitants with silver hair.
IV. One-third of those with silver hair have green eyes.
CONCLUSION: There are more golden-eyed beings on Zeinon than green-eyed ones.
A. The conclusion is proved by sentences I-IV.
B. The conclusion is disproved by sentences I-IV.
C. The facts are not sufficient to prove or disprove the conclusion.

33. In this question, select the choice that is MOST relevant to the conclusion. 33.____
John and Kevin are leaving Amaranth to go to school in Bethany. They've decided to rent a small truck to move their possessions. Joe's Truck Rental charges $100 plus 30¢ a mile. National Movers charges $50 more but gives free mileage for the first 100 miles. After the first 100 miles, they charge 25¢ a mile.
CONCLUSION: John and Kevin rent their truck from National Movers because it is cheaper.
A. The conclusion is proved by the facts in the above paragraph.
B. The conclusion is disproved by the facts in the above paragraph.
C. The facts are not sufficient to prove or disprove the conclusion.

34. For this question, select the choice that supports the information given in the passage. 34.____
Municipalities in Country X are divided into villages, towns, and cities. A village has a population of 5,000 or less. The population of a town ranges from 5,001 to 15,000. In order to be incorporated as a city, the municipality must have a population over 15,000. If, after a village becomes a town, or a town becomes a city, the population drops below the minimum required (for example, the population of a city goes below 15,000), and stays below the minimum for more than ten years, it loses its current status, and drops to the next category. As soon as a municipality rises in population to the next category (village to town, for example), however, it is immediately reclassified to the next category.
In the 2000 census, Plainfield had a population of 12,000. Between 2000 and 2010, Plainfield grew 10%, and between 2010 and 2020 Plainfield grew another 20%. The population of Springdale doubled from 2000 to 2010, and increased 25% from 2010 to 2020. The city of Smallville's population, 20,283, has not changed significantly in recent years. Granton had a population of 25,000 people in1990, and has decreased 25% in each ten year period since then. Ellenville had a population of 4,283 in 1990, and grew 5% in each ten year period since 1990.

In 2020,

A. Plainfield, Smallville, and Granton are cities.
B. Smallville is a city, Granton is a town, and Ellenville is a village.
C. Springdale, Granton, and Ellenville are towns.
D. Plainfield and Smallville are cities, and Ellenville is a town.

35. For this question, select the choice that is MOST relevant to the conclusion. 35.____

A study was done for a major food-distributing firm to determine if there is any difference in the kind of caffeine containing products used by people of different ages. A sample of one thousand people between the ages of twenty and fifty were drawn from selected areas in the country. They were divided equally into three groups.

Those individuals who were 20-29 were designated Group A, those 30-39 were Group B, and those 40-50 were placed in Group C.

It was found that on the average, Group A drank 1.8 cups of coffee, Group B 3.1, and Group C 2.5 cups of coffee daily. Group A drank 2.1 cups of tea, Group B drank 1.2, and Group C drank 2.6 cups of tea daily. Group A drank 3 1.8 ounces glasses of cola, Group B drank 1.9, and Group C drank 1.5 glasses of cola daily.

CONCLUSION: According to the study, the average person in the 20-29 age group drinks less tea daily than the average person in the 40-50 age group, but drinks more coffee daily than the average person in the 30-39 age group drinks cola.

A. The conclusion is proved by the facts in the above paragraph.
B. The conclusion is disproved by the facts in the above paragraph.
C. The facts are not sufficient to prove or disprove the conclusion.

36. For this question, select the choice that is MOST relevant to the conclusion 36.____

I. Mary is taller than Jane but shorter than Dale.
II. Fred is taller than Mary but shorter than Steven.
III. Dale is shorter than Steven but taller than Elizabeth.
IV. Elizabeth is taller than Mary but not as tall as Fred.

CONCLUSION: Dale is taller than Fred.

A. The conclusion is proved by sentences I-IV.
B. The conclusion is disproved by sentences I-IV.
C. The facts are not sufficient to prove or disprove the conclusion.

37. For this question, select the choice that is MOST relevant to the conclusion. 37.____

I. Main Street is between Spring Street and Glenn Blvd.
II. Hawley Avenue is one block south of Spring Street and three blocks north of Main Street.
III. Glenn Street is five blocks south of Elm and four blocks south of Main.
IV. All the streets mentioned are parallel to one another.

CONCLUSION: Elm Street is between Hawley Avenue and Glenn Blvd.

A. The conclusion is proved by the facts in sentences I-IV.
B. The conclusion is disproved by the facts in sentences I-IV.
C. The facts are not sufficient to prove or disprove the conclusion.

38. For this question, select the choice that is MOST relevant to the conclusion. 38.____
   I. Train A leaves the town of Hampshire every day at 5:50 A.M. and arrives in New London at 6:42 A.M.
   II. Train A leaves New London at 7:00 A.M. and arrives in Kellogsville at 8:42 A.M.
   III. Train B leaves Kellogsville at 8:00 A.M. and arrives in Hampshire at 10:45 A.M.
   IV. Due to the need for repairs, there is just one railroad track between New London and Hampshire.

   CONCLUSION: It is impossible for Train A and Train B to follow these schedules without colliding.
   A. The conclusion is proved by the facts in sentences I-IV.
   B. The conclusion is disproved by the facts in sentences I-IV.
   C. The facts are not sufficient to prove or disprove the conclusion.

KEY (CORRECT ANSWERS)

1.	D	11.	C	21.	D	31.	C
2.	B	12.	C	22.	A	32.	A
3.	E	13.	D	23.	C	33.	C
4.	B	14.	B	24.	B	34.	B
5.	C	15.	E	25.	E	35.	B
6.	A	16.	B	26.	C	36.	C
7.	D	17.	A	27.	B	37.	A
8.	B	18.	B	28.	E	38.	B
9.	B	19.	D	29.	B		
10.	B	20.	E	30.	D		

SOLUTIONS TO QUESTIONS

1. The answer is D. This statement weakens the conclusion, but does not disprove it. If a new branch of the community college opened in September, it could possibly bring in new business for Mr. Bryant. Since it states in the conclusion that Mr. Bryant felt there would not be enough new business to support the additional stores, this would tend to disprove the conclusion. Choice C would not be correct because it's possible that he felt that the students would not have enough additional money to support his new venture, or would not be interested in his clothing styles. It's also possible that the majority of the students already live in the area, so that they wouldn't really be a new customer population. This type of question is tricky, and can initially be very confusing, so don't feel badly if you missed it. Most people need to practice with a few of these types of questions before they feel comfortable recognizing exactly what they're being asked to do.

2. The answer is B. It supports the conclusion because the closing of the factory would probably take money and customers out of the town, causing Mr. Bryant to lose some of his present business. It doesn't prove the conclusion, however, because we don't know how large the factory was. It's possible that only a small percentage of the population was employed there, or that they found other jobs.

3. The answer is E. The fact that the number of children per household dropped slightly nationwide in the decade is irrelevant. Statistics showing a drop nationwide doesn't mean that there was a drop in the number of children per household in Mr. Bryant's hometown. This is a tricky question, as choice B, supporting the conclusion but not proving it, may seem reasonable. If the number of children per household declined nationwide, then it may not seem unreasonable to feel that this would support Mr. Bryant's decision not to expand his business. However, we're preparing you for promotional exams, not "real life." One of the difficult things about taking exams is that sometimes you're forced to make a choice between two statements that both seem like they could be the possible answer. What you need to do in that case is choose the best choice. Becoming annoyed or frustrated with the question won't really help much. If there's a review of the exam, you can certainly appeal the question. There have been many cases where, after an appeal, two possible choices have been allowed as correct answers. We've included this question, however, to help you see what to do should you get a question like this. It's most important not to get rattled, and to select the BEST choice. In this case, the connection between the statistical information and Mr. Bryant's decision is pretty remote. If the question had said that the number of children in Mr. Bryant's town had decreased, then choice B would have been a more reasonable choice. It could also help in this situation to visualize the situation. Picture Mr. Bryant in his armchair reading that, nationwide, the average number of children per household has declined slightly. How likely would this be to influence his decision, especially since he sells men's and women's clothing? It would take a while for this decline in population to show up, and we're not even sure if it applies to Mr. Bryant's hometown. Don't feel badly if you missed this; it was tricky. The more of these you do, the more comfortable you'll feel.

4. The answer is B. If a new clothing boutique specializing in casual women's clothing were to open soon, this would lend support to Mr. Bryant's decision not to expand, but would not prove that he had actually made the decision to expand. A new women's clothing boutique would most likely be in competition with his existing business, thus making any possible expansion a riskier venture. We can't be sure from this, however, that he didn't go ahead and expand his business despite the increased competition. Choice A, proves the conclusion, would only be the answer if we could be absolutely sure from the statement that Mr. Bryant had actually <u>not</u> expanded his business.

5. The answer is C. This statement disproves the conclusion. In order for his sister to buy several items for her baby at Mr. Bryant's store, he would have to have changed his business to include children's clothing.

6. The answer is A. It definitely proves the conclusion. The passage states that Mr. Bryan's store had been in business since 1920. A pie baked in honor of his store's 100th anniversary would have to be presented sometime in 2020. The conclusion states that he made his decision not to expand on November 7, 2018. If, more than a year later Mrs. MacIntyre comments that his store has maintained the same look and feel over the years, it could not have been expanded, or otherwise significantly changed.

7. The answer is D. If Mr. Bryant's aunt lent him $50,000 in October, this would tend to weaken the conclusion, which took place in November. Because it was stated that Mr. Bryant would need to borrow money in order to expand his business, it would be logical to assume that if he borrowed money he had decided to expand his business, weakening the conclusion. The reason C, disproves the conclusion, is not the correct answer is because we can't be sure Mr. Bryant didn't borrow the money for another reason.

8. The answer is B. If Mr. Bryant's town is eligible for federal funds to encourage the location of new businesses in the central district, this would tend to support his decision not to expand his business. Funds to encourage new business would increase the likelihood of there being additional competition for Mr. Bryant's store to contend with. Since we can't say for sure that there would be direct competition from a new business, however, choice A would be incorrect. Note that this is also a tricky question. You might have thought that the new funds weakened the conclusion because it would mean that Mr. Bryant could easily get the money he needed. Mr. Bryant is expanding his present business, not creating a <u>new</u> business. Therefore, he is not eligible for the funding.

9. The answer is B. This is a very tricky question. It's stated that 59% of car occupants don't use seat belts. The legislature is considering the use of air bags because of safety issues. The advantage of air bags over seat belts is that they inflate upon impact, and don't require car occupants to do anything with them ahead of time. Since the population has strongly resisted using seat belts, the air bags could become even more important in saving lives. Since saving lives is the purpose of the proposed legislation, the information that a small percentage of people use seat belts could be helpful to the passage of the legislation. We can't be sure that this is reason enough for the legislature to vote for the legislation, however, so choice A in incorrect.

10. The answer is B, as the information that 5,900 lives could be saved would tend to support the conclusion. Saving that many lives through the use of air bags could be a very persuasive reason to vote for the legislation. Since we don't know for sure that it's enough of a compelling reason for the legislature to vote for the legislation, however, choice A could not be the answer.

11. The answer is C, disproves the conclusion. If the legislation had been passed as stated in the conclusion, there would be no reason to appoint someone head of an advisory committee six days later to analyze the "feasibility of the proposed legislation." The key word here is "proposed." If it has been proposed, it means it hasn't been passed. This contradicts the conclusion and, therefore, disproves it.

12. The answer is C, disproves the conclusion. If the legislation had passed, there would be no reason for supporters of the legislation to accuse the legislature of rejecting the legislation for political reasons. This question may have seemed so obvious that you might have thought there was a trick to it. Exams usually have a few obvious questions, which will trip you up if you begin reading too much into them.

13. The answer is D, as this would tend to disprove the conclusion. A projected dramatic rise in imported cars could be very harmful to the country's economy and could be a very good reason for some legislators to vote against the proposed legislation. It would be assuming too much to choose C, however, because we don't know if they actually did vote against it.

14. The answer is B. This information would tend to support the passage of the legislation. The estimate of the cost of the air bags is $800 less than the cost estimated by opponents, and it's stated that the protection would be more reliable than any other type of seat belt. Both of these would be good arguments in favor of passing the legislation. Since we don't know for sure, however, how persuasive they actually were, choice A would not be the correct choice.

15. The answer is E, as this is irrelevant information. It really doesn't matter whether auto sales in 2001 have increased slightly over the previous year. If the air bag legislation were to go into effect in 2004, that might make the information somehow more relevant. But the air bag legislation would not take effect until 2009, so the information is irrelevant, since it tells us nothing about the state of the auto industry then.

16. The answer is B, supports the conclusion. This is a tricky question. While at first it might seem to prove the conclusion, we can't be sure that the air bag legislation is responsible for the drop in automobile deaths. It's possible air bags came into popular use without the legislation, or with different legislation. There's no way we can be sure that it was the proposed legislation mandating the use of air bags that was responsible.

17. The answer is A. If, in June of 2009, the lobbyist received a bonus "for her work on the air bag legislation," we can be sure that the legislation passed. This proves the conclusion.

18. The answer is B. This is another tricky question. A three-fold stock increase would strongly suggest that the legislation had been passed, but it's possible that factors other than the air bag legislation caused the increase. Note that the stock is in "crash protection

equipment." Nowhere in the statement does it say air bags. Seat belts, motorcycle helmets, and collapsible bumpers are all crash protection equipment and could have contributed to the increase. This is just another reminder to read carefully because the questions are often designed to mislead you.

19. The answer is D. This would tend to weaken the conclusion because Joan is very fond of her mother and she would not want to upset her unnecessarily. It does not prove it, however, because if Joan strongly feels she is right, she probably wouldn't let her mother's opinion sway her. Choice E would also not be correct, because we cannot assume that Joan's mother's opinion is of so little importance to her as to be considered irrelevant.

20. The answer is E. The statement is irrelevant. We are told that Joan's income has doubled but we are not old why. The phrase "six months after the interview" can be misleading in that it leads us to assume that the increase and the interview are related. Her income could have doubled because she regained her popularity but it could also have come from stocks or some other business venture. Because we are not given any reason for her income doubling, it would be impossible to say whether or not this statement proves or disproves the conclusion. Choice E is the best choice of the five possible choices. One of the problems with promotional exams is that sometimes you need to select a choice you're not crazy about. In this case, "not having enough information to made a determination" would be the best choice. However, that's not an option, so you're forced to work with what you've got. On these exams it's sometimes like voting for President; you have to pick the "lesser of the two evils" or the least awful choice. In this case, the information is more irrelevant to the conclusion than it is anything else.

21. The answer is D, weakens the conclusion. We've been told that Joan's agent feels that she should apologize. If he is pleased with her interview, then it would tend to weaken the conclusion but not disprove it. We can't be sure that he hasn't had a change of heart, or that there weren't other parts of the interview he liked so much that they outweighed her unwillingness to apologize.

22. The answer is A. The conclusion states that Joan will donate $1 to the Cellulite Prevention League for every pound the actress loses. Joan's sister's financial report on the League's activities directly supports and proves the conclusion.

23. The answer is C, disproves the conclusion. If the magazine receives many letters commending Joan for her courage in apologizing, this directly contradicts the conclusion, which states that Joan didn't apologize.

24. The answer is B. It was stated in the passage that two of Joan's performances were cancelled after the controversy first occurred. The cancellation of another performance immediately after her interview was published would tend to support the conclusion that she refused to apologize. Because we can't be sure, however, that her performance wasn't cancelled for another reason, choice A would be incorrect.

25. The answer is E, as this information is irrelevant. Postponing the article an extra week does not affect Joan's decision or the public's reaction to it.

26. The answer is C. If 500 new employees are hired to handle the "increased paperwork created by the new tax on DVDs," this would directly contradict the conclusion, which states that the legislature defeated both bills. (They should all be this easy.)

27. The answer is B. The results of the study would support the conclusion. If implementing the legislation was going to be so costly, it is likely that the legislature would vote against it. Choice A is not the answer, however, because we can't be sure that the legislature didn't pass it anyway.

28. The answer is E. It's irrelevant to the conclusion that 80% of all those working in the entertainment industry own DVD recorders. Sometimes if you're not sure about these, it can help a lot to try and visualize the situation. Why would someone voting on this legislation care about this fact? It doesn't seem to be the kind of information that would make any difference or impact upon the conclusion.

29. The answer is B. The head of the law enforcement agency's statement that the legislation would be unenforceable would support the conclusion. It's possible that many legislators would question why they should bother to pass legislation that would be impossible to enforce. Choice A would be incorrect, however, because we can't be sure that the legislation wasn't passed in spite of his statement.

30. The answer is D. This would tend to weaken the conclusion because the prospect of several large companies going bankrupt would seem to be a good argument in favor of the legislation. The possible loss of jobs and businesses would be a good reason for some people to vote for the legislation. We can't be sure, however, that this would be a competing enough reason to ensure passage of the legislation so choice C is incorrect.

This concludes our section on the "Validity of Conclusion" type of questions. We hope these weren't too horrible for you. It's important to keep in mind <u>exactly</u> what you've been given and <u>exactly</u> what they want you to do with it. It's also necessary to remember that you may have to choose between two possible answers. In that case, you must choose the one that seems the best. Sometimes you may think there is no good answer. You will probably be right, but you can't let that upset you. Just choose the one you dislike the least.

We want to repeat that it is unlikely that this exact format will appear on the exam. The skills required to answer these questions, however, are the same as those you'll need for the exam so we suggest that you review this section before taking the actual exam.

31. The answer is C. This next set of questions requires you to "switch gears" slightly, and get used to different formats. In this type of question, you have to decide whether the conclusion is proved by the facts give, disproved by the facts given, or neither because note enough information has been provided. Fortunately, unlike the previous questions, you don't have to decide whether particular facts support or don't support the conclusion. This type of question is more straight forward, but the reasoning behind it is the same. We are told that the Bills have won two games less than the Patriots, and that the Patriots are in first place and the Bills are in second place. We are also told that there are two games left to play, and that they won't play each other again. The conclusion states that the Bills won the division. Is there anything in the four statements that would prove this? We have

no idea what the outcome of the last two games of the season was. The Bills and Patriots could have ended up tied at the end of the season, or the Bills could have lost both or one of their last games while the Patriots did the same. There might even be another team tied for first or second place with the Bills or Patriots. Since we don't know for sure, Choice A is incorrect. Choice B is trickier. It might seem at first glance that the best the Bills could do would be to tie the Patriots if the Patriots lost their last two games and the Bills won their last two games. But it would be too much to assume that there is no procedure for a tiebreaker that wouldn't give the Bills the division championship. Since we don't know what the rules are in the event of a tie (for example, what if a tie was decided on the results of what happened when the two teams had played each other, or on the best record in the division, or on most points scored?), we can't say for sure that it would be impossible for the Bills to win their division. For this reason, choice C is the answer, as we don't have enough information to prove or disprove the conclusion. This question looked more difficult than it actually was. It's important to disregard any factors outside of the actual question, and to focus only on what you've been given. In this case, as on all of these types of questions, what you know or don't know about a subject is actually irrelevant. It's best to concentrate only on the actual facts given.

32. The answer is A. The conclusion is proved by the facts given.
In this type of problem, it is usually best to pull as many facts as possible from the sentences and then put them into a simpler form. The phrasing and the order of exam questions are designed to be confusing so you need to restate things as clearly as possible by eliminating the extras.
Sentence I tells us that there are only two possible colors for eyes and two for hair. Looking at the other sentences we learn that eyes are either green or gold and that hair is either silver or purple. If half the beings with purple hair have golden eyes, then the other half must have green eyes since it is the only other eye color. Likewise, if one-third of those with silver hair have green eyes, the other two-thirds must have golden eyes.
This information makes it clear that there are more golden-eyed beings on Zeinon than green-eyed ones. It doesn't matter that we don't know exactly how many are actually living on the planet. The number of those with gold eyes (1/2 plus 2/3) will always be greater than the number of those with green eyes (1/2 plus 1/3), no matter what the actual figures might be. Sentence III is totally irrelevant because even if there were more silver-haired inhabitants it would not affect the conclusion.

33. The answer is C. The conclusion is neither proved nor disproved by the facts because we don't know how many miles Bethany is from Amoranth.
With this type of question, if you're not sure how to approach it, you can always substitute in a range of "real numbers" to see what the result would be. If they were 200 miles apart, Joe's Truck Rental would be cheaper because they would charge a total of $160 while National Movers would charge $175.
Joe's - $100 plus .30 x 200 (or $60) = $160
National - $150 plus .25 x 100 (or $25) = $175
If the towns were 600 miles apart, however, National Movers would be cheaper. The cost of renting from National would be $275 compared to the $280 charged by Joe's Trucking.
Joe's - $100 plus .30 x 600 (or $180) = $280
National - $150 plus .25 x 500 (or $125) = $275

34. The answer is B. We've varied the format once more, but the reasoning is similar. This is a tedious question that is more like a math question, but we wanted to give you some practice with this type, just in case. You won't be able to do this question if you've forgotten how to do percents. Many exams require this knowledge, so if you feel you need a review we suggest you read Booklets 1, 2 or 3 in this series.

The only way to attack this problem is to go through each choice until you find the one that is correct. Choice A states that Plainfield, Smallville, and Granton are cities. Let's begin with Plainfield. The passage states that in 1990 Plainfield had a population of 12,000, and that it grew 10% between 1990 and 2000, and another 20% between 2000 and 2010. Ten percent of 12,000 is 1200 (12,000 x .10 = 1200). Therefore, the population grew from 12,000 in 1990 to 12,000 + 1200 between 1990 and 2000. At the time of the 2000 Census, Plainfield's population was 13,200. It then grew another 20% between 2000 and 2010, so, 13,200 x .20 = 2640. 13,200 plus the additional increase of 2640 would make the population of Plainfield 15,840. This would qualify it as a city, since its population is over 15,000. Since a change upward in the population of a municipality is re-classified immediately, Plainfield would have become a city right away. So far, statement A is true. The passage states that Smallville's population has not changed significantly in the last twenty years. Since Smallville's population was 20,283, Smallville would still be a city. Granton had a population of 25,000 (what a coincidence that so any of these places have such nice, even numbers) in 1980. The population has decreased 25% in each ten year period since that time. So from 1980 to 1990, the population decreased 25%. 25,000 x .25 = 6,250. 25,000 minus 6,250 = 18,750. So the population of Granton in 1990 would have been 18,750. (Or, you could have saved a step and multiplied 25,000 by .75 to get 18,750.) The population from 1990 to 2000 decreased an additional 25%. So: 18,750 x .25 = 4,687.50. 18,750 minus 4,687.50 = 14,062.50. Or: 18,750 x .75 = 14,062.50. (Don't let the fact that a half of a person is involved confuse you; these are exam questions, not real life.) From 2000 to 2010 the population decreased an additional 25%. This would mean that Granton's population was below 15,000 for more than ten years, so it's status as a city would have changed to that of a town, which would make choice A incorrect.

Choice B states that Smallville is a city and Granton is a town, which we know to be true from the information above. Choice B is correct so far. We next need to determine if Ellenville is a village. Ellenville had a population of 4,283 in 1980, and increased 5% in each ten year period since 1980. 4,283 x .05 = 214.15. 4,283 plus 214.15 = 4,497.15, so Ellenville's population from 1980 to 1990 increased to 4,497.15. (Or: 4,283 x 1.05 – 4,497.15.) From 1990 to 2000 Ellenville's population increased another 5%: 4,497.15 x .05 = 224.86. 4,497.15 plus 224.86 = 4,772.01 (or: 4,497.15 x 1.05 = 4,722.01.) From 2000 to 2010, Ellenville's population increased another 5%: 4,722.01 x .05 = 236.10. 4,722.01 plus 236.10 = 4,958.11. (Or: 4,722.01 x 1.05 = 4,958.11.).

Ellenville's population is still under 5,000 in 2010, so it would continue to be classified as a village. Since all three statements in choice B are true, choice B must be the answer. However, we'll go through the other choices. Choice C states that Springdale is a town. The passage tells us that the population of Springdale doubled from 1990 to 2000, and increased 25% from 2000 to 2010. It doesn't give us any actual population figures, however, so it's impossible to know what the population of Springdale is, making choice C incorrect. Choice C also states that Granton is a town, which is true, and that Ellenville is a town, which is false (from choice B we know it's a village). Choice D states that Plainfield and Smallville are cities, which is information we already know is true, and that Ellenville is a town. Since Ellenville is a village, choice D is also incorrect.

This was a lot of work for just one question and we doubt you'll get one like this on this section of the exam, but we included it just in case. On an exam, you can always put a check mark next to a question like this and come back to it later, if you feel you're pressed for time and cold spend your time more productively on other, less time-consuming problems.

35. The answer is B. This question requires very careful reading. It's best to break the conclusion down into smaller parts in order to solve the problem. The first half of the conclusion states that the average person in the 20-29 age group (Group A) drinks less tea daily than the average person in the 40-50 age group (Group C). The average person in Group A drinks 2.1 cups of tea daily, while the average person in Group C drinks 2.6 cups of tea daily. Since 2.1 is less than 2.6, the conclusion is correct so far. The second half of the conclusion states that the average person in Group A drinks more coffee daily than the average person in the 30-39 age group (Group B) drinks cola. The average person in Group A drinks 1.8 cups of coffee daily, while the average person in Group B drinks 1.9 glasses of cola. This disproves the conclusion, which states that the average person in Group A drinks more coffee daily than the average person in Group B drinks cola.

36. The answer is C. The easiest way to approach a problem that deals with the relationship between a number of different people or things is to set up a diagram. This type of problem is usually too confusing to do in your head. For this particular problem, the "diagram" could be a line, one end of which would be labeled tall and the other end labeled short. Then, taking one sentence at a time, place the people on the line to see where they fall in relation to one another.

The diagram of the first sentence would look like this:

Mary is taller than Jane but shorter than Dale, so she would fall somewhere between the two of them. We have placed tall on the left and labeled it left just to make the explanation easier. You could just as easily have reversed the position.

The second sentence places Fred somewhere to the left of Mary because he is taller than she is. Steven would be to the left of Fred for the same reason. At this point we don't know whether Steven and Fred are taller or shorter than Dale. The new diagram would look like this:

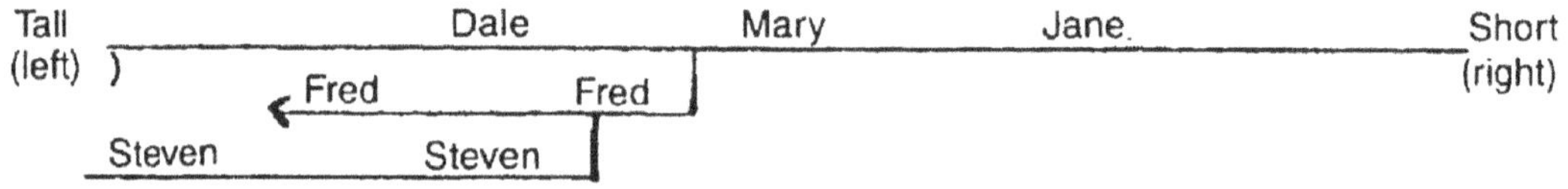

The third sentence introduces Elizabeth, presenting a new problem. Elizabeth can be anywhere to the right of Dale. Don't make the mistake of assuming she falls between Dale and Mary. At this point we don't know where she fits in relation to Mary, Jane, or even Fred.

We do get information about Steven, however. He is taller than Dale so he would be to the left of Dale. Since he is also taller than Fred (see sentence II), we know that Steven is the tallest person thus far. The diagram would now look like this:

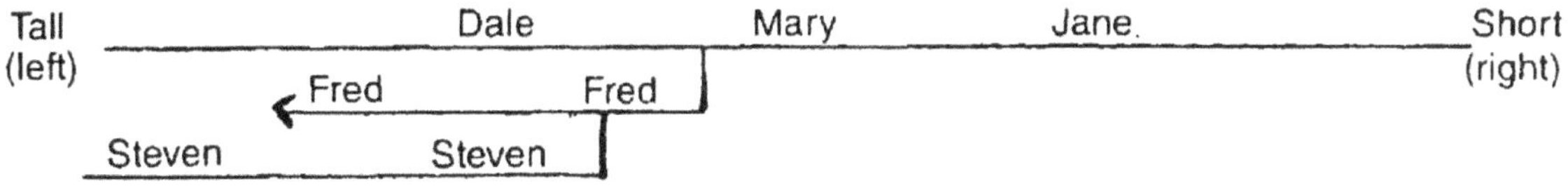

Fred's height is somewhere between Steven and Mary, Elizabeth's anywhere between Dale and the end of the line.

The fourth sentence tells us where Elizabeth stands, in relation to Fred and the others in the problem. The fact that she is taller than Mary means she is also taller than Jane. The final diagram would look like this:

We still don't know whether Dale or Fred is taller, however. Therefore, the conclusion that Dale is taller than Fred can't be proved. It also can't be disproved because we don't know for sure that he isn't. The answer has to be choice C, as the conclusion can't be proved or disproved.

37. The answer is A. This is another problem that is easiest for most people if they make a diagram. Sentence I states that Main Street is between Spring Street and Glenn Blvd. At this point we don't know if they are next to each other or if they are separated by a number of streets. Therefore, you should leave space between streets as you plot your first diagram.

The order of the streets could go either:

Spring St. Main St. Glenn Blvd.	or	Glenn Blvd. Main St. Spring St.

Sentence II states that Hawley Street is one block south of Spring Street and 3 blocks north of Main Street. Because most people think in terms of north as above and south as below and because it was stated that Hawley is one block south of Spring Street and three blocks north of Main Street, the next diagram could look like this:

18 (#1)

Spring
Hawley
______
______
Main
Glenn

The third sentence states that Glenn Street is five blocks south of Elm and four blocks south of Main. It could look like this:

Spring
Hawley
______
Elm
Main
____
____
____
Glenn

The conclusion states that Elm Street is between Hawley Avenue and Glenn Blvd. From the above diagram, we can see that this is the case.

38. The answer is B. For most people, the best way to do this problem is to draw a diagram, plotting the course of both trains. Sentence I states that Train A leaves Hampshire at 5:50 A.M. and reaches New London at 6:42. Your first diagram might look like this:

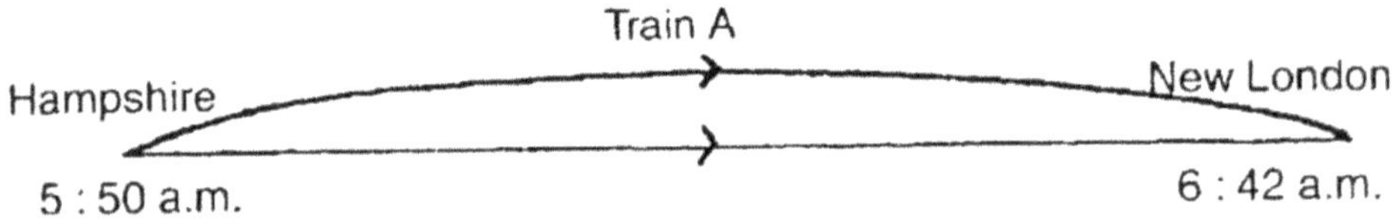

Sentence II states that the train leaves New London at 7:00 a.m. and arrives in Kellogsville at 8:42 a.m. The diagram might now look like this:

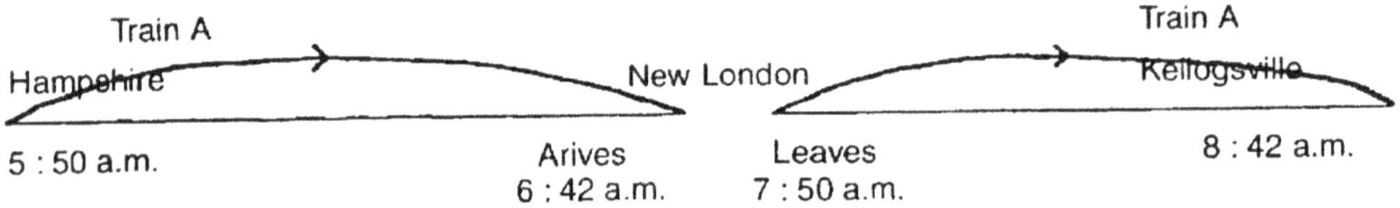

Sentence III gives us the rest of the information that must be included in the diagram. It introduces Train B, which moves in the opposite direction, leaving Kellogsville at 8:00 a.m. and arriving at Hampshire at 10:42 a.m. The final diagram might look like this:

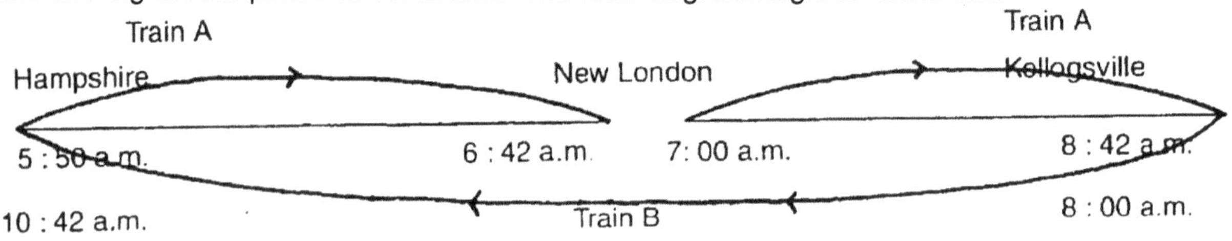

19 (#1)

As you can see from the diagram, the routes of the two trains will overlap somewhere between Kellogsville and New London. If you read sentence IV quickly and assumed that that was the section with only one track, you probably would have assumed that there would have had to be a collision. Sentence IV states, however, that there is only one railroad track between New London and Hampshire. That is the only section, then, where the two trains could collide. By the time Train B gets to that section, however, Train A will have passed it. The two trains will pass each other somewhere between New London and Kellogsville, not New London and Hampshire.

REPORT WRITING

EXAMINATION SECTION

TEST 1

DIRECTIONS: Each question or incomplete statement is followed by several suggested answers or completions. Select the one that BEST answers the question or completes the statement. *PRINT THE LETTER OF THE CORRECT ANSWER IN THE SPACE AT THE RIGHT.*

1. Following are six steps that should be taken in the course of report preparation: 1.____
   I. Outlining the material for presentation in the report
   II. Analyzing and interpreting the facts
   III. Analyzing the problem
   IV. Reaching conclusions
   V. Writing, revising, and rewriting the final copy
   VI. Collecting data

   According to the principles of good report writing, the CORRECT order in which these steps should be taken is:
   A. VI, III, II, I, IV, V
   B. III, VI, II, IV, I, V
   C. III, VI, II, I, IV, V
   D. VI, II, III, IV, I, V

2. Following are three statements concerning written reports: 2.____
   I. Clarity is generally more essential in oral reports than in written reports.
   II. Short sentences composed of simple words are generally preferred to complex sentences and difficult words.
   III. Abbreviations may be used whenever they are customary and will not distract the attention of the reader.

   Which of the following choices correctly classifies the above statements in to those which are valid and those which are not valid?
   A. I and II are valid, but III is not valid
   B. I is valid, but II and III are not valid.
   C. II and III are valid, but I is not valid.
   D. III is valid, but I and II are not valid.

3. In order to produce a report written in a style that is both understandable and effective, an investigator should apply the principles of unit, coherence, and emphasis. 3.____
   The one of the following which is the BEST example of the principle of coherence is
   A. interlinking sentences so that thoughts flow smoothly
   B. having each sentence express a single idea to facilitate comprehension
   C. arranging important points in prominent positions so they are not overlooked
   D. developing the main idea fully to insure complete consideration

4. Assume that a supervisor is preparing a report recommending that a standard work procedure be changed. 4.____
Of the following, the MOST important information that he should include in this report is
   A. a complete description of the present procedure
   B. the details and advantages of the recommended procedure
   C. the type and amount of retraining needed
   D. the percentage of men who favor the change

5. When you include in your report on an inspection some information which you have obtained from other individuals, it is MOST important that 5.____
   A. this information have no bearing on the work these other people are performing
   B. you do not report as fact the opinions of other individuals
   C. you keep the source of the information confidential
   D. you do not tell the other individuals that their statements will be included in your report

6. Before turning in a report of an investigator of an accident, you discover some additional information you did not know about when you wrote the report. 6.____
Whether or not you re-write your report to include this additional information should depend MAINLY on the
   A. source of this additional information
   B. established policy covering the subject matter of the report
   C. length of the report and the time it would take you to re-write it
   D. bearing this additional information will have on the conclusions in the report

7. The MOST desirable *first* step in the planning of a written report is to 7.____
   A. ascertain what necessary information is readily available in the files
   B. outline the methods you will employ to get the necessary information
   C. determine the objectives and uses of the report
   D. estimate the time and cost required to complete the report

8. In writing a report, the practice of taking up the least important points and the most important points last is a 8.____
   A. *good* technique since the final points made in a report will make the greatest impression on the reader
   B. *good* technique since the material is presented in a more logical manner and will lead directly to the conclusions
   C. *poor* technique since the reader's time is wasted by having to review irrelevant information before finishing the report
   D. *poor* technique since it may cause the reader to lose interest in the report and arrive at incorrect conclusions about the report

9. Which one of the following serves as the BEST guideline for you to follow for effective written reports? 9.____
Keep sentences
   A. short and limit sentences to one thought
   B. short and use as many thoughts as possible
   C. long and limit sentences to one thought
   D. long and use as many thoughts as possible

10. One method by which a supervisor might prepare written reports to management is to begin with the conclusions, results, or summary, and to follow this with the supporting data. 10.____
The BEST reason why management may *prefer* this form of report is that
   A. management lacks the specific training to understand the data
   B. the data completely supports the conclusions
   C. time is saved by getting to the conclusions of the report first
   D. the data contains all the information that is required for making the conclusions

11. When making written reports, it is MOST important that they be 11.____
   A. well-worded
   B. accurate as to the facts
   C. brief
   D. submitted immediately

12. Of the following, the MOST important reason for a supervisor to prepare good written reports is that 12.____
   A. a supervisor is rated on the quality of his reports
   B. decisions are often made on the basis of the reports
   C. such reports take less time for superiors to review
   D. such reports demonstrate efficiency of department operations

13. Of the following, the BEST test of a good report is whether it 13.____
   A. provides the information needed
   B. shows the good sense of the writer
   C. is prepared according to a proper format
   D. is grammatical and neat

14. When a supervisor writes a report, he can BEST show that he has a understanding of the subject of the report by 14.____
   A. including necessary facts and omitting nonessential details
   B. using statistical data
   C. giving his conclusions but not the data on which they are based
   D. using a technical vocabulary

15. Suppose you and another supervisor on the same level are assigned to work together on a report. You disagree strongly with one of the recommendations the other supervisor wants to include in the report but you cannot change his views. 15.____

Of the following, it would be BEST that
A. you refuse to accept responsibility for the report
B. you ask that someone else be assigned to this project to replace you
C. each of you state his own ideas about this recommendation in the report
D. you give in to the other supervisor's opinion for the sake of harmony

16. Standardized forms are often provided for submitting reports. 16.____
Of the following, the MOST important advantage of using standardized forms for reports is that
A. they take less time to prepare than individually written reports
B. the person making the report can omit information he considers unimportant
C. the responsibility for preparing these reports can be turned over to subordinates
D. necessary information is less likely to be omitted

17. A report which may BEST be classed as a *periodic* report is one which 17.____
A. requires the same type of information at regular intervals
B. contains detailed information which is to be retained in permanent records
C. is prepared whenever a special situation occurs
D. lists information in graphic form

18. In the writing of reports or letters, the ideas presented in a paragraph are usually of unequal importance and require varying degrees of emphasis. 18.____
All of the following are methods of placing extra stress on an idea EXCEPT
A. repeating it in a number of forms
B. placing it in the middle of the paragraph
C. placing it either at the beginning or at the end of a paragraph
D. underlining it

Questions 19-25.

DIRECTIONS: Questions 19 through 25 concern the subject of report writing and are based on the information and incidents described in the following paragraph. (In answering these questions, assume that the facts and incidents in the paragraph are true.)

On December 15, at 8 A.M., seven Laborers reported to Foreman Joseph Meehan in the Greenbranch Yard in Queens. Meehan instructed the men to load some 50-pound boxes of books on a truck for delivery to an agency building in Brooklyn. Meehan told the men that, because the boxes were rather heavy, two men should work together, helping each other lift and load each box. Since Michael Harper, one of the Laborers, was without a partner, Meehan helped him with the boxes for a while. When Meehan was called to the telephone in a nearby building, however, Harper decided to lift a box himself. He appeared able to lift the box, but, as he got the box halfway up, he cried out that he had a sharp pain in his back. Another Laborer, Jorge Ortiz, who was passing by, ran over to help Harper put the box down. Harper suddenly dropped the box, which fell on Ortiz' right foot. By this time, Meehan had come out of the building. He immediately helped get the box off Ortiz' foot and had both men lie down. Meehan covered the men with blankets and called an ambulance, which arrived a half hour later. At the hospital, the doctor said that the X-ray results showed that Ortiz' right foot was broken in three places.

19. What would be the BEST term to use in a report describing the injury of Jorge Ortiz? 19.____
    A. Strain B. Fracture C. Hernia D. Hemorrhage

20. Which of the following would be the MOST accurate summary for the Foreman to put in his report of the incident? 20.____
    A. Ortiz attempted to help Harper carry a box which was too heavy for one person, but Harper dropped it before Ortiz got there.
    B. Ortiz tried to help Harper carry a box but Harper got a pain in his back and accidentally dropped the box on Ortiz' foot.
    C. Harper refused to follow Meehan's orders and lifted a box too heavy for him; he deliberately dropped it when Ortiz tried to help him carry it.
    D. Harper lifted a box and felt a pain in his back; Ortiz tried to help Harper put the box down but Harper accidentally dropped it on Ortiz' foot.

21. One of the Laborers at the scene of the accident was asked his version of the incident. 21.____
    Which information obtained from this witness would be LEAST important for including in the accident report?
    A. His opinion as to the cause of the accident
    B. How much of the accident he saw
    C. His personal opinion of the victims
    D. His name and address

22. What should be the MAIN objective of writing a report about the incident described in the above paragraph? To 22.____
    A. describe the important elements in the accident situation
    B. recommend that such Laborers as Ortiz be advised not to interfere in another's work unless given specific instructions
    C. analyze the problems occurring when there are not enough workers to perform a certain task
    D. illustrate the hazards involved in performing routine everyday tasks

23. Which of the following is information *missing* from the above passage but which *should* be included in a report of the incident? The 23.____
    A. name of the Laborer's immediate supervisor
    B. contents of the boxes
    C. time at which the accident occurred
    D. object or action that caused the injury to Ortiz' foot

24. According to the description of the incident, the accident occurred because 24.____
    A. Ortiz attempted to help Harper who resisted his help
    B. Harper failed to follow instructions given him by Meehan
    C. Meehan was not supervising his men as closely as he should have
    D. Harper was not strong enough to carry the box once he lifted it

25. Which of the following is MOST important for a foreman to avoid when writing up an official accident report? 25.____
    A. Using technical language to describe equipment involved in the accident
    B. Putting in details which might later be judged unnecessary
    C. Giving an opinion as to conditions that contributed to the accident
    D. Recommending discipline for employees who, in his opinion, caused the accident

---

KEY (CORRECT ANSWERS)

1.	B	11.	B
2.	C	12.	B
3.	A	13.	A
4.	B	14.	A
5.	B	15.	C
6.	D	16.	D
7.	C	17.	A
8.	D	18.	B
9.	A	19.	B
10.	C	20.	D

21.	C
22.	A
23.	C
24.	B
25.	D

TEST 2

DIRECTIONS: Each question or incomplete statement is followed by several suggested answers or completions. Select the one that BEST answers the question or completes the statement. *PRINT THE LETTER OF THE CORRECT ANSWER IN THE SPACE AT THE RIGHT.*

1. Lieutenant X is preparing a report to submit to his commanding officer in order to get approval of a plan of operation he has developed. 1.____
The report starts off with the statement of the problem and continues with the details of the problem. It contains factual information gathered with the help of field and operational personnel. It contains a final conclusion and recommendation for action. The recommendation is supplemented by comments from other precinct staff members on how the recommendations will affect their areas of responsibility. The report also includes directives and general orders ready for the commanding officer's signature. In addition, it has two statements of objections presented by two precinct staff members.
Which one of the following, if any, is either an item that Lieutenant X should have included in his report and which is not mentioned above, or is an item which Lieutenant X improperly did include in his report?
   A. Considerations of alternative courses of action and their consequences should have been covered in the report.
   B. The additions containing undocumented objections to the recommended course of action should not have been included as part of the report.
   C. A statement on the qualifications of Lieutenant X, which would support his expertness in the field under consideration, should have been included in the report.
   D. The directives and general orders should not have been prepared and included in the report until the commanding officer had approved the recommendations.
   E. None of the above, since Lieutenant X's report was both proper and complete.

2. During a visit to a section, the district supervisor criticizes the method being used by the assistant foreman to prepare a certain report and orders him to modify the method. This change ordered by the district supervisor is in direct conflict with the specific orders of the foreman. 2.____
In this situation, it would be BEST for the assistant foreman to
   A. change the method and tell the foreman about the change at the first opportunity
   B. change the method and rely on the district supervisor to notify the foreman
   C. report the matter to the foreman and delay the preparation of the report
   D. ask the district supervisor to discuss the matter with the foreman but use the old method for the time being

3. A department officer should realize that the MOST usual reason for writing a report is to 3.____
   A. give orders and follow up their execution
   B. establish a permanent record
   C. raise questions
   D. supply information

4. A very important report which is being prepared by a department officer will soon be due on the desk of the district supervisor. No typing help is available at this time for the officer. 4.____
   For the officer to write out this report in longhand in such a situation would be
   A. *bad*; such a report would not make the impression a typed report would
   B. *good*; it is important to get the report in on time
   C. *bad*; the district supervisor should not be required to read longhand reports
   D. *good*; it would call attention to the difficult conditions under which this section must work

5. In a well-written report, the length of each paragraph in the report should be 5.____
   A. varied according to the content
   B. not over 300 words
   C. pretty nearly the same
   D. gradually longer as the report is developed and written

6. A clerk in the headquarters office complains to you about the way in which you are filing out a certain report. 6.____
   It would be BEST for you to
   A. tell the clerk that you are following official procedures in filling out the report
   B. ask to be referred to the clerk's superior
   C. ask the clerk exactly what is wrong with the way in which you are filling out the report
   D. tell the clerk that you are following the directions of the district supervisor

7. The use of an outline to help in writing a report is 7.____
   A. *desirable*, in order to insure good organization and coverage
   B. *necessary*, so it can be used as an introduction to the report itself
   C. *undesirable*, since it acts as a straightjacket and may result in an unbalanced report
   D. *desirable*, if you know your immediate supervisor reads reports with extreme care and attention

8. It is advisable that a department officer do his paper work and report writing as soon as he has completed an inspection MAINLY because 8.____
   A. there are usually deadlines to be met
   B. it insures a steady work-flow
   C. he may not have time for this later
   D. the facts are then freshest in his mind

9. Before you turn in a report you have written of an investigation that you have made, you discover some additional information you didn't know about before. Whether or not you re-write the report to include this additional information should depend MAINLY on the 9.____
   A. amount of time remaining before the report is due
   B. established policy of the department covering the subject matter of the report
   C. bearing this information will have on the conclusions of the report
   D. number of people who will eventually review the report

10. When a supervisory officer submits a periodic report to the district supervisor, he should realize that the CHIEF importance of such a report is that it 10.____
    A. is the principal method of checking on the efficiency of the supervisor and his subordinates
    B. is something to which frequent reference will be made
    C. eliminates the need for any personal follow-up or inspection by higher echelons
    D. permits the district supervisor to exercise his functions of direction, supervision, and control better

11. Conclusions and recommendations are usually placed at the end rather than at the beginning of a report because 11.____
    A. the person preparing the report may decide to change some of the conclusions and recommendations before he reaches the end of the report
    B. they are the most important part of the report
    C. they can be judged better by the person to whom the report is sent after he reads the facts and investigators which come earlier in the report
    D. they can be referred to quickly when needed without reading the rest of the report

12. The use of the same method of record-keeping and reporting by all agency sections is 12.____
    A. *desirable*, MAINLY because it saves time in section operations
    B. *undesirable*, MAINLY because it kills the initiative of the individual section foreman
    C. *desirable*, MAINLY because it will be easier for the administrator to evaluate and compare section operations
    D. *undesirable*, MAINLY because operations vary from section to section and uniform record-keeping and reporting is not appropriate

13. The GREATEST benefit the section officer will have from keeping complete and accurate records and reports of section operations is that 13.____
    A. he will find it easier to run his section efficiently
    B. he will need less equipment
    C. he will need less manpower
    D. the section will run smoothly when he is out

14. You have prepared a report to your superior and are ready to send it forward. But on re-reading it, you think some parts are not clearly expressed and your superior ay have difficulty getting your point. Of the following, it would be BEST for you to 14.____
   A. give the report to one of your men to read, and if he has no trouble understanding it send it through
   B. forward the report and call your superior the next day to ask whether it was all right
   C. forward the report as is; higher echelons should be able to understand any report prepared by a section officer
   D. do the report over, re-writing the sections you are in doubt about

15. The BEST of the following statements concerning reports is that 15.____
   A. a carelessly written report may give the reader an impression of inaccuracy
   B. correct grammar and English are unimportant if the main facts are given
   C. every man should be required to submit a daily work report
   D. the longer and more wordy a report is, the better it will read

16. In writing a report, the question of whether or not to include certain material could be determined BEST by considering the 16.____
   A. amount of space the material will occupy in the report
   B. amount of time to be spent in gathering the material
   C. date of the material
   D. value of the material to the superior who will read the report

17. Suppose you are submitting a fairly long report to your superior. The one of the following sections that should come FIRST in this report is a 17.____
   A. description of how you gathered material
   B. discussion of possible objections to your recommendations
   C. plan of how your recommendations can be put into practice
   D. statement of the problem dealt with

Questions 18-20.

DIRECTIONS: A foreman is asked to write a report on the incident described in the following passage. Answer Questions 18 through 20 based on the following information.

On March 10, Henry Moore, a laborer, was in the process of transferring some equipment from the machine shop to the third floor. He was using a dolly to perform this task and, as he was wheeling the material through the machine shop, laborer Bob Greene called to him. As Henry turned to respond to Bob, he jammed the dolly into Larry Mantell's leg, knocking Larry down in the process and causing the heavy drill that Larry was holding to fall on Larry's foot. Larry started rubbing his foot and then, infuriated, jumped up and punched Henry in the jaw. The force of the blow drove Henry's head back against the wall. Henry did not fight back; he appeared to be dazed. An ambulance was called to take Henry to the hospital, and the ambulance attendant told the foreman that it appeared likely that Henry had suffered a concussion. Larry's injuries consisted of some bruises, but he refused medical attention.

18. An adequate report of the above incident should give as minimum information the names of the persons involved, the names of the witnesses, the date and the time that each event took place, and the 18.____
    A. names of the ambulance attendants
    B. names of all the employees working in the machine shop
    C. location where the accident occurred
    D. nature of the previous safety training each employee had been given

19. The only one of the following which is NOT a fact is 19.____
    A. Bob called to Henry
    B. Larry suffered a concussion
    C. Larry rubbed his foot
    D. the incident took place in the machine shop

20. Which of the following would be the MOST accurate summary of the incident for the foreman to put in his report of the accident? 20.____
    A. Larry Mantell punched Henry Moore because a drill fell on his foot and he was angry. Then Henry fell and suffered a concussion.
    B. Henry Moore accidentally jammed a dolly into Larry Mantell's foot, knocking Larry down. Larry punched Henry, pushing him into the wall and causing him to bang his head against the wall.
    C. Bob Greene called Henry Moore. A dolly than jammed into Larry Mantell and knocked him down. Larry punched Henry who tripped and suffered some bruises. An ambulance was called.
    D. A drill fell on Larry Mantell's foot. Larry jumped up suddenly and punched Henry Moore and pushed him into the wall. Henry may have suffered a concussion as a result of falling.

Questions 21-25.

DIRECTIONS: Questions 21 through 25 are to be answered ONLY on the basis of the information provided in the following passage.

A written report is a communication of information from one person to another. It is an account of some matter especially investigated, however routine that matter may be. The ultimate basis of any good written report is facts, which become known through observation and verification. Good written reports may seem to be no more than general ideas and opinions. However, in such cases, the facts leading to these opinions were gathered, verified, and reported earlier, and the opinions are dependent upon these facts. Good style, proper form, and emphasis cannot make a good written report out of unreliable information and bad judgment; but, on the other hand, solid investigation and brilliant thinking are not likely to become very useful until they are effectively communicated to others. If a person's work calls for written reports, then his work is often no better than his written reports.

21. Based on the information in the above passage, it can be concluded that opinions expressed in a report should be 21.____
   A. based on facts which are gathered and reported
   B. emphasized repeatedly when they result from a special investigation
   C. kept to a minimum
   D. separated from the body of the report

22. In the above passage, the one of the following which is mentioned as a way of establishing facts is 22.____
   A. authority
   B. communication
   C. reporting
   D. verification

23. According to the above passage, the characteristic shared by ALL written reports is that they are 23.____
   A. accounts of routine matters
   B. transmissions of information
   C. reliable and logical
   D. written in proper form

24. Which of the following conclusions can logically be drawn from the information given in the above passage? 24.____
   A. Brilliant thinking can make up for unreliable information in a report.
   B. One method of judging an individual's work is the quality of the written reports he is required to submit.
   C. Proper form and emphasis can make a good report out of unreliable information.
   D. Good written reports that seem to be no more than general ideas should be rewritten.

25. Which of the following suggested titles would be MOST appropriate for this passage? 25.____
   A. Gathering and Organizing Facts
   B. Techniques of Observation
   C. Nature and Purpose of Reports
   D. Reports and Opinions: Differences and Similarities

KEY (CORRECT ANSWERS)

1. A
2. A
3. D
4. B
5. A

6. C
7. A
8. D
9. C
10. D

11. C
12. C
13. A
14. D
15. A

16. D
17. D
18. C
19. B
20. B

21. A
22. D
23. B
24. B
25. C

TEST 3

DIRECTIONS: Each question or incomplete statement is followed by several suggested answers or completions. Select the one that BEST answers the question or completes the statement. *PRINT THE LETTER OF THE CORRECT ANSWER IN THE SPACE AT THE RIGHT.*

Questions 1-5.

DIRECTIONS: The following is an accident report similar to those used in departments for reporting accidents. Questions 1 through 5 are be answered using ONLY the information given in this report.

ACCIDENT REPORT

FROM: John Doe	**DATE OF REPORT:** June 23	
TITLE: Sanitation Worker		
DATE OF ACCIDENT: June 22 time 3 ~~AM~~ PM	**CITY:** Metropolitan	
PLACE: 1489 Third Avenue		
VEHICLE NO. 1	**VEHICLE NO. 2**	
OPERATOR: John Doe, <u>Sanitation Worker</u> Title	**OPERATOR:** Richard Roe	
VEHICLE CODE NO: 14-238	**ADDRESS:** 498 High Street	
LICENSE NO.: 0123456	**OWNER:** Henry Roe **ADDRESS:**786 E.83 St.	**LIC. NO.:** 5N1492
DESCRIPTION OF ACCIDENT: Light green Chevrolet sedan while trying to pass drove in to rear side of sanitation truck which had stopped to collect garbage. No one was injured but there was property damage.		
NATURE OF DAMAGE TO PRIVATE VEHICLE: Right front fender crushed, bumper bent		
DAMAGE TO CITY VEHICLE: Front of left rear fender pushed in. Paint scraped.		
NAME OF WITNESS: Frank Brown	**ADDRESS:** 48 Kingsway	
SIGNATURE OF PERSON MAKING THIS REPORT *John Doe*		**BADGE NO.:** 428

1. Of the following, the one which has been omitted from this accident report is the 1.____
   A. location of the accident
   B. drivers of the vehicles involved
   C. traffic situation at the time of the accident
   D. owners of the vehicles involved

2. The address of the driver of Vehicle No. 1 is not required because he 2.____
   A. is employed by the department B. is not the owner of the vehicle
   C. reported the accident D. was injured in the accident

3. The report indicates that the driver of Vehicle No. 2 was PROBABLY 3.____
   A. passing on the wrong side of the truck
   B. not wearing his glasses
   C. not injured in the accident
   D driving while intoxicated

4. The number of people *specifically* referred to in this report is 4.____
   A. 3 B. 4 C. 5 D. 6

5. The license number of Vehicle No. 1 is 5.____
   A. 428 B. 5N1492 C. 14-238 D. 0123456

6. In a report of unlawful entry into department premises, it is LEAST important to include the 6.____
   A. estimated value of the property missing
   B. general description of the premises
   C. means used to get into the premises
   D. time and date of entry

7. In a report of an accident, it is LEAST important to include the 7.____
   A. name of the insurance company of the person injured in the accident
   B. probable cause of the accident
   C. time and place of the accident
   D. names and addresses of all witnesses of the accident

8. Of the following, the one which is NOT required in the preparation of a weekly functional expense report is the 8.____
   A. hourly distribution of the time by proper heading in accordance with the actual work performed
   B. signatures of officers not involved in the preparation of the report
   C. time records of the men who appear on the payroll of the respective locations
   D. time records of men working in other districts assigned to this location

KEY (CORRECT ANSWERS)

1.	C	5.	D
2.	A	6.	B
3.	C	7.	A
4.	B	8.	B

READING COMPREHENSION
UNDERSTANDING AND INTERPRETING WRITTEN MATERIAL

EXAMINATION SECTION
TEST 1

DIRECTIONS: Each question or incomplete statement is followed by several suggested answers or completions. Select the one that BEST answers the question or completes the statement. *PRINT THE LETTER OF THE CORRECT ANSWER IN THE SPACE AT THE RIGHT.*

Questions 1-5.

DIRECTIONS: Questions 1 through 5 are based on the following passage. You are to answer the questions which follow based SOLELY upon the information in the passage.

More than 700 dolphins and whales piled up on France's Atlantic coast last February and March. Most were common dolphins, but the toll also included striped and bottlenose dolphins — even a few harbor porpoises and fin, beaked, pilot, and minke whales. Many victims had ropes around their tails or had heads or tails cut off; some had been partly butchered for food. To scientists the cause is obvious: These marine mammals were seen as waste, *byaatah,* to the fishermen who snared them in their nets while seeking commercial fish.

Mid-water trawlers are responsible for this, not drift nets, says Anne Collet, a French biologist who examined the carcasses. The European Union has banned large drift nets. Two other European treaties call for bycatch reduction by vessels using huge trawls for hake and other species. But the Bay of Biscay falls beyond the treaties, a painfully obvious loophole.

1. What killed the dolphins and whales at the Bay of Biscay? 1.____

   A. The propellers of recreational motorboats
   B. Fishermen using drift nets to catch commercial fish
   C. Fishermen seeking commercial fish
   D. Fishermen seeking their tails and heads as trophies

2. What is *bycatch?* 2.____

   A. Animals accidentally caught in the same nets used to catch other types of fish
   B. Animals which typically gather close to certain types of fish, allowing fishermen to hunt more than one species at a time
   C. Those parts of animals and fish discarded by fishermen after the catch
   D. Those fish which exceed the fisherman's specified limit and must be thrown back

3. The dolphins and whales were killed around the Bay of Biscay because the 3.____

   A. treaties which protect these species of dolphins and whales do not reach the Bay of Biscay
   B. bodies of the animals were dumped at the Bay of Biscay, but scientists do not know where they were killed
   C. treaties which limit the use of drift nets do not reach the Bay of Biscay
   D. treaties which limit the use of trawls do not reach the Bay of Biscay

4. Where is the Bay of Biscay located? 4.____

   A. France's Pacific coast
   B. France's Atlantic coast
   C. The European Union's Atlantic coast
   D. The French Riviera

5. What types of fish are mid-water trawlers usually used for? 5.____

   A. Common, striped, and bottlenose dolphins
   B. Common dolphins, harbor porpoises, and pilot whales
   C. Hake and pilot, minke, fin, and beaked whales
   D. Hake and other species

Questions 6-10.

DIRECTIONS: Questions 6 through 10 are based on the following passage. You are to answer the questions which follow based SOLELY upon the information in the passage.

Malaria once infected 9 out of 10 people in North Borneo, now known as Brunei. In 1955, the World Health Organization (WHO) began spraying the island with dieldrin (a DDT relative) to kill malaria-carrying mosquitoes. The program was so successful that the dread disease was virtually eliminated.

Other, unexpected things began to happen, however. The dieldrin also killed other insects, including flies and cockroaches living in houses. At first, the islanders applauded this turn of events, but then small lizards that also lived in the houses died after gorging themselves on dieldrin-contaminated insects. Next, cats began dying after feeding on the lizards. Then, in the absence of cats, rats flourished and overran the villages. Now that the people were threatened by sylvatic plague carried by rat fleas, WHO parachuted healthy cats onto the island to help control the rats.

Then the villagers' roofs began to fall in. The dieldrin had killed wasps and other insects that fed on a type of caterpillar that either avoided or was not affected by the insecticide. With most of its predators eliminated, the caterpillar population exploded, munching its way through its favorite food: the leaves used in thatched roofs.

Ultimately, this episode ended happily: Both malaria and the unexpected effects of the spraying program were brought under control. Nevertheless, the chain of unforeseen events emphasizes the unpredictability of interfering in an ecosystem.

6. The World Health Organization (WHO) began spraying dieldrin on North Borneo in order to 6.____

   A. kill the bacteria which causes malaria
   B. kill the mosquitoes that carry malaria
   C. disrupt the foodchain so that malaria-carrying mosquitoes would die
   D. kill the mosquitoes, flies, and cockroaches that carry malaria

7. Which of the following did the dieldrin kill? 7.____

   A. Mosquitoes
   B. Rats
   C. Caterpillars
   D. All of the above

8. The villagers' roofs caved in because the dieldrin killed 8.____

   A. mosquitoes, flies, rats, and cats
   B. the trees whose leaves are used in thatched roofs
   C. the caterpillar that eats the leaves used in thatched roofs
   D. the predators of the caterpillar that eats the leaves used in thatched roofs

9. Which of the following was NOT a side effect of spraying dieldrin on Borneo? 9.____

   A. Malaria was virtually eliminated.
   B. The rat population exploded.
   C. The cat population exploded.
   D. The caterpillar population exploded.

10. Why did the World Health Organization (WHO) deliver healthy cats to Borneo without trying to replenish the other animals and insects which had been wiped out by the dieldrin? The 10.____

   A. presence of a healthy cat population was all that was required to restore the balanced ecosystem
   B. rats that cats preyed upon carried an illness threatening to humans
   C. other insects and animals killed by the dieldrin were nuisances and the villagers were happy to be free of them
   D. villagers' had become attached to cats as domestic pets

Questions 11-15.

DIRECTIONS: Questions 11 through 15 are based on the following passage. You are to answer the questions which follow based SOLELY upon the information in the passage.

Historically, towns and cities grew as a natural byproduct of people choosing to live in certain areas for agricultural, business, or recreational reasons. Beginning in the 1920s, private and governmental planners began to think about how an ideal town would be planned. These communities would be completely built before houses were offered for sale. This concept of preplanning, designing, and building an ideal town was not fully developed until the 1960s. By 1976, about forty-three towns could be classified as planned *new towns.*

One example of a new town is Reston, Virginia, located about 40 kilometers west of Washington, D.C. Reston began to accept residents in 1964 and has a projected population of eighty thousand. Because developers tried to preserve the great natural beauty of the area and the high quality of architectural design of its buildings, Reston has attracted much attention. Reston also has innovative programs in education, government, transportation, and recreation. For example, the stores in Reston are within easy walking distance of the residential parts of the community, and there are many open spaces for family activities. Because Reston is not dependent upon the automobile, noise and air pollution have been greatly reduced. Recent research indicates that the residents of Reston have rated their community much higher than residents of less well-planned suburbs.

11. When did the concept of first building a town and then offering houses for sale fully develop? 11.____

A. 1920s B. 1950s C. 1960s D. 1970s

12. The goal of planners who develop and build ideal towns and suburbs is to 12.____

A. eliminate the tendency of towns and cities to naturally develop around business or recreational centers
B. control population growth
C. regulate the resources devoted to housing and recreation
D. cut down on suburban sprawl by developing communities where residents are not dependent on cars to maintain a high quality of living

13. Which of the following goals did developers have in mind when planning the community of Reston? 13.____

I. Preservation of natural beauty
II. Communal living spaces
III. Communal recreational spaces
IV. High standards of architectural design

The CORRECT answer is:

A. I, II, III, IV B. I, III, IV
C. II, III, IV D. I, II, IV

14. The fact that stores in Reston are within easy walking distance of the residential parts of the community is an example of innovation in 14.____

A. transportation B. recreation
C. education D. all of the above

15. What are the environmental advantages to towns like Reston? 15.____

A. Uniform architecture
B. Individual recreational spaces cut down on the overuse of resources
C. Decreased noise and air pollution
D. Ability to control the number and type of residents

Questions 16-20.

DIRECTIONS: Questions 16 through 20 are based on the following passage. You are to answer the questions which follow based SOLELY upon the information in the passage.

Lead is one of the most common toxic (harmful or poisonous) metals in the intercity environment. It is found, to some extent, in all parts of the urban environment (e.g., air, soil, and older pipes and paint) and in all biological systems, including people. There is no apparent biologic need for lead, but it is sufficiently concentrated in the blood and bones of children living in inner cities to cause health and behavior problems. In some populations over 20% of the children have levels of lead concentrated in their blood above that believed safe. Lead affects nearly every system of the body. Acute lead toxicity may be characterized by a variety of symptoms, including anemia, mental retardation, palsy, coma, seizures, apathy, uncoordination, subtle loss of recently acquired skills, and bizarre behavior. Lead toxicity is particularly a problem for young children who tend to be exposed to higher concentrations in some urban areas and apparently are more susceptible to lead poisoning than are adults. Following exposure to lead and having acute toxic response, some children manifest aggressive, difficult to manage behavior.

The occurrence of lead toxicity or lead poisoning has cultural, political, and sociological implications. Over 2,000 years ago, the Roman Empire produced and used tremendous amounts of lead for a period of several hundred years. Production rates were as high as 55,000 metric tons per year. Romans had a wide variety of uses for lead, including pots in which grapes were crushed and processed into a syrup for making wine, cups, and goblets from which the wine was drunk, as a base for cosmetics and medicines, and finally for the wealthy class of people who had running water in their homes, lead was used to make the pipes that carried the water. It has been argued by some historians that gradual lead poisoning among the upper class in Rome was partly responsible for Rome's eventual fall.

16. In which parts of the urban environment can lead be found? 16.____

I. Air
II. Water
III. Adults
IV. Children

The CORRECT answer is:

A. I, II, III
B. I, III, IV
C. II, III, IV
D. All of the above

17. Lead toxicity has the most powerful effect on which of the following? 17.____

A. Mentally retarded children
B. Young children
C. Anemic women
D. Children who suffer from seizures

18. Romans used lead in which of the following? 18.____

A. Cosmetics
B. Paint
C. Wine
D. Clothes

19. Humans require a certain level of lead in the bloodstream in order to avoid which of the following? 19.____

A. Anemia
B. Uncoordination
C. Seizures
D. Scientists have found no biological need for lead among humans

20. Which of the following would most directly support the theory that lead poisoning was partially responsible for the fall of Rome? 20.____

A. Evidence of bizarre behavior among ancient Roman leaders
B. Evidence of lead in the drinking water of ancient Rome
C. Studies analyzing the lead content of bones of ancient Romans which detect increased levels of lead
D. Evidence of lead in the environment of ancient Rome

Questions 21-25.

DIRECTIONS: Questions 21 through 25 are based on the following passage. You are to answer the questions which follow based SOLELY upon the information in the passage.

The city of Venice, Italy has been known to be slowly sinking, but for a long time no one knew the cause or a solution. Floods were becoming more and more common, especially during the winter storms when the winds drove waters from the Adriatic Sea into the city's streets. Famous for its canals and architectural beauty, Venice was in danger of being destroyed by the very lagoon that had sustained its commerce for more than a thousand years. Then the reason that the city was sinking was discovered: groundwater in the region was being pumped out and used; the depletion of the water table, over time, caused the soil to compress under the weight of the city above it. The wells that influenced Venice, which were located on the Italian mainland as well as on the islands that make up Venice, supplied water to nearly industrial and domestic users.

Once the cause was discovered, the wells were capped .and other sources of water were found; as a result the city has stopped sinking. This is an example of the application of scientific research on the environment to achieve a solution helpful to a major city.

21. What causes the winter floods in Venice? 21.____

A. The disintegration of the canals that used to protect the city from the floods
B. Storms that drive waters from the wells into the streets
C. The flawed canal system for which the city is famous
D. Storms that drive waters from the Adriatic Sea into the streets

22. Venice was sinking because of depletion of the 22.____

A. lagoon upon which the city was founded
B. wells used to flood the lagoons
C. water table beneath the city
D. soil beneath the city

23. What was the water beneath Venice used for? 23.____

A. Wastewater
B. To supply water to the famous canals
C. To supply drinking water to Venetians
D. To supply local industrial users

24. How was the problem remedied? 24.____

A. City leaders regulated use of the wells and found other sources of water.
B. The wells were capped.
C. Flood water was diverted back to the Adriatic Sea.
D. The wells were used to supply water to nearby industrial and domestic users.

25. How were scientists able to restore Venice to its proper (and previous) elevation? 25.____

A. Venice was not restored to its previous elevation
B. By diverting water back into the soil beneath Venice
C. By capping the wells and finding other sources of water
D. By restoring the water table

KEY (CORRECT ANSWERS)

1. C
2. A
3. D
4. B
5. D
6. B
7. A
8. D
9. C
10. B
11. C
12. D
13. B
14. A
15. C
16. D
17. B
18. A
19. D
20. C
21. D
22. C
23. D
24. B
25. A

TEST 2

DIRECTIONS: Each question or incomplete statement is followed by several suggested answers or completions. Select the one that BEST answers the question or completes the statement. *PRINT THE LETTER OF THE CORRECT ANSWER IN THE SPACE AT THE RIGHT.*

Questions 1-5.

DIRECTIONS: Questions 1 through 5 are based on the following passage. You are to answer the questions which follow based SOLELY upon the information in the passage.

China, with one-fifth of the world's population, is the most populous country in the world. Between 1980 and 1995, China's population grew by 200 million people — about three-fourths of the population of the United States — to reach 1.2 billion. Although its growth rate is expected to slow somewhat in the coming decades, population experts predict that there will be 1.5 billion Chinese by 2025. But can China's food production continue to keep pace with its growing population? Should China develop a food deficit, it may need to import more grain from other countries than those countries can spare from their own needs.

To give some idea of the potential impact of China on the world's food supply, consider the following examples. All of the grain produced by Norway would be needed to supply two more beers to each person in China. If the Chinese were to eat as much fish as the Japanese do, China would consume the entire world fish catch. Food for all the chickens required for China to reach its goal of 200 eggs per person per year by 2010 will equal all the grain exported by Canada — the world's second largest grain exporter. Increased demand by China for world grain supplies could result in dramatic increases in food prices and precipitate famines in other areas of the world.

1. China's population increased between 1980 and 1995 by 1.____

   A. 200 million people
   B. 1.2 billion people
   C. 1.5 billion people
   D. one-fifth of the world's population

2. If China developed a food deficit, which of the following would most negatively affect the world's supply of food? 2.____

   A. Famines resulting from the increased price of grain
   B. Domestic increase in the production of grain to meet the needs of the Chinese people
   C. International increase in the production of grain to meet China's need
   D. Importing more grain from other countries than those countries could spare

3. Which of the following was a goal the Chinese government hoped to reach by 2010? 3.____

   A. Importing Canada's entire supply of grain
   B. Supplying 200 eggs annually to every citizen
   C. A population of 1.5 billion people
   D. Supplying enough fish to each citizen to match Japan's consumption

4. Which of the following countries exports the most grain? 4.____

A. China B. Norway C. Canada D. Japan

5. Which of the following groups contains 200 million people? 5.____

A. The current population of the United States
B. Three-quarters of the population of the United States
C. China's current population
D. Three-quarters of the population of China

Questions 6-10.

DIRECTIONS: Questions 6 through 10 are based on the following passage. You are to answer the questions which follow based SOLELY upon the information in the passage.

On Tuesday, 16 June 1987, the last dusky seaside sparrow *(Ammo-dramus maratimus nigrescens)* died in captivity at Walt Disney World's Discovery Island Zoological Park in Orlando, Florida. The bird was a male that was probably about twelve years old. Originally, this subspecies and several other subspecies were found in the coastal salt marshes on the Atlantic coast of Florida. (A subspecies is a distinct population of a species that has several characteristics that distinguish it from other populations.) One other subspecies, the Smyrna seaside sparrow *(Ammodramus maratimus pelonata)*, is believed to have become extinct several years ago, and a third subspecies, the Cape Sable seaside sparrow *(Ammodramus maratimus mirabilis)*, was listed as an endangered species in 1967. Before the deaths of the last remaining dusky seaside sparrows, a few males were crossed with another subspecies, Scott's seaside sparrow *(Ammodramus maratimus peninsulae)*. Thus, the hybrid offspring between these two subspecies contain some of the genes that made the dusky seaside sparrow unique.

The endangerment and extinction of these different birds was a direct result of the land development and drainage that destroyed the salt-marsh habitat to which they were adapted. The development of Cape Canaveral as a major center for the U.S. space program also resulted in the modification of much of the birds' original habitat and was a partial cause of their extinction.

6. Which of the following subspecies is NOT yet extinct? 6.____

A. Dusky seaside sparrow
B. Cape Sable seaside sparrow
C. Smyrna seaside sparrow
D. All of the listed subspecies are extinct

7. A subspecies is a population 7.____

A. within a species that has been crossed with another population within the same species in order to avoid extinction
B. within a subspecies that has distinguishing characteristics
C. that has distinguishing characteristics
D. within a species that has distinguishing characteristics

8. What was the dusky seaside sparrow's natural habitat? 8.____

A. Coastal salt marshes of Florida
B. Man-made parks and zoos such as Discovery Land
C. Flat, desert-like plains around Cape Canaveral
D. Areas of land development

9. A hybrid is an animal that 9.____

A. cannot reproduce
B. is extinct
C. is the result of a cross between two subspecies
D. is the result of a cross between two species

10. What caused the extinction of the dusky seaside sparrow? 10.____

A. An overabundance of predators caused by human influence and development
B. Destruction of its natural habitat by human development
C. Inability to reproduce in captivity
D. All of the above

Questions 11-15.

DIRECTIONS: Questions 11 through 15 are based on the following passage. You are to answer the questions which follow based SOLELY upon the information in the passage.

For more than 600 years only Adelie penguins lived along the chilly shores of the Western Antarctic Peninsula in the Palmer region. Ornithologist and paleontologist Steven Emslie of the University of North Carolina, Wilmington, found Adelie bones in nests near Palmer Station dating from as early as the 14th century.

But two other penguin species have moved in, apparently as the result of a 50-year warming trend that has seen winter temperatures rise seven to nine degrees F and lessened the amount of ice around the peninsula. *Adelies require the edges of pack ice for foraging,* Emslie says. As the ice shrinks, he believes, their numbers decline. Chinstrap penguins, which forage in the open ocean and aren't affected by ice breakup, began to arrive in the 1950s. Gentoos, normally a subantarctic species, first appeared here in 1975. The two newcomers now form a major portion of the region's penguin population.

11. When did new penguin species begin arriving in the Palmer region? 11.____

A. 1400s B. 1950s C. 1975 D. 1990s

12. Which of the following penguin species are NOT affected by ice breakup? 12.____

A. Adelie B. Gentoos C. Chinstrap D. Emslie

13. What has caused the new penguin species to move into the Palmer region? 13.____

A. A warming trend
B. An increase in the amount of pack ice around the peninsula
C. An increase in the availability of food
D. All of the above

14. Adelie penguins have lived in the Palmer region since 14.____

A. the 14th century
B. the early 1900s
C. the 1950s
D. 1975

15. What effect does the decrease in the amount of pack ice have on Adelie penguins? 15.____

A. Decreased ability to fight off predators
B. Increased ability to fight off predators
C. Increased ability to forage for food
D. Decreased ability to forage for food

Questions 16-20.

DIRECTIONS: Questions 16 through 20 are based on the following passage. You are to answer the questions which follow based SOLELY upon the information in the passage.

The price of a liter of gasoline is determined by two major factors: (1) the cost of purchasing and processing crude oil into gasoline, and (2) various taxes. Most of the differences in gasoline prices between countries are a result of the differences in taxes and reflect differences in government policy toward motor vehicle transportation.

A major objective of governments is to collect money to build and repair roads, and governments often charge the user by taxing the fuel used by the car or truck. Governments can also discourage the use of automobiles by increasing the cost of fuel. An increase in fuel costs also creates a demand for increased fuel efficiency in all forms of motor transport.

Many European countries raise more money from fuel taxes than they spend on building and repairing roads, while the United States raises approximately 60 percent of the moneys needed for roads from fuel taxes. The relatively low cost of fuel in the United States encourages more travel and increases road repair costs. The cost of taxes to the United States consumer is about 20 percent of the cost of fuel, while in Japan and many European countries, the percentage is 60 to 75 percent.

16. Which of the following is likely to result from an increase in the cost of fuel? 16.____

A. *Decreased* fuel efficiency
B. *Increased* fuel efficiency
C. *Increased* travel
D. *Increased* road repair costs

17. Which of the following affects the price of gasoline? 17.____

A. Cost of purchasing crude oil
B. Cost of processing crude oil
C. Taxes
D. All of the above

18. Most governments tax car and truck fuel in order to 18.____

A. finance the costs of repairing roads
B. discourage motor travel as much as possible

C. finance various social welfare programs
D. finance public transportation systems

19. Differences in _______ accounts for the differences in gasoline prices between countries. 19.____

A. the cost of purchasing a car
B. the amount of crude oil each country exports
C. government taxes
D. the number of automobiles imported by individual countries

20. Which of the following is most likely to discourage travel? 20.____

A. *Decrease* in fuel tax
B. *Increase* in fuel tax
C. *Decrease* in fuel efficiency
D. *Increase* in road repair

Questions 21-25.

DIRECTIONS: Questions 21 through 25 are based on the following passage. You are to answer the questions which follow based SOLELY upon the information in the passage.

Wyoming rancher Jack Turnell is one of a new breed of cowpuncher who gets along with environmentalists. He talks about riparian ecology and biodiversity as fluently as he talks about cattle. *I guess I have learned how to bridge the gap between the environmentalists, the bureaucracies, and the ranching industry.*

Turnell grazes cattle on his 32,000-hectare (80,000 acre) ranch south of Cody, Wyoming, and on 16,000 hectares (40,000 acres) of Forest Service land on which he has grazing rights. For the first decade after he took over the ranch, he punched cows the conventional way. Since then, he's made some changes.

Turnell disagrees with the proposals by environmentalists to raise grazing fees and remove sheep and cattle from public rangeland. He believes that if ranchers are kicked off the public range, ranches like his will be sold to developers and chopped up into vacation sites, irreversibly destroying the range for wildlife and livestock alike.

At the same time, he believes that ranches can be operated in more ecologically sustainable ways. To demonstrate this, Turnell began systematically rotating his cows away from the riparian areas, gave up most uses of fertilizers and pesticides, and crossed his Hereford and Angus cows with a French breed that tends to congregate less around water. Most of his ranching decisions are made in consultation with range and wildlife scientists, and changes in range condition are carefully monitored with photographs.

The results have been impressive. Riparian areas on the ranch and Forest Service land are lined with willows and other plant life, providing lush habitat for an expanding population of wildlife, including pronghorn antelope, deer, moose, elk, bear, and mountain lions. And this *eco-rancher* now makes more money because the higher-quality grass puts more meat on his cattle. He frequently talks to other ranchers about sustainable range management; some of them probably think he has been chewing locoweed.

21. The fact that Turnell's decision-making process involves range and wildlife scientists is an example of 21.____

    A. successful government oversight
    B. enforced government regulation
    C. conventional ranching
    D. successful sustainable ranching

22. What is the environmental drawback to removing grazing animals from government range land? 22.____

    A. The loss of ranches which rely on public ranges to real-estate developers
    B. The loss of public range land to real-estate developers
    C. Under-use of public range land
    D. Increased vulnerability to forest fires due to under-use

23. Which of the following is a result of Turnell's decision to rotate his cattle? 23.____

    A. The production of cattle which tend to congregate less around water
    B. Increased bio-diversity which attracts and supports several animal species
    C. The production of beefier, more profitable cattle
    D. All of the above

24. Which of the following is an example of sustainable ranching? 24.____

    A. The use of pesticides to control disease
    B. Non-use of, and non-reliance on, public grazing lands
    C. Rotation of cattle away from riparian areas
    D. Independent decision-making

25. Which of the following is an effect of the increased diversity of plant life on the grazing land that Turnell uses? 25.____

    A. Production of leaner cattle
    B. Production of larger, meatier cattle
    C. Production of more abundant but less nutritious grasses
    D. Less reliance on pesticides

KEY (CORRECT ANSWERS)

1. A
2. D
3. B
4. C
5. B
6. B
7. D
8. A
9. C
10. B
11. B
12. C
13. A
14. A
15. D
16. B
17. D
18. A
19. C
20. B
21. D
22. A
23. B
24. C
25. B

READING COMPREHENSION
UNDERSTANDING AND INTERPRETING WRITTEN MATERIAL

EXAMINATION SECTION

TEST 1

DIRECTIONS: Each question or incomplete statement is followed by several suggested answers or completions. Select the one that BEST answers the question or completes the statement. *PRINT THE LETTER OF THE CORRECT ANSWER IN THE SPACE AT THE RIGHT.*

Questions 1-3.

DIRECTIONS: Questions 1 through 3 are to be answered SOLELY on the basis of the information contained in the following passage.

It is common knowledge that ability to do a particular job and performance on the job do not always go hand in hand. Persons with great potential abilities sometimes fall down on the job because of laziness or lack of interest in the job, while persons with mediocre talents have often achieved excellent results through their industry and their loyalty to the interests of their employers. It is clear, therefore, that in a balanced personnel program, measures of employee ability need to be supplemented by measures of employee performance, for the final test of any employee is his performance on the job.

1. The MOST accurate of the following statements, on the basis of the above passage, is that 1.____
   A. employees who lack ability are usually not industrious
   B. an employee's attitudes are more important than his abilities
   C. mediocre employees who are interested in their work are preferable to employees who possess great ability
   D. superior capacity for performance should be supplemented with proper attitudes

2. On the basis of the above passage, the employee of most value to his employer is NOT necessarily the one who 2.____
   A. best understands the significance of his duties
   B. achieves excellent results
   C. possesses the greatest talents
   D. produces the greatest amount of work

3. According to the above passage, an employee's efficiency is BEST determined by an 3.____
   A. appraisal of his interest in his work
   B. evaluation of the work performed by him
   C. appraisal of his loyalty to his employer
   D. evaluation of his potential ability to perform his work

Questions 4-5.

DIRECTIONS: Questions 4 and 5 are to be answered SOLELY on the basis of the information contained in the following passage.

The cabinet shall be *fabricated* entirely of 22-gage stainless steel with #4 satin finish on all exposed surfaces. The face trim shall be one-piece construction with no mitres or welding, 1" wide and ¼" to the wall. All doors shall be mounted on heavy-duty stainless steel piano hinges and have a concealed lock.

4. As used in the above passage, the word *fabricated* means MOST NEARLY 4.____
   A. made B. designed C. cut D. plated

5. According to the above passage, a satin finish is to be used on surfaces 5.____
   A. to be welded
   B. that are visible
   C. on which the hinges are mounted
   D. that are to be covered

Questions 6-10.

DIRECTIONS: Questions 6 through 10 are to be answered SOLELY on the basis of the information contained in the following passage.

Many people still think accidents just happen—that they are due to bad luck. Nothing could be further from the truth.

Evidence of this is in the drop in accidents among employees of the City since the Safety Program started.

The one-out-of-a-hundred accidents that cannot be prevented might be called "Acts of God." They are things like lightning, earthquakes, tornadoes, and tidal waves that we are powerless to prevent—although we can take precautions against them which will cut down the accident rate.

The other ninety-nine percent of the accidents clearly have a man-made cause. If you trace back far enough, you'll find that somewhere, somehow, someone could have done something to prevent these accidents. For just about every accident, there is some fellow who fouled up. He didn't protect himself, he didn't use the right equipment, he wasn't alert, he lost his temper, he didn't have his mind on his work, he was "kidding around," or he took a shortcut because he was just too lazy.

We must all work together to improve safety and prevent injury and death.

6. The one of the following titles which BEST describes the subject matter of the above passage is: 6.____
   A. Acts of God
   B. The Importance of Safety Consciousness
   C. Safety in the City
   D. Working Together

7. After the City began to operate a safety program, it was found that 7.____
   A. the number of accidents was reduced
   B. production decreased
   C. accidents stayed the same but employees were more careful
   D. the element of bad luck did not change

8. One cause of accidents that is NOT mentioned in the above passage is 8.____
   A. failure to keep alert
   B. taking a shortcut
   C. using the wrong equipment
   D. working too fast

9. The number of accidents caused by such things as hurricanes can be 9.____
   A. changed only by an "Act of God"
   B. eliminated by strict adherence to safety rules
   C. increased by being too careful
   D. reduced by proper safety precautions

10. The percentage of accidents that occur as a result of things that cannot be prevented is APPROXIMATELY _____ percent. 10.____
   A. 1
   B. 10
   C. 50
   D. 99

Questions 11-15.

DIRECTIONS: Questions 11 through 15 are to be answered SOLELY on the basis of the information contained in the following passage.

The most effective control mechanism to prevent gross incompetence on the part of public employees is a good personnel program. The personnel officer in the line departments and the central personnel agency should exert positive leadership to raise levels of performance. Although the key factor is the quality of the personnel recruited, staff members other than personnel officers can make important contributions to efficiency. Administrative analysts, now employed in many agencies, make detailed studies of organization and procedures, with the purpose of eliminating delays, waste, and other inefficiencies. Efficiency is, however, more than a question of good organization and procedures; it is also the product of the attitudes and values of the public employees. Personal motivation can provide the will to be efficient. The best management studies will not result in substantial improvement of the performance of those employees who feel no great urge to work up to their abilities.

11. The passage indicates that the *key* factor in preventing gross incompetence of public employees is the 11.____
   A. hiring of administrative analysts to assist personnel people
   B. utilization of effective management studies
   C. overlapping of responsibility
   D. quality of the employees hired

12. According to the above passage, the central personnel agency staff should 12.____
   A. work more closely with administrative analysts in the line departments than with personnel officers
   B. make a serious effort to avoid jurisdictional conflicts with personnel officers in line departments

C. contribute to improving the quality of work of public employees
D. engage in a comprehensive program to change the public's negative image of public employees

13. The author of the passage believes that efficiency in an organization can BEST be brought about by 13.____
A. eliminating ineffective control mechanisms
B. instituting sound organizational procedures
C. promoting competent personnel
D. recruiting people with desire to do good work

14. According to the passage, the purpose of administrative analysis in a public agency is to 14.____
A. prevent injustice to the public employee
B. promote the efficiency of the agency
C. protect the interests of the public
D. ensure the observance of procedural due process

15. The passage *implies* that a considerable rise in the quality of work of public employees can be brought about by 15.____
A. encouraging positive employee attitudes toward work
B. controlling personnel officers who exceed their powers
C. creating warm personal associations among public employees in an agency
D. closing loopholes in personnel organizations and procedures

Questions 16-25.

DIRECTIONS: Questions 16 through 25 are to be answered SOLELY on the basis of the following instructions.

INSTRUCTIONS FOR PREPARATION AND PLACEMENT OF RAT BAITS

a. Fresh baits are the most acceptable to rats, so mix only enough bait for current needs. Use a binder of molasses or of vegetable, mineral or fish oil in cereal or dry baits to hold the poison and the dry bait together and to aid in mixing.

b. Mix an emetic, usually tartar emetic, with zinc phosphide and other more toxic bait formulations to protect animals other than rodents, even though acceptability of such baits to the rodents is thereby reduced.

c. Mix bait as directed. Too much poison may give the bait a strong taste or odor. Too little will not kill but may result in "bait shyness." Excessive amounts of poison increase the danger to man and to domestic animals.

d. Mix baits well. Poor mixing results in non-uniform baits and poor kills and speeds development of bait shyness. Mechanical bait-mixing equipment is necessary where large quantities of bait are mixed routinely.

e. Clearly label poisons and mixing equipment. Do no use bait-mixing equipment for other purposes. Lock up poisons and mixing equipment when not in use. Treat all poisons with respect. Read and follow all label instructions. Avoid inhaling powders or getting poisons on hands, clothes, or utensils from which they may reach the mouth. Wear rubber gloves when handling poisons. Always mix poisons in a well-ventilated place, particularly when mixing dry ingredients.

f. If anti-coagulant baits are used, they should be placed in paper, metal, or plastic pie plates or in permanent bait stations. Be liberal in baiting. For anti-coagulants to be fully effective, repeated doses must be consumed by every rodent at a given location for a period of five or more consecutive days.

g. Protect animals other than domestic rodents, and shield baits from the weather under shelter or with bait boxes, boards, pipes, or cans.

h. Note locations of all bait container so that inspections can be made rapidly and the bait that has been consumed can be quickly replaced. (Bait consumption is generally heavy right after initial placement, making daily inspection and replacement advisable for the first 3 days after regular feeding begins.)

i. At each inspection, smooth the surface of the baits so that new signs of feeding will show readily. Replace moldy, wet, caked, or insect-infested baits with fresh ones. If a bait remains undisturbed for several successive inspections, move it to an area showing fresh rodent signs.

j. Use shallow bait containers fastened to the floor, or containers of sufficient weight to prevent the rodents from overturning them or dragging them to their burrows. A roofing tack driven through metal or fiber containers into the floor reduces spillage.

k. When single-dose poisons are used, wrap one-shot poison foot baits in 4" x 4" paper squares to form "torpedoes" about the size of a large olive. These may be tossed readily into otherwise inaccessible places. If several types of bait such as meat, fish, or cereal are to be distributed at the same time, a different color of paper should be used for each of the various types of bait.

l. Be generous with baits. Too few baits, or poorly-placed baits, may miss many rodents. Bait liberally where signs of rat activity are numerous and recent. In light or moderate infestations, torpedoes containing a single-dose poison, such as reds quill, have given good control when applied at a minimum rate of 20 baits per private residence. As many as 100 to 200 baits may be required for premises with heavy rodent infestations.

m. Place baits in hidden sites out of reach of children and pets.

n. Inspect and rebait as needed, using another poison and another bait material when the rats become shy of the original baits.

16. According to the above instructions, if you find, upon inspection, that your baits are overrun with insects, you should 16.____
    A. replace the baits with fresh baits
    B. move the baits to another station
    C. add more rodenticide to the baits and re-mix them
    D. apply the appropriate insecticide to the baits

17. According to the above instructions, if you want to make sure you do NOT get poor kills, you should 17.____
    A. mix large quantities of baits routinely
    B. stick to one poison
    C. mix the baits well
    D. use deep bait containers that cannot be easily overturned

18. According to the above instructions, the equipment which is used for mixing bait should be 18.____
    A. cleaned routinely
    B. mechanically easy to handle
    C. easily disposable
    D. labeled clearly

19. According to the above instructions, making the surface of the bait smooth every time that you inspect the bait containers is 19.____
    A. *proper*, because it disturbs the insect infestation of the bait
    B. *improper*, because it will make the bait less uniform if it was already mixed poorly
    C. *proper*, because it will help you determine if new signs of feeding are present
    D. *improper*, because it increases the presence of human odor on the bait and discourages rodents

20. According to the above instructions, if you are making a bait with zinc phosphide, it is MOST important to 20.____
    A. prepare a generous amount so you can bait liberally where signs of rat activity are numerous
    B. use molasses to insure that the bait will be uniform
    C. shield the bait from the weather
    D. mix an emetic with the bait

21. According to the above instructions, you should substitute one poison for another poison when the 21.____
    A. bait consumption is heavy after initial placement
    B. rodents become shy of the original baits
    C. poison is dangerous to domestic animals
    D. rodents are able to drag the baits to their burrows

22. According to the above instructions, when you handle poisons, you should 22.____
    A. use mechanical bait-making equipment
    B. wear rubber gloves
    C. never place them in paper plates
    D. always mix them with moist ingredients

23. According to the above instructions, if you plan to distribute several types of bait at the same time in the form of "torpedoes," you should 23.____
    A. select only anti-coagulant baits for this purpose
    B. reduce the possibility of bait spillage by driving a roofing tack through the container into the floor
    C. use a different color of paper for each of the various types of bait
    D. make sure that the rodent does not consume repeated doses for more than a period of five consecutive days at the same location

24. According to the above instructions, mixing too much poison in the bait 24.____
    A. may bring about bait shyness
    B. permits you to make less frequent re-inspections
    C. increases the danger to other life
    D. may be necessary when anti-coagulants are used

25. According to the above instructions, if grain is to be used as bait, 25.____
    A. rodents will not accept it if it is mixed with fish oil
    B. you will only be able to make "torpedoes"
    C. it will not be necessary to check the bait for fresh rodent signs
    D. a binder should also be used to aid in mixing

KEY (CORRECT ANSWERS)

1.	D	11.	D
2.	C	12.	C
3.	B	13.	D
4.	A	14.	B
5.	B	15.	A
6.	B	16.	A
7.	A	17.	C
8.	D	18.	D
9.	D	19.	C
10.	A	20.	D

21.	B
22.	B
23.	C
24.	C
25.	D

TEST 2

DIRECTIONS: Each question or incomplete statement is followed by several suggested answers or completions. Select the one that BEST answers the question or completes the statement. *PRINT THE LETTER OF THE CORRECT ANSWER IN THE SPACE AT THE RIGHT.*

Questions 1-4.

DIRECTIONS: Questions 1 through 4 are to be answered SOLELY on the basis of the information contained in the following passage.

Cylindrical surfaces are the most common form of finished surfaces found on machine parts, although flat surfaces are also very common; hence, many metal-cutting processes are for the purpose of producing either cylindrical or flat surfaces. The machines used for cylindrical or flat shapes may be, and often are, utilized also for forming the various irregular or special shapes required on many machine parts. Because of the prevalence of cylindrical and flat surfaces, the student of manufacturing practice should learn first about the machines and methods employed to produce these surfaces. The cylindrical surfaces may be internal as in holes and cylinders. Any one part may, of course, have cylindrical sections of different diameters and lengths and include flat ends or shoulders and, frequently, there is a threaded part or possibly some finished surface that is not circular in cross-section. The prevalence of cylindrical surfaces on machine parts explains why lathes are found in all machine shops. It is important to understand the various uses of the lathe because many of the operations are the same fundamentally as those performed on other types of machine tools.

1. According to the above passage, the MOST common form of finished surfaces found on machine parts is 1.____
   A. cylindrical B. elliptical C. flat D. square

2. According to the above passage, any one part of cylindrical surfaces may have 2.____
   A. chases B. shoulders C. keyways D. splines

3. According to the above passage, lathes are found in all machine shops because cylindrical surfaces on machine parts are 3.____
   A. scarce B. internal C. common D. external

4. As used in the above passage, the word *processes* means 4.____
   A. operations B. purposes C. devices D. tools

Questions 5-6.

DIRECTIONS: Questions 5 and 6 are to be answered SOLELY on the basis of the information contained in the following passage.

The principle of interchangeability requires manufacture to such specification that component parts of a device may be selected at random and assembled to fit and operate satisfactorily. Interchangeable manufacture, therefore, requires that parts be made to definite limits of error, and to fit gages instead of mating parts. Interchangeability does not necessarily involve a high degree of precision; stove lids, for example, are interchangeable but are not particularly accurate, and carriage bolts and nuts are not precision products but are completely interchangeable. Interchangeability may be employed in unit-production as well as mass-production systems of manufacture.

5. According to the above passage, in order for parts to be interchangeable, they must be 5.____
   A. precision-machined
   B. selectively-assembled
   C. mass-produced
   D. made to fit gages

6. According to the above passage, carriage bolts are interchangeable because they are 6.____
   A. precision-made
   B. sized to specific tolerances
   C. individually matched products
   D. produced in small units

Questions 7-9.

DIRECTIONS: Questions 7 through 9 are to be answered SOLELY on the basis of the information contained in the following passage.

The soda-acid fire extinguisher is the commonest type of water-solution extinguisher in which pressure is used to expel the water. The chemicals used are sodium bicarbonate (baking soda) and sulfuric acid. The sodium bicarbonate is dissolved in water, and this solution is the extinguishing agent. The extinguishing value of the stream is that of an equal quantity of water.

7. According to the above paragraph, the soda-acid extinguisher, compared to others of the same type, is the 7.____
   A. most widely used
   B. most effective in putting out fire
   C. cheapest to operate
   D. easiest to operate

8. In the soda-acid extinguisher, the fire is put out by a solution of sodium bicarbonate and 8.____
   A. sulfuric acid
   B. baking soda
   C. soda-acid
   D. water

9. According to the above passage, the sodium bicarbonate solution, compared to water, is 9.____
   A. more effective in putting out fires
   B. less effective in putting out fires
   C. equally effective in putting out fires
   D. more or less effective, depending upon the type of fire

Questions 10-12.

DIRECTIONS: Questions 10 through 12 are to be answered SOLELY on the basis of the information contained in the following passage.

Some gases which may be inhaled have an irritant effect on the respiratory tract. Among them are ammonia fumes, hydrogen sulfide, nitrous fumes, and phosgene. Persons who have been exposed to irritant gases must lie down at once and keep absolutely quiet until the doctor arrives. The action of some of these gases may be delayed, and at first the victim may show few or no symptoms.

10. According to the above passage, the part of the body that is MOST affected by irritant gases is the 10.____
    A. heart B. lungs C. skin D. nerves

11. According to the above passage, a person who has inhaled an irritant gas should be 11.____
    A. given artificial respiration
    B. made to rest
    C. wrapped in blankets
    D. made to breathe smelling salts

12. A person is believed to have come in contact with an irritant gas but he does not become sick immediately. 12.___
    According to the above passage, we may conclude that the person
    A. did not really come in contact with the gas
    B. will become sick later
    C. came in contact with a small amount of gas
    D. may possibly become sick later

Questions 13-17.

DIRECTIONS: Questions 13 through 17 are to be answered SOLELY on the basis of the information contained in the following passage.

At one time people thought that in the interview designed primarily to obtain information, the interviewer had to resort to clever and subtle lines of questioning in order to accomplish his ends. Some people still believe that this is necessary, but it is not so. An example of the "tricky" approach may be seen in the work of a recent study. The study deals with materials likely to be buried beneath deep defenses. Interviewers utilized methods of questioning which, in effect, trapped the interviewee and destroyed his defenses. Doubtless, these methods succeeded in bringing out items of information which straightforward questions would have missed. Whether they missed more information than they obtained and whether they obtained the most important facts, must remain unanswered questions. In defense of the "clever" approach, it is often said that, in many situations, the interviewee is motivated to conceal information or to distort what he chooses to report.

Technically, it is likely that a highly skilled interviewer can, given the time and the inclination, penetrate the interviewee's defenses and get information which the latter intended to keep hidden. It is unlikely that the interviewer could successfully elicit all of the information that might be relevant. If, for example, he found that an applicant for financial assistance was heavily in debt to gamblers, he might not care about getting any other information. There are situations in which one item, if answered in the "wrong" way is enough. Ordinarily, this is not true. The usual situation is that there are many considerations and that the plus and minus features must be weighed before a decision may be made. It is, therefore, important to obtain complete information.

13. According to the above passage, it was generally believed that an interviewer would have difficulty in obtaining the information he sought from a person if he 13.____
   A. were tricky in his methods
   B. were open and frank in his approach
   C. were clever in his questioning
   D. utilized carefully prepared questions

14. The passage does NOT reveal whether the type of questions used 14.____
   A. trapped those being interviewed
   B. elicited facts which an open method of questioning might miss
   C. elicited the most important acts that were sought
   D. covered matters which those interviewed were reluctant to talk about openly

15. An argument in favor of the "tricky" or "clever" interviewing technique is that, unless this approach is used, the person interviewed will NOT 15.____
   A. offer to furnish all pertinent information
   B. answer questions concerning routine data
   C. clearly understand what is being sought
   D. want to continue the interview

16. According to the above passage, in favorable circumstances, a talented interviewer would be able to obtain from the person interviewed information 16.____
   A. which the person regards as irrelevant
   B. which the person intends to conceal
   C. about the person's family background
   D. which the person would normally have forgotten

17. According to the above passage, a highly skilled interviewer should concentrate, in most cases, on getting 17.____
   A. one outstanding fact about the interviewee which would do away with the need for prolonged questioning
   B. facts which the interviewee wanted to conceal because these would be the most relevant in making a decision
   C. all the facts so that he can consider their relative values before reaching any conclusion
   D. information about any bad habits of the interviewee, such as gambling, which would make further questioning unnecessary

Questions 18-22.

DIRECTIONS: Questions 18 through 22 are to be answered SOLELY on the basis of the information contained in the following passage.

For a period of nearly fifteen years, beginning in the mid-1950's, higher education sustained a phenomenal rate of growth. The factors principally responsible were continuing improvement in the rate of college entrance by high school graduates, a 50-percent increase in the size of the college-age (eighteen to twenty-one) group, and—until about 1967—a rapid expansion of university research activity supported by the federal government.

Today, as one looks ahead fifteen years to the year 2020, it is apparent that each of these favorable stimuli will either be abated or turn into a negative factor. The rate of growth of the college-age group has already diminished, and from 2010 to 2015 the size of the college-age group will shrink annually almost as fast as it grew from 1965 to 1970. From 2015 to 2020, this annual decrease will slow down so that by 2020 the age group will be about the same size a it was in 2019. This substantial net decrease in the size of the college-age group over the next fifteen years will dramatically affect college enrollments since, currently, 83 percent of undergraduates are twenty-one and under, and another 11 percent are twenty-two to twenty-four.

18. Which one of the following factors is NOT mentioned in the above passage as contributing to the high rate of growth of higher education? 18.____
   A. A large increase in the size of the eighteen to twenty-one age group
   B. The equalization of educational opportunities among socio-economic groups
   C. The federal budget impact on research and development spending in the higher education sector
   D. The increasing rate at which high-school graduates enter college

19. Based on the information in the above passage, the size of the college-age group in 2020 will be 19.____
   A. larger than it was in 2019
   B. larger than it was in 2005
   C. smaller than it was in 2015
   D. about the same as it was in 2010

20. According to the above passage, the tremendous rate of growth of higher education started around 20.____
   A. 1950
   B. 1955
   C. 1960
   D. 1965

21. The percentage of undergraduates who are over age 25 is MOST NEARLY 21.____
   A. 6%
   B. 8%
   C. 11%
   D. 17%

22. Which one of the following conclusions can be substantiated by the information given in the above passage? The 22.____
   A. college-age group will be about the same size in 2010 as it was in 1965
   B. annual decrease in the size of the college-age group from 2010 to 2015 will be about the same as the annual increase from 1965 to 1970
   C. overall decrease in the size of the college-age group from 2010 to 2015 will be followed by an overall increase in its size from 2015 to 2020
   D. size of the college-age group will decrease at a fairly constant rate from 2005 to 2020

Questions 23-25.

DIRECTIONS: Questions 23 through 25 are to be answered SOLELY on the basis of the information contained in the following passage.

A fire of undetermined origin started in the warehouse shed of a flour mill. Although there was some delay in notifying the fire department, they practically succeeded in bringing the fire under control when a series of dust explosions occurred which caused the fire to spread and the main building was destroyed. The fire department's efforts were considerably handicapped because it was undermanned, and the water pressure in the vicinity was inadequate.

23. From the information contained in the above passage, it is MOST accurate to state that the cause of the fire was   23.____
    A. suspicious   B. unknown
    C. accidental   D. arson
    E. spontaneous combustion

24. In the fire described above, the MOST important cause of the fire spreading to the main building was the   24.____
    A. series of dust explosions
    B. delay in notifying the fire department
    C. inadequate water pressure
    D. lack of manpower
    E. wooden construction of the building

25. In the fire described above, the fire department's efforts were handicapped CHIEFLY by   25.____
    A. poor leadership
    B. outdated apparatus
    C. uncooperative company employees
    D. insufficient water pressure
    E. poorly trained men

Questions 26-30.

DIRECTIONS: Questions 26 through 30 are to be answered SOLELY on the basis of the information contained in the following passage.

Upon the death of a member or former member of the retirement system there shall be paid to his estate, or to the person he had nominated by written designation, his accumulated deductions. In addition, if he is a member who is in city service, there shall be paid a sum consisting of: an amount equal to the compensation he earned while a member during the three months immediately preceding his death, or, if the total number of years allowable service exceeds five there shall be paid an amount equal to the compensation he earned while a member during the six months immediately preceding his death; and the reserve-for-increased-take-home-pay, if any.

Payment for the expense of burial, not exceeding two hundred and fifty dollars, may be made to a relative or friend who, in the absence or failure of the designated beneficiary, assumes this responsibility.

Until the first retirement benefit payment has been made, where a member has not selected an option, the member will be considered to be in city service, and the death benefits provided above will be paid instead of the retirement allowance. The member, or upon his death, his designated beneficiary, may provide that the actuarial equivalent of the benefit otherwise payable in a lump sum shall be paid in the form of an annuity payable in installments; the amount of such annuity is determined at the time of the member's death on the basis of the age of the beneficiary at that time.

26. Suppose that a member who has applied for retirement benefits without selecting an option dies before receiving any payments. 26.____
According to the information in the above passage, his member's beneficiary would be entitled to receive
   A. an annuity based on the member's age at the time of his death
   B. a death benefit only
   C. the member's retirement allowance only
   D. the member's retirement allowance, plus a death-benefit payment in a lump sum

27. Suppose that a member died on June 15, 2007, while still in city service. 27.____
He had joined the retirement system in March 1990. During the year preceding his death, he earned $75,000.
Based on the information in the above passage, the designated beneficiary of this member would be entitled to receive all of the following EXCEPT
   A. a payment of $37,500
   B. payment of burial expense up to $250
   C. the member's accumulated deductions
   D. the reserve-for-increased-take-home-pay, if any

28. According to the information in the above passage, the amount of the benefit payable upon the death of a member is based, in part, on the 28.____
   A. length of city service during which the deceased person was a member
   B. number of beneficiaries the deceased member had nominated
   C. percent of the deceased member's deductions for social security
   D. type of retirement plan to which the deceased member belonged

29. According to the information in the above passage, which one of the following statements concerning the payment of death benefits is CORRECT? 29.____
   A. In order for a death benefit to be paid, the deceased member must have previously nominated, in writing, someone to receive the benefit.
   B. Death benefits are paid upon the death of members who are in city service.
   C. A death benefit must be paid in one lump sum.
   D. When a retired person dies, his retirement allowance is replaced by a death-benefit payment.

30. According to the information in the above passage, the amount of annuity payments made to a beneficiary in monthly installments in lieu of a lump-sum payment is determined by the 30.____
   A. length of member's service at the time of his death
   B. age of the beneficiary at the time of the member's death
   C. member's age at retirement
   D. member's age at the time of his death

KEY (CORRECT ANSWERS)

1.	A	11.	B	21.	A
2.	B	12.	D	22.	B
3.	C	13.	B	23.	B
4.	A	14.	C	24.	A
5.	D	15.	A	25.	D
6.	B	16.	B	26.	B
7.	A	17.	C	27.	B
8.	D	18.	B	28.	A
9.	C	19.	C	29.	B
10.	B	20.	B	30.	B

PRINCIPLES AND PRACTICES, OF ADMINISTRATION, SUPERVISION AND MANAGEMENT

TABLE OF CONTENTS

PRINCIPLES AND PRACTICES, OF ADMINISTRATION, SUPERVISION AND MANAGEMENT

Most people are inclined to think of administration as something that only a few persons are responsible for in a large organization. Perhaps this is true if you are thinking of Administration with a capital *A*, but administration with a lower case *a* is a responsibility of supervisors at all levels each working day.

All of us feel we are pretty good supervisors and that we do a good job of administering the workings of our agency. By and large, this is true, but every so often it is good to check up on ourselves. Checklists appear from time to time in various publications which psychologists say tell whether or not a person will make a good wife, husband, doctor, lawyer, or supervisor.

The following questions are an excellent checklist to test yourself as a supervisor and administrator.

Remember, Administration gives direction and points the way but administration carries the ideas to fruition. Each is dependent on the other for its success. Remember, too, that no unit is too small for these departmental functions to be carried out. These statements apply equally as well to the Chief Librarian as to the Department Head with but one or two persons to supervise.

GENERAL ADMINISTRATION: General Responsibilities of Supervisors

1. Have I prepared written statements of functions, activities, and duties for my organizational unit?
2. Have I prepared procedural guides for operating activities?
3. Have I established clearly in writing, lines of authority and responsibility for my organizational unit?
4. Do I make recommendations for improvements in organization, policies, administrative and operating routines and procedures, including simplification of work and elimination of non-essential operations?
5. Have I designated and trained an understudy to function in my absence?
6. Do I supervise and train personnel within the unit to effectively perform their assignments?
7. Do I assign personnel and distribute work on such a basis as to carry out the organizational unit's assignment or mission in the most effective and efficient manner?
8. Have I established administrative controls by:

   a. Fixing responsibility and accountability on all supervisors under my direction for the proper performance of their functions and duties.

b. Preparations and submitting periodic work load and progress reports covering the operations of the unit to my immediate superior.

c. Analysis and evaluation of such reports received from subordinate units.

d. Submission of significant developments and problems arising within the organizational unit to my immediate superior.

e. Conducting conferences, inspections, etc., as to the status and efficiency of unit operations.

9. Do I maintain an adequate and competent working force?

10. Have I fostered good employee-department relations, seeing that established rules, regulations, and instructions are being carried out properly?

11. Do I collaborate and consult with other organizational units performing related functions to insure harmonious and efficient working relationships?

12. Do I maintain liaison through prescribed channels with city departments and other governmental agencies concerned with the activities of the unit?

13. Do I maintain contact with and keep abreast of the latest developments and techniques of administration (professional societies, groups, periodicals, etc.) as to their applicability to the activities of the unit?

14. Do I communicate with superiors and subordinates through prescribed organizational channels?

15. Do I notify superiors and subordinates in instances where bypassing is necessary as soon thereafter as practicable?

16. Do I keep my superior informed of significant developments and problems?

SEVEN BASIC FUNCTIONS OF THE SUPERVISOR

I. PLANNING

This means working out goals and means to obtain goals. What needs to be done, who will do it, how, when, and where it is to be done.

SEVEN STEPS IN PLANNING

A. Define job or problem clearly.
B. Consider priority of job.
C. Consider time-limit—starting and completing.
D. Consider minimum distraction to, or interference with, other activities.
E. Consider and provide for contingencies—possible emergencies.
F. Break job down into components.

G. Consider the 5 W's and H:
WHY..........is it necessary to do the job? (Is the purpose clearly defined?)
WHAT........needs to be done to accomplish the defined purpose?
.........is needed to do the job? (Money, materials, etc.)
WHO..........is needed to do the job?
..........will have responsibilities?
WHERE......is the work to be done?
WHEN........is the job to begin and end? (Schedules, etc.)
HOW..........is the job to bed done? (Methods, controls, records, etc.)

II. ORGANIZING

This means dividing up the work, establishing clear lines of responsibility and authority and coordinating efforts to get the job done.

III. STAFFING

The whole personnel function of bringing in and training staff, getting the right man and fitting him to the right job—the job to which he is best suited.

In the normal situation, the supervisor's responsibility regarding staffing normally includes providing accurate job descriptions, that is, duties of the jobs, requirements, education and experience, skills, physical, etc.; assigning the work for maximum use of skills; and proper utilization of the probationary period to weed out unsatisfactory employees.

IV. DIRECTING

Providing the necessary leadership to the group supervised. Important work gets done to the supervisor's satisfaction.

V. COORDINATING

The all-important duty of inter-relating the various parts of the work.
The supervisor is also responsible for controlling the coordinated activities. This means measuring performance according to a time schedule and setting quotas to see that the goals previously set are being reached. Reports from workers should be analyzed, evaluated, and made part of all future plans.

VI. REPORTING

This means proper and effective communication to your superiors, subordinates, and your peers (in definition of the job of the supervisor). Reports should be read and information contained therein should be used, not be filed away and forgotten. Reports should be written in such a way that the desired action recommended by the report is forthcoming.

VII. BUDGETING
This means controlling current costs and forecasting future costs. This forecast is based on past experience, future plans and programs, as well as current costs.

You will note that these seven functions can fall under three topics:

Planning) Organizing) Make a plan	Staffing) Directing) Controlling) Get things done	Reporting) Budgeting) Watch it work

PLANNING TO MEET MANAGEMENT GOALS

I. WHAT IS PLANNING?

A. Thinking a job through before new work is done to determine the best way to do it
B. A method of doing something
C. Ways and means for achieving set goals
D. A means of enabling a supervisor to deliver with a minimum of effort, all details involved in coordinating his work

II. WHO SHOULD MAKE PLANS?

Everybody!
All levels of supervision must plan work. (Top management, heads of divisions or bureaus, first line supervisors, and individual employees.) The higher the level, the more planning required.

III. WHAT ARE THE RESULTS OF POOR PLANNING?

A. Failure to meet deadline
B. Low employee morale
C. Lack of job coordination
D. Overtime is frequently necessary
E. Excessive cost, waste of material and manhours

IV. PRINCIPLES OF PLANNING

A. Getting a clear picture of your objectives. What exactly are you trying to accomplish?
B. Plan the whole job, then the parts, in proper sequence.
C. Delegate the planning of details to those responsible for executing them.
D. Make your plan flexible.
E. Coordinate your plan with the plans of others so that the work may be processed with a minimum of delay.
F. Sell your plan before you execute it.
G. Sell your plan to your superior, subordinate, in order to gain maximum participation and coordination.
H. Your plan should take precedence. Use knowledge and skills that others have brought to a similar job.
I. Your plan should take account of future contingencies; allow for future expansion.
J. Plans should include minor details. Leave nothing to chance that can be anticipated.
K. Your plan should be simple and provide standards and controls. Establish quality and quantity standards and set a standard method of doing the job. The controls will indicate whether the job is proceeding according to plan.
L. Consider possible bottlenecks, breakdowns, or other difficulties that are likely to arise.

V. Q. WHAT ARE THE YARDSTICKS BY WHICH PLANNING SHOULD BE MEASURED?
A. Any plan should:
—Clearly state a definite course of action to be followed and goal to be achieved, with consideration for emergencies.
— Be realistic and practical.
— State what's to be done, when it's to be done, where, how, and by whom.
— Establish the most efficient sequence of operating steps so that more is accomplished in less time, with the least effort, and with the best quality results.
— Assure meeting deliveries without delays.
— Establish the standard by which performance is to be judged.

Q. WHAT KINDS OF PLANS DOES EFFECTIVE SUPERVISION REQUIRE?
A. Plans should cover such factors as:
— Manpower: right number of properly trained employees on the job
— Materials: adequate supply of the right materials and supplies
— Machines: full utilization of machines and equipment, with proper maintenance
— Methods: most efficient handling of operations
— Deliveries: making deliveries on time
— Tools: sufficient well-conditioned tools
— Layout: most effective use of space
— Reports: maintaining proper records and reports
— Supervision: planning work for employees and organizing supervisor's own time

MANAGEMENT PRINCIPLES

I. MANAGEMENT
Q. What do we mean by management?
A. Getting work done through others.

Management could also be defined as planning, directing, and controlling the operations of a bureau or division so that all factors will function properly and all persons cooperate efficiently for a common objective.

II. MANAGEMENT PRINCIPLES

A. There should be a hierarchy—wherein authority and responsibility run upward and downward through several levels—with a broad base at the bottom and a single head at the top.

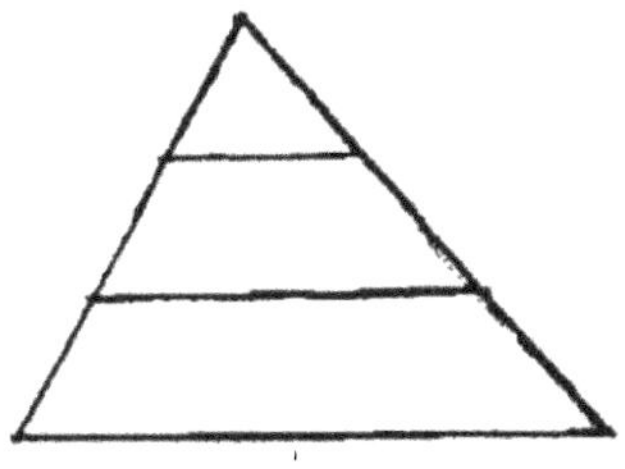

B. Each and every unit or person in the organization should be answerable ultimately to the manager at the apex. In other words, *The buck stops here!*

C. Every necessary function involved in the bureau's objectives is assigned to a unit in that bureau.

D. Responsibilities assigned to a unit are specifically clear-cut and understood.

E. Consistent methods of organizational structure should be applied at each level of the organization.

F. Each member of the bureau from top to bottom knows: to whom he reports and who reports to him.

G. No member of one bureau reports to more than one supervisor. No dual functions.

H. Responsibility for a function is matched by authority necessary to perform that function. Weight of authority.

I. Individuals or units reporting to a supervisor do not exceed the number which can be feasibly and effectively coordinated and directed. Concept of *span of control.*

J. Channels of command (management) are not violated by staff units, although there should be staff services to facilitate and coordinate management functions.

K. Authority and responsibility should be decentralized to units and individuals who are responsible for the actual performance of operations.
Welfare – down to Welfare Centers
Hospitals – down to local hospitals

L. Management should exercise control through attention to policy problems of exceptional performance, rather than through review of routine actions of subordinates.

M. Organizations should never be permitted to grow so elaborate as to hinder work accomplishments.

III. ORGANIZATION STRUCTURE

Types of Organizations
The purest form is a leader and a few followers, such as:

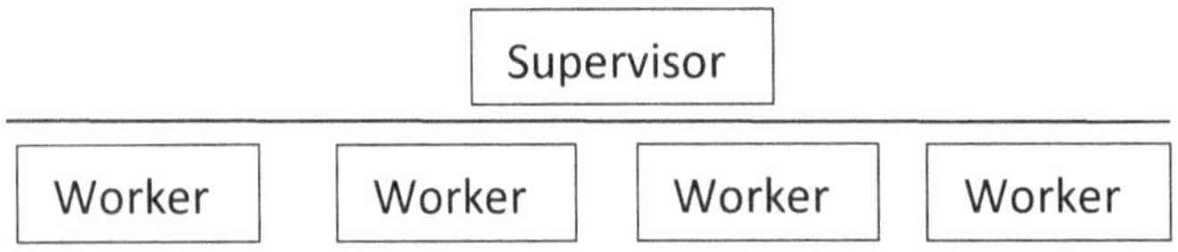

(Refer to organization chart) from supervisor to workers.

The line of authority is direct, The workers know exactly where they stand in relation to their boss, to whom they report for instructions and direction.

Unfortunately, in our present complex society, few organizations are similar to this example of a pure line organization. In this era of specialization, other people are often needed in the simplest of organizations. These specialists are known as staff. The sole purpose for their existence (staff) is to assist, advise, suggest, help or counsel line organizations. Staff has no authority to direct line people—nor do they give them direct instructions.

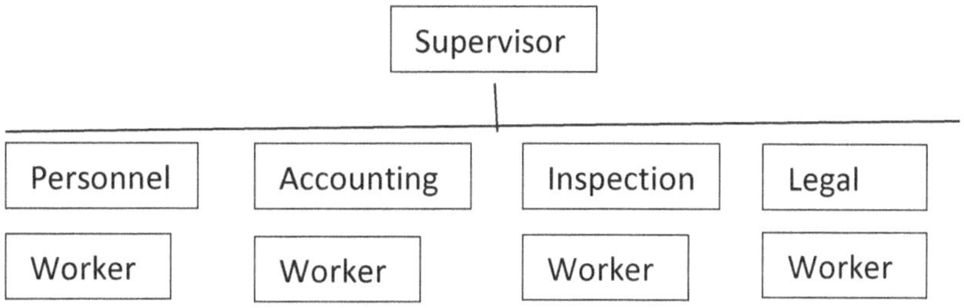

<u>Line Functions</u>

1. Directs
2. Orders
3. Responsibility for carrying out activities from beginning to end
4. Follows chain of command
5. Is identified with what it does
6. Decides when and how to use staff advice
7. Line executes

<u>Staff Functions</u>

1. Advises
2. Persuades and sells
3. Staff studies, reports, recommends but does not carry out
4. May advise across department lines
5. May find its ideas identified with others
6. Has to persuade line to want its advice
7. Staff: Conducts studies and research. Provides advice and instructions in technical matters. Serves as technical specialist to render specific services.

<u>Types and Functions of Organization Charts</u>

An organization chart is a picture of the arrangement and inter-relationship of the subdivisions of an organization.

A. Types of Charts:
    1. Structural: basic relationships only
    2. Functional: includes functions or duties
    3. Personnel: positions, salaries, status, etc.
    4. Process Chart: work performed
    5. Gantt Chart: actual performance against planned
    5. Flow Chart: flow and distribution of work

B. Functions of Charts:
    1. Assist in management planning and control
    2. Indicate duplication of functions
    3. Indicate incorrect stressing of functions
    4. Indicate neglect of important functions
    5. Correct unclear authority
    6. Establish proper span of control

C. Limitations of Charts:
1. Seldom maintained on current basis
2. Chart is oversimplified
3. Human factors cannot adequately be charted

D. Organization Charts should be:
1. Simple
2. Symmetrical
3. Indicate authority
4. Line and staff relationship differentiated
5. Chart should be dated and bear signature of approving officer
6. Chart should be displayed, not hidden

ORGANIZATION

There are four basic principles of organization:
1. Unity of command
2. Span of control
3. Uniformity of assignment
4. Assignment of responsibility and delegation of authority

I. UNITY OF COMMAND

Unity of command means that each person in the organization should receive orders from one, and only one, supervisor. When a person has to take orders from two or more people, (a) the orders may be in conflict and the employee is upset because he does not know which he should obey, or (b) different orders may reach him at the same time and he does not know which he should carry out first.

Equally as bad as having two bosses is the situation where the supervisor is bypassed. Let us suppose you are a supervisor whose boss bypasses you (deals directly with people reporting to you). To the worker, it is the same as having two bosses; but to you, the supervisor, it is equally serious. Bypassing on the part of your boss will undermine your authority, and the people under you will begin looking to your boss for decisions and even for routine orders.

You can prevent bypassing by telling the people you supervise that if anyone tries to give them orders, they should direct that person to you.

II. SPAN OF CONTROL

Span of control on a given level involves:
A. The number of people being supervised
B. The distance
C The time involved in supervising the people. (One supervisor cannot supervise too many workers effectively.)

Span of control means that a supervisor has the right number (not too many and not too few) of subordinates that he can supervise well.

III. UNIFORMITY OF ASSIGNMENT

In assigning work, you as the supervisor should assign to each person jobs that are similar in nature. An employee who is assigned too many different types of jobs will waste time in going from one kind of work to another. It takes time for him to get to top production in one kind of task and, before he does so, he has to start on another.
When you assign work to people, remember that:

A. Job duties should be definite. Make it clear from the beginning what they are to do, how they are to do it, and why they are to do it. Let them know how much they are expected to do and how well they are expected to do it.
B. Check your assignments to be certain that there are no workers with too many unrelated duties, and that no two people have been given overlapping responsibilities. Your aim should be to have every task assigned to a specific person with the work fairly distributed and with each person doing his part.

IV. ASSIGNMENT OF RESPONSIBILITY AND DELEGATION OF AUTHORITY

A supervisor cannot delegate his final responsibility for the work of his department. The experienced supervisor knows that he gets his work done through people. He can't do it all himself. So he must assign the work and the responsibility for the work to his employees. Then they must be given the authority to carry out their responsibilities.

By assigning responsibility and delegating authority to carry out the responsibility, the supervisor builds in his workers initiative, resourcefulness, enthusiasm, and interest in their work. He is treating them as responsible adults. They can find satisfaction in their work, and they will respect the supervisor and be loyal to the supervisor.

PRINCIPLES OF ORGANIZATION

I. DEFINITION

Organization is the method of dividing up the work to provide the best channels for coordinated effort to get the agency's mission accomplished.

II. PURPOSE OF ORGANIZATION

A. To enable each employee within the organization to clearly know his responsibilities and relationships to his fellow employees and to organizational units
B. To avoid conflicts of authority and overlapping of jurisdiction.
C. To ensure teamwork.

III. BASIC CONSIDERATIONS IIN ORGANIZATIONAL PLANNING

A. The basic plans and objectives of the agency should be determined, and the organizational structure should be adapted to carry out effectively such plans and objectives.
B. The organization should be built around the major functions of the agency and not individuals or groups of individuals.

C. The organization should be sufficiently flexible to meet new and changing conditions which may be brought about from within or outside the department.
D. The organizational structure should be as simple as possible and the number of organizational units kept at a minimum.
E. The number of levels of authority should be kept at a minimum. Each additional management level lengthens the chain of authority and responsibility and increases the time for instructions to be distributed to operating levels and for decisions to be obtained from higher authority.
F. The form of organization should permit each executive to exercise maximum initiative within the limits of delegated authority.

IV. BASES FOR ORGANIZATION

A. Purpose (Examples: education, police, sanitation)
B. Process (Examples: accounting, legal, purchasing)
C. Clientele (Examples: welfare, parks, veteran)
D. Geographic (Examples: borough offices, precincts, libraries)

V. ASSIGNMENTS OF FUNCTIONS

A. Every function of the agency should be assigned to a specific organizational unit. Under normal circumstances, no single function should be assigned to more than one organizational unit.
B. There should be no overlapping, duplication, or conflict between organizational elements.
C. Line functions should be separated from staff functions, and proper emphasis should be placed on staff activities.
D. Functions which are closely related or similar should normally be assigned to a single organizational unit.
E. Functions should be properly distributed to promote balance, and to avoid overemphasis of less important functions and underemphasis of more essential functions.

VI. DELEGATION OF AUTHORITY AND RESPONSIBILITY

A. Responsibilities assigned to a specific individual or organizational unit should carry corresponding authority, and all statements of authority or limitations thereof should be as specific as possible.
B. Authority and responsibility for action should be decentralized to organizational units and individuals responsible for actual performance to the greatest extent possible, without relaxing necessary control over policy or the standardization of procedures. Delegation of authority will be consistent with decentralization of responsibility but such delegation will not divest an executive in higher authority of his overall responsibility.
C. The heads of organizational units should concern themselves with important matters and should delegate to the maximum extent details and routines performed in the ordinary course of business.
D. All responsibilities, authorities, and relationships should be stated in simple language to avoid misinterpretation.
E. Each individual or organizational unit charged with a specific responsibility will be held responsible for results.

VII. EMPLOYEE RELATIONSHIPS

A. The employees reporting to one executive should not exceed the number which can be effectively directed and coordinated. The number will depend largely upon the scope and extent of the responsibilities of the subordinates.
B. No person should report to more than one supervisor. Every supervisor should know who reports to him, and every employee should know to whom he reports. Channels of authority and responsibility should not be violated by staff units.
C. Relationships between organizational units within the agency and with outside organizations and associations should be clearly stated and thoroughly understood to avoid misunderstanding.

DELEGATING

I. WHAT IS DELEGATING?
Delegating is assigning a job to an employee, giving him the authority to get that job done, and giving him the responsibility for seeing to it that the job is done.

A. What To Delegate
   1. Routine details
   2. Jobs which may be necessary and take a lot of time, but do not have to be done by the supervisor personally (preparing reports, attending meetings, etc.)
   3. Routine decision-making (making decisions which do not require the supervisor's personal attention)

B. What Not To Delegate
   1. Job details which are *executive functions* (setting goals, organizing employees into a good team, analyzing results so as to plan for the future)
   2. Disciplinary power (handling grievances, preparing service ratings, reprimands, etc.)
   3. Decision-making which involves large numbers of employees or other bureaus and departments
   4. Final and complete responsibility for the job done by the unit being supervised

C. Why Delegate?
   1. To strengthen the organization by developing a greater number of skilled employees
   2. To improve the employee's performance by giving him the chance to learn more about the job, handle some responsibility, and become more interested in getting the job done
   3. To improve a supervisor's performance by relieving him of routine jobs and giving him more time for *executive functions* (planning, organizing, controlling, etc.) which cannot be delegated

II. TO WHOM TO DELEGATE
People with abilities not being used. Selection should be based on ability, not on favoritism.

REPORTS

I. DEFINITION
A report is an orderly presentation of factual information directed to a specific reader for a specific purpose

II. PURPOSE
The general purpose of a report is to bring to the reader useful and factual information about a condition or a problem. Some specific purposes of a report may be:

A. To enable the reader to appraise the efficiency or effectiveness of a person or an operation
B. To provide a basis for establishing standards
C. To reflect the results of expenditures of time, effort, and money
D. To provide a basis for developing or altering programs

III. TYPES

A. Information Report: Contains facts arranged in sequence
B. Summary (Examination) Report: Contains facts plus an analysis or discussion of the significance of the facts. Analysis may give advantages and disadvantages or give qualitative and quantitative comparisons
C. Recommendation Report: Contains facts, analysis, and conclusion logically drawn from the facts and analysis, plus a recommendation based upon the facts, analysis, and conclusions

IV. FACTORS TO CONSIDER BEFORE WRITING REPORT

A. Why write the report?: The purpose of the report should be clearly defined.
B. Who will read the report?: What level of language should be used? Will the reader understand professional or technical language?
C. What should be said?: What does the reader need or want to know about the subject?
D. How should it be said?: Should the subject be presented tactfully? Convincingly? In a stimulating manner?

V. PREPARATORY STEPS

A. Assemble the facts: Find out who, why, what, where, when, and how.
B. Organize the facts: Eliminate unnecessary information
C. Prepare an outline: Check for orderliness, logical sequence
D. Prepare a draft: Check for correctness, clearness, completeness, conciseness, and tone
E. Prepare it in final form: Check for grammar, punctuation, appearance

VI. OUTLINE FOR A RECOMMENDATION REPORT

Is the report:
A. Correct in information, grammar, and tone?
B. Clear?
C. Complete?

D. Concise?
E. Timely?
F. Worth its cost?

Will the report accomplish its purpose?

MANAGEMENT CONTROLS

I. CONTROL

What is control? What is controlled? Who controls?

The essence of control is action which adjusts operations to predetermined standards, and its basis is information in the hands of managers. Control is checking to determine whether plans are being observed and suitable progress toward stated objectives is being made, and action is taken, if necessary, to correct deviations.

We have a ready-made model for this concept of control in the automatic systems which are widely used for process control in the chemical land petroleum industries. A process control system works this way. Suppose, for example, it is desired to maintain a constant rate of flow of oil through a pipe at a predetermined or set-point value. A signal, whose strength represents the rate of flow, can be produced in a measuring device and transmitted to a control mechanism. The control mechanism, when it detects any deviation of the actual from the set-point signal, will reposition the value regulating flow rate.

II. BASIS FOR CONTROL

A process control mechanism thus acts to adjust operations to predetermined standards and does so on the basis of information it receives. In a parallel way, information reaching a manager gives him the opportunity for corrective action and is his basis for control. He cannot exercise control without such information, and he cannot do a complete job of managing without controlling.

III. POLICY

What is policy?

Policy is simply a statement of an organization's intention to act in certain ways when specified types of circumstances arise. It represents a general decision, predetermined and expressed as a principle or rule, establishing a normal pattern of conduct for dealing with given types of business events—usually recurrent. A statement is therefore useful in economizing the time of managers and in assisting them to discharge their responsibilities equitably and consistently.

Policy is not a means of control, but policy does generate the need for control.

Adherence to policies is not guaranteed nor can it be taken on faith. It has to be verified. Without verification, there is no basis for control. Policy and procedures, although closely related and interdependent to a certain extent, are not synonymous. A policy may be adopted, for example, to maintain a materials inventory not to exceed one million dollars.

A procedure for inventory control could interpret that policy and convert it into methods for keeping within that limit, with consideration, too, of possible but foreseeable expedient deviation.

IV. PROCEDURE

What is procedure?

A procedure specifically prescribes:
A. What work is to be performed by the various participants
B. Who are the respective participants
C. When and where the various steps in the different processes are to be performed
D. The sequence of operations that will insure uniform handling of recurring transactions
E. The paper that is involved, its origin, transition, and disposition

Necessary appurtenances to a procedure are:
A. Detailed organizational chart
B. Flow charts
C. Exhibits of forms, all presented in close proximity to the text of the procedure

V. BASIS OF CONTROL – INFORMATION IN THE HANDS OF MANAGERS

If the basis of control is information in the hands of managers, then reporting is elevated to a level of very considerable importance.

Types of reporting may include:
A. Special reports and routine reports
B. Written, oral, and graphic reports
C. Staff meetings
D. Conferences
E. Television screens
F. Non-receipt of information, as where management is by exception
G. Any other means whereby information is transmitted to a manager as a basis for control action

FRAMEWORK OF MANAGEMENT

I. ELEMENTS

A. Policy: It has to be verified, controlled.

B. Organization is part of the giving of an assignment. The organizational chart gives to each individual in his title, a first approximation of the nature of his assignment and orients him as being accountable to a certain individual. Organization is not in a true sense a means of control. Control is checking to ascertain whether the assignment is executed as intended and acting on the basis of that information.

C. Budgets perform three functions:
   1. They present the objectives, plans, and programs of the organization in financial terms.

2. They report the progress of actual performance against these predetermined objectives, plans, and programs.
3. Like organizational charts, delegations of authority, procedures, and job descriptions, they define the assignments which have flowed from the Chief Executive. Budgets are a means of control in the respect that they report progress of actual performance against the program. They provide information which enables managers to take action directed toward bringing actual results into conformity with the program.

D. Internal Check provides in practice for the principle that the same person should not have responsibility for all phases of a transaction. This makes it clearly an aspect of organization rather than of control. Internal Check is static, or built-in.

E. Plans, Programs, Objectives
People must know what they are trying to do. Objectives fulfill this need. Without them, people may work industriously and yet, working aimlessly, accomplish little. Plans and Programs complement Objectives, since they propose how and according to what time schedule the objectives are to be reached.

F. Delegations of Authority
Among the ways we have for supplementing the titles and lines of authority of an organizational chart are delegations of authority. Delegations of authority clarify the extent of authority of individuals and in that way serve to define assignments. That they are not means of control is apparent from the very fact that wherever there has been a delegation of authority, the need for control increases. This could hardly be expected to happen if delegations of authority were themselves means of control.

II. MANAGER'S RESPONSIBILITY

Control becomes necessary whenever a manager delegates authority to a subordinate because he cannot delegate and then simply sit back and forget4 about it. A manager's accountability to his own superior has not diminished one whit as a result of delegating part of his authority to a subordinate. The manager must exercise control over actions taken under the authority so delegated. That means checking serves as a basis for possible corrective action.

Objectives, plans, programs, organizational charts, and other elements of the managerial system are not fruitfully regarded as either controls or means of control. They are pre-established standards or models of performance to which operations are adjusted by the exercise of management control. These standards or models of performance are dynamic in character for they are constantly altered, modified, or revised. Policies, organizational set-up, procedures, delegations, etc. are constantly altered but, like objectives and plans, they remain in force until they are either abandoned or revised. All of the elements (or standards or models of performance), objectives, plans, and programs, policies, organization, etc. can be regarded as a *framework of management*.

III. CONTROL TECHNIQUES

Examples of control techniques:

A. Compare against established standards
B. Compare with a similar operation
C. Compare with past operations
D. Compare with predictions of accomplishment

IV. WHERE FORECASTS FIT

Control is after-the-fact while forecasts are before. Forecasts and projections are important for setting objectives and formulating plans.

Information for aiming and planning does not have to be before-the-fact. It may be an after-the-fact analysis proving that a certain policy has been impolitic in its effect on the relation of the company or department with customer, employee, taxpayer, or stockholder; or that a certain plan is no longer practical, or that a certain procedure is unworkable.

The prescription here certainly would not be in control (in these cases, control would simply bring operations into conformity with obsolete standards) but the establishment of new standards, a new policy, a new plan, and a new procedure to be controlled too.

Information is, of course, the basis for all communication in addition to furnishing evidence to management of the need for reconstructing the framework of management.

PROBLEM SOLVING

The accepted concept in modern management for problem solving is the utilization of the following steps:

A. Identify the problem
B. Gather data
C. List possible solutions
D. Test possible solutions
E. Select the best solution
F. Put the solution into actual practice

Occasions might arise where you would have to apply the second step of gathering data before completing the first step.

You might also find that it will be necessary to work on several steps at the same time.

I. IDENTIFY THE PROBLEM

Your first step is to define as precisely as possible the problem to be solved. While this may sound easy, it is often the most difficult part of the process.

It has been said of problem solving that you are halfway to the solution when you can write out a clear statement of the problem itself.

Our job now is to get below the surface manifestations of the trouble and pinpoint the problem. This is usually accomplished by a logical analysis, by going from the general to the particular; from the obvious to the not-so-obvious cause.

Let us say that production is behind schedule. WHY? Absenteeism is high. Now, is absenteeism the basic problem to be tackled, or is it merely a symptom of low morale among the workforce? Under these circumstances, you may decide that production is not the problem; the problem is *employee morale*.

In trying to define the problem, remember there is seldom one simple reason why production is lagging, or reports are late, etc.

Analysis usually leads to the discovery that an apparent problem is really made up of several subproblems which must be attacked separately.

Another way is to limit the problem, and thereby ease the task of finding a solution, and concentrate on the elements which are within the scope of your control.

When you have gone this far, write out a tentative statement of the problem to be solved.

II. GATHER DATA

In the second step, you must set out to collect all the information that might have a bearing on the problem. Do not settle for an assumption when reasonable fact and figures are available.

If you merely go through the motions of problem-solving, you will probably shortcut the information-gathering step. Therefore, do not stack the evidence by confining your research to your own preconceived ideas.

As you collect facts, organize them in some form that helps you make sense of them and spot possible relationships between them. For example, plotting cost per unit figures on a graph can be more meaningful than a long column of figures.

Evaluate each item as you go along. Is the source material absolutely, reliable, probably reliable, or not to be trusted.

One of the best methods for gathering data is to go out and look the situation over carefully. Talk to the people on the job who are most affected by this problem.

Always keep in mind that a primary source is usually better than a secondary source of information.

III. LIST POSSIBLE SOLUTIONS

This is the creative thinking step of problem solving. This is a good time to bring into play whatever techniques of group dynamics the agency or bureau might have developed for a joint attack on problems.

Now the important thing for you to do is: Keep an open mind. Let your imagination roam freely over the facts you have collected. Jot down every possible solution that occurs to you. Resist the temptation to evaluate various proposals as you go along. List seemingly absurd ideas along with more plausible ones. The more possibilities you list during this step, the less risk you will run of settling for merely a workable, rather than the best, solution.

Keep studying the data as long as there seems to be any chance of deriving additional ideas, solutions, explanations, or patterns from it.

IV. TEST POSSIBLE SOLUTIONS

Now you begin to evaluate the possible solutions. Take pains to be objective. Up to this point, you have suspended judgment but you might be tempted to select a solution you secretly favored all along and proclaim it as the best of the lot.

The secret of objectivity in this phase is to test the possible solutions separately, measuring each against a common yardstick. To make this yardstick try to enumerate as many specific criteria as you can think of. Criteria are best phrased as questions which you ask of each possible solution. They can be drawn from these general categories:

Suitability – Will this solution do the job?
Will it solve the problem completely or partially?
Is it a permanent or a stopgap solution?

Feasibility - Will this plan work in actual practice?
Can we afford this approach?
How much will it cost?

Acceptability - Will the boss go along with the changes required in the plan?
Are we trying to drive a tack with a sledge hammer?

V. SELECT THE BEST SOLUTION

This is the area of executive decision.

Occasionally, one clearly superior solution will stand out at the conclusion of the testing process. But often it is not that simple. You may find that no one solution has come through all the tests with flying colors.

You may also find that a proposal, which flunked miserably on one of the essential tests, racked up a very high score on others.

The best solution frequently will turn out to be a combination.

Try to arrange a marriage that will bring together the strong points of one possible solution with the particular virtues of another. The more skill and imagination that you apply, the greater is the likelihood that you will come out with a solution that is not merely adequate and workable, but is the best possible under the circumstances.

VI. PUT THE SOLUTION INTO ACTUAL PRACTICE

As every executive knows, a plan which works perfectly on paper may develop all sorts of bugs when put into actual practice.

Problem-solving does not stop with selecting the solution which looks best in theory. The next step is to put the chosen solution into action and watch the results. The results may point towards modifications.

If the problem disappears when you put your solution into effect, you know you have the right solution.

If it does not disappear, even after you have adjusted your plan to cover unforeseen difficulties that turned up in practice, work your way back through the problem-solving solutions.

Would one of them have worked better?
Did you overlook some vital piece of data which would have given you a different slant on the whole situation? Did you apply all necessary criteria in testing solutions? If no light dawns after this much rechecking, it is a pretty good bet that you defined the problem incorrectly in the first place.

You came up with the wrong solution because you tackled the wrong problem.

Thus, step six may become step one of a new problem-solving cycle.

COMMUNICATION

I. WHAT IS COMMUNICATION?
We communicate through writing, speaking, action, or inaction. In speaking to people face-to-face, there is opportunity to judge reactions and to adjust the message. This makes the supervisory chain one of the most, and in many instances the most, important channels of communication.

In an organization, communication means keeping employees informed about the organization's objectives, policies, problems, and progress. Communication is the free interchange of information, ideas, and desirable attitudes between and among employees and between employees and management.

II. WHY IS COMMUNICATION NEEDED?

A. People have certain social needs
B. Good communication is essential in meeting those social needs
C. While people have similar basic needs, at the same time they differ from each other
D. Communication must be adapted to these individual differences

An employee cannot do his best work unless he knows why he is doing it. If he has the feeling that he is being kept in the dark about what is going on, his enthusiasm and productivity suffer.

Effective communication is needed in an organization so that employees will understand what the organization is trying to accomplish; and how the work of one unit contributes to or affects the work of other units in the organization and other organizations.

III. HOW IS COMMUNICATION ACHIEVED?

Communication flows downward, upward, sideways.

A. Communication may come from top management down to employees. This is downward communication.

Some means of downward communication are:
1. Training (orientation, job instruction, supervision, public relations, etc.)
2. Conferences
3. Staff meetings
4. Policy statements
5. Bulletins
6. Newsletters
7. Memoranda
8. Circulation of important letters

In downward communication, it is important that employees be informed in advance of changes that will affect them.

B. Communications should also be developed so that the ideas, suggestions, and knowledge of employees will flow upward to top management.

Some means of upward communication are:
1. Personal discussion conferences
2. Committees
3. Memoranda
4. Employees suggestion program
5. Questionnaires to be filled in giving comments and suggestions about proposed actions that will affect field operations.

Upward communication requires that management be willing to listen, to accept, and to make changes when good ideas are present. Upward communication succeeds when there is no fear of punishment for speaking out or lack of interest at the top. Employees will share their knowledge and ideas with management when interest is shown and recognition is given.

C. The advantages of downward communication:
1. It enables the passing down of orders, policies, and plans necessary to the continued operation of the station.
2. By making information available, it diminishes the fears and suspicions which result from misinformation and misunderstanding.
3. It fosters the pride people want to have in their work when they are told of good work.
4. It improves the morale and stature of the individual to be *in the know.*

5. It helps employees to understand, accept, and cooperate with changes when they know about them in advance.

D. The advantages of upward communication:
   1. It enables the passing upward of information, attitudes, and feelings.
   2. It makes it easier to find out how ready people are to receive downward communication.
   3. It reveals the degree to which the downward communication is understood and accepted.
   4. It helps to satisfy the basic social needs.
   5. It stimulates employees to participate in the operation of their organization.
   6. It encourage employees to contribute ideas for improving the efficiency and economy of operations.
   7. It helps to solve problem situations before they reach the explosion point.

IV. WHY DOES COMMUNICATION FAIL?

A. The technical difficulties of conveying information clearly
B. The emotional content of communication which prevents complete transmission
C. The fact that there is a difference between what management needs to say, what it wants to day, and what it does say
D. The fact that there is a difference between what employees would like to say, what they think is profitable or safe to say, and what they do say

V. HOW TO IMPROVE COMMUNICATION

As a supervisor, you are a key figure in communication. To improve as a communicator, you should:
A. Know: Knowing your subordinates will help you to recognize and work with individual differences.
B. Like: If you like those who work for you and those for whom you work, this will foster the kind of friendly, warm, work atmosphere that will facilitate communication.
C. Trust: Showing a sincere desire to communicate will help to develop the mutual trust and confidence which are essential to the free flow of communication.
D. Tell: Tell your subordinates and superiors *what's doing*. Tell your subordinates *why* as well as *how*.
E. Listen: By listening, you help others to talk and you create good listeners. Don't forget that listening implies action.
F. Stimulate: Communication has to be stimulated and encouraged. Be receptive to ideas and suggestions and motivate your people so that each member of the team identifies himself with the job at hand.
G. Consult: The most effective way of consulting is to let your people participate, insofar as possible, in developing determinations which affect them or their work.

VI. HOW TO DETERMINE WHETHER YOU ARE GETTING ACROSS

A. Check to see that communication is received and understood
B. Judge this understanding by actions rather than words
C. Adapt or vary communication, when necessary
D. Remember that good communication cannot cure all problems

VII. THE KEY ATTITUDE

Try to see things from the other person's point of view. By doing this, you help to develop the permissive atmosphere and the shared confidence and understanding which are essential to effective two-way communication.

Communication is a two-way process:

A. The basic purpose of any communication is to get action.
B. The only way to get action is through acceptance.
C. In order to get acceptance, communication must be humanly satisfying as well as technically efficient.

HOW ORDERS AND INSTRUCTIONS SHOULD BE GIVEN

I. CHARACTERISTICS OF GOOD ORDERS AND INSTRUCTIONS

A. Clear
Orders should be definite as to
—What is to be done
—Who is to do it
—When it is to be done
—Where it is to be done
—How it is to be done

B. Concise
Avoid wordiness. Orders should be brief and to the point.

C. Timely
Instructions and orders should be sent out at the proper time and not too long in advance of expected performance.

D. Possibility of Performance
Orders should be feasible:
1. Investigate before giving orders
2. Consult those who are to carry out instructions before formulating and issuing them

E. Properly Directed
Give the orders to the people concerned. Do not send orders to people who are not concerned. People who continually receive instructions that are not applicable to them get in the habit of neglecting instructions generally.

F. Reviewed Before Issuance
Orders should be reviewed before issuance:
1. Test them by putting yourself in the position of the recipient
2. If they involve new procedures, have the persons who are to do the work review them for suggestions.

G. Reviewed After Issuance
Persons who receive orders should be allowed to raise questions and to point out unforeseen consequences of orders.

H. Coordinated
Orders should be coordinated so that work runs smoothly.

I. Courteous
Make a request rather than a demand. There is no need to continually call attention to the fact that you are the boss.

J. Recognizable as an Order
Be sure that the order is recognizable as such.

K. Complete
Be sure recipient has knowledge and experience sufficient to carry out order. Give illustrations and examples.

A DEPARTMENTAL PERSONNEL OFFICE IS RESPONSIBLE FOR THE FOLLOWING FUNCTIONS

1. Policy
2. Personnel Programs
3. Recruitment and Placement
4. Position Classification
5. Salary and Wage Administration
6. Employee performance Standards and Evaluation
7. Employee Relations
8. Disciplinary Actions and Separations
9. Health and Safety
10. Staff Training and Development
11. Personnel Records, Procedures, and Reports
12. Employee Services
13. Personnel Research

SUPERVISION

I. LEADERSHIP

All leadership is based essentially on authority. This comes from two sources: It is received from higher management or it is earned by the supervisor through his methods of supervision. Although effective leadership has always depended upon the leader's using his authority in such a way as to appeal successfully to the motives of the people supervised, the conditions for making this appeal are continually changing. The key to today's problem of leadership is flexibility and resourcefulness on the part of the leader in meeting changes in conditions as they occur.

Three basic approaches to leadership are generally recognized:

A. The Authoritarian Approach
   1. The methods and techniques used in this approach emphasize the *I* in leadership and depend primarily on the formal authority of the leader. This authority is sometimes exercised in a hardboiled manner and sometimes in a benevolent

manner, but in either case the dominating role of the leader is reflected in the thinking, planning, and decisions of the group.

2. Group results are to a large degree dependent on close supervision by the leader. Usually, the individuals in the group will not show a high degree of initiative or acceptance of responsibility and their capacity to grow and develop probably will not be fully utilized. The group may react with resentment or submission, depending upon the manner and skill of the leader in using his authority.
3. This approach develops as a natural outgrowth of the authority that goes with the leader's job and his feeling of sole responsibility for getting the job done. It is relatively easy to use and does not require must resourcefulness.
4. The use of this approach is effective in times of emergencies, in meeting close deadline as a final resort, in settling some issues, in disciplinary matters, and with dependent individuals and groups.

B. The Laissez-Faire or Let 'em Alone Approach
1. This approach generally is characterized by an avoidance of leadership responsibility by the leader. The activities of the group depend largely on the choice of its members rather than the leader.
2. Group results probably will be poor. Generally, there will be disagreements over petty things, bickering, and confusion. Except for a few aggressive people, individuals will not show much initiative and growth and development will be retarded. There may be a tendency for informal leaders to take over leadership of the group.
3. This approach frequently results from the leader's dislike of responsibility, from his lack of confidence, from failure of other methods to work, from disappointment or criticism. It is usually the easiest of the three to use and requires both understanding and resourcefulness on the part of the leader.
4. This approach is occasionally useful and effective, particularly in forcing dependent individuals or groups to rely on themselves, to give someone a chance to save face by clearing his own difficulties, or when action should be delayed temporarily for good cause.

C. The Democratic Approach
1. The methods and techniques used in this approach emphasize the *we* in leadership and build up the responsibility of the group to attain its objectives. Reliance is placed largely on the earned authority of the leader.
2. Group results are likely to be good because most of the job motives of the people will be satisfied. Cooperation and teamwork, initiative, acceptance of responsibility, and the individual's capacity for growth probably will show a high degree of development.
3. This approach grows out of a desire or necessity of the leader to find ways to appeal effectively to the motivation of his group. It is the best approach to build up inside the person a strong desire to cooperate and apply himself to the job. It is the most difficult to develop, and requires both understanding and resourcefulness on the part of the leader.
4. The value of this approach increases over a long period where sustained efficiency and development of people are important. It may not be fully effective in all situations, however, particularly when there is not sufficient time to use it properly or where quick decisions must be made.

All three approaches are used by most leaders and have a place in supervising people. The extent of their use varies with individual leaders, with some using one approach predominantly. The leader who uses these three approaches, and varies their use with time and circumstance, is probably the most effective. Leadership which is used predominantly with a democratic approach requires more resourcefulness on the part of the leader but offers the greatest possibilities in terms of teamwork and cooperation.

The one best way of developing democratic leadership is to provide a real sense of participation on the part of the group, since this satisfies most of the chief job motives. Although there are many ways of providing participation, consulting as frequently as possible with individuals and groups on things that affect them seems to offer the most in building cooperation and responsibility. Consultation takes different forms, but it is most constructive when people feel they are actually helping in finding the answers to the problems on the job.

There are some requirements of leaders in respect to human relations which should be considered in their selection and development. Generally, the leader should be interested in working with other people, emotionally stable, self-confident, and sensitive to the reactions of others. In addition, his viewpoint should be one of getting the job done through people who work cooperatively in response to his leadership. He should have a knowledge of individual and group behavior, but, most important of all, he should work to combine all of these requirements into a definite, practical skill in leadership.

II. NINE POINTS OF CONTRAST BETWEEN *BOSS* AND *LEADER*

A. The boss drives his men; the leader coaches them.
B. The boss depends on authority; the leader on good will.
C. The boss inspires fear; the leader inspires enthusiasm.
D. The boss says I; the leader says *We.*
E. The boss says *Get here on time*; the leader gets there ahead of time.
F. The boss fixes the blame for the breakdown; the leader fixes the breakdown.
G. The boss knows how it is done; the leader shows how.
H. The boss makes work a drudgery; the leader makes work a game.
I. The boss says *Go*; the leader says *Let's go.*

EMPLOYEE MORALE

Employee morale is the way employees feel about each other, the organization or unit in which they work, and the work they perform.

I. SOME WAYS TO DEVELOP AND MAINTAIN GOOD EMPLYEE MORALE

A. Give adequate credit and praise when due.
B. Recognize importance of all jobs and equalize load with proper assignments, always giving consideration to personality differences and abilities.
C. Welcome suggestions and do not have an *all-wise* attitude. Request employees' assistance in solving problems and use assistants when conducting group meetings on certain subjects.
D. Properly assign responsibilities and give adequate authority for fulfillment of such assignments.

E. Keep employees informed about matters that affect them.
F. Criticize and reprimand employees privately.
G. Be accessible and willing to listen.
H. Be fair.
I. Be alert to detect training possibilities so that you will not miss an opportunity to help each employee do a better job, and if possible with less effort on his part.
J. Set a good example.
K. Apply the golden rule.

II. SOME INDICATIONS OF GOOD MORALE

A. Good quality of work
B. Good quantity
C. Good attitude of employees
D. Good discipline
E. Teamwork
F. Good attendance
G. Employee participation

MOTIVATION

DRIVES

A drive, stated simply, is a desire or force which causes a person to do or say certain things. These are some of the most usual drives and some of their identifying characteristics recognizable in people motivated by such drives:

A. Security (desire to provide for the future)
Always on time for work
Works for the same employer for many years
Never takes unnecessary chances
Seldom resists doing what he is told

B. Recognition (desire to be rewarded for accomplishment)
Likes to be asked for his opinion
Becomes very disturbed when he makes a mistake
Does things to attract attention
Likes to see his name in print

C. Position (desire to hold certain status in relation to others)
Boasts about important people he knows
Wants to be known as a key man
Likes titles
Demands respect
Belongs to clubs, for prestige

D. Accomplishment (desire to get things done)
Complains when things are held up
Likes to do things that have tangible results
Never lies down on the job
Is proud of turning out good work

E. Companionship (desire to associate with other people)
Likes to work with others
Tells stories and jokes
Indulges in horseplay
Finds excuses to talk to others on the job

F. Possession (desire to collect and hoard objects)
Likes to collect things
Puts his name on things belonging to him
Insists on the same location

Supervisors may find that identifying the drives of employees is a helpful step toward motivating them to self-improvement and better job performance. For example: An employee's job performance is below average. His supervisor, having previously determined that the employee is motivated by a drive for security, suggests that taking training courses will help the employee to improve, advance, and earn more money. Since earning more money can be a step toward greater security, the employee's drive for security would motivate him to take the training suggested by the supervisor. In essence, this is the process of charting an employee's future course by using his motivating drives to positive advantage.

EMPLOYEE PARTICIPATION

I. WHAT IS PARTICIPATION

Employee participation is the employee's giving freely of his time, skill, and knowledge to an extent which cannot be obtained by demand.

II. WHY IS IT IMPORTANT?

The supervisor's responsibility is to get the job done through people. A good supervisor gets the job done through people who work willingly and well. The participation of employees is important because:

A. Employees develop a greater sense of responsibility when they share in working out operating plans and goals.
B. Participation provides greater opportunity and stimulation for employees to learn, and to develop their ability.
C. Participation sometimes provides better solutions to problems because such solutions may combine the experience and knowledge of interested employees who want the solutions to work.
D. An employee or group may offer a solution which the supervisor might hesitate to make for fear of demanding too much.

E. Since the group wants to make the solution work, they exert pressure in a constructive way on each other.
F. Participation usually results in reducing the need for close supervision.

II. HOW MAY SUPERVISORS OBTAIN IT?

Participation is encouraged when employees feel that they share some responsibility for the work and that their ideas are sincerely wanted and valued. Some ways of obtaining employee participation are:

A. Conduct orientation programs for new employees to inform them about the organization and their rights and responsibilities as employees.
B. Explain the aims and objectives of the agency. On a continuing basis, be sure that the employees know what these aims and objectives are.
C. Share job successes and responsibilities and give credit for success.
D. Consult with employees, both as individuals and in groups, about things that affect them.
E. Encourage suggestions for job improvements. Help employees to develop good suggestions. The suggestions can bring them recognition. The city's suggestion program offers additional encouragement through cash awards.

The supervisor who encourages employee participation is not surrendering his authority. He must still make decisions and initiate action, and he must continue to be ultimately responsible for the work of those he supervises. But, through employee participation, he is helping his group to develop greater ability and a sense of responsibility while getting the job done faster and better.

STEPS IN HANDLING A GRIEVANCE

1. Get the Facts
   a. Listen sympathetically
   b. Let him talk himself out
   c. Get his story straight
   d. Get his point of view
   e. Don't argue with him
   f. Give him plenty of time
   g. Conduct the interview privately
   h. Don't try to shift the blame or pass the buck

2. Consider the Facts
   a. Consider the employee's viewpoint
   b. How will the decision affect similar cases
   c. Consider each decision as a possible precedent
   d. Avoid snap judgments—don't jump to conclusions

3. Make or Get a Decision
   a. Frame an effective counter-proposal
   b. Make sure it is fair to all
   c. Have confidence in your judgment
   d. Be sure you can substantiate your decision

4. Notify the Employee of Your Decision
Be sure he is told; try to convince him that the decision is fair and just.

5. Take Action When Needed and If Within Your Authority
Otherwise, tell employee that the matter will be called to the attention of the proper person or that nothing can be done, and why it cannot.

6. Follow through to see that the desired result is achieved.

7. Record key facts concerning the complaint and the action taken.

8. Leave the way open to him to appeal your decision to a higher authority.

9. Report all grievances to your superior, whether they are appealed or not.

DISCIPLINE

Discipline is training that develops self-control, orderly conduct, and efficiency.

To discipline does not necessarily mean to punish.

To discipline does mean to train, to regulate, and to govern conduct.

I. THE DISCIPLINARY INTERVIEW

Most employees sincerely want to do what is expected of them. In other words, they are self-disciplined. Some employees, however, fail to observe established rules and standards, and disciplinary action by the supervisor is required.

The primary purpose of disciplinary action is to improve conduct without creating dissatisfaction, bitterness, or resentment in the process.

Constructive disciplinary action is more concerned with causes and explanations of breaches of conduct than with punishment. The disciplinary interview is held to get at the causes of apparent misbehavior and to motivate better performance in the future.

It is important that the interview be kept on an impersonal a basis as possible. If the supervisor lets the interview descend to the plane of an argument, it loses its effectiveness.

II. PLANNING THE INTERVIEW

Get all pertinent facts concerning the situation so that you can talk in specific terms to the employee.

Review the employee's record, appraisal ratings, etc.

Consider what you know about the temperament of the employee. Consider your attitude toward the employee. Remember that the primary requisite of disciplinary action is fairness.

Don't enter upon the interview when angry.

Schedule the interview for a place which is private and out of hearing of others.

III. CONDUCTING THE INTERVIEW

A. Make an effort to establish accord.
B. Question the employee about the apparent breach of discipline. Be sure that the question is not so worded as to be itself an accusation.
C. Give the employee a chance to tell his side of the story. Give him ample opportunity to talk.
D. Use understanding—listening except where it is necessary to ask a question or to point out some details of which the employee may not be aware. If the employee misrepresents facts, make a plain, accurate statement of the facts, but don't argue and don't engage in personal controversy.
E. Listen and try to understand the reasons for the employee's (mis)conduct. First of all, don't assume that there has been a breach of discipline. Evaluate the employee's reasons for his conduct in the light of his opinions and feelings concerning the consistency and reasonableness of the standards which he was expected to follow. Has the supervisor done his part in explaining the reasons for the rule? Was the employee's behavior unintentional or deliberate? Does he think he had real reasons for his actions? What new facts is he telling? Do the facts justify his actions? What causes, other than those mentioned, could have stimulated the behavior?
F. After listening to the employee's version of the situation, and if censure of his actions is warranted, the supervisor should proceed with whatever criticism is justified. Emphasis should be placed on future improvement rather than exclusively on the employee's failure to measure up to expected standards of job conduct.
G. Fit the criticism to the individual. With one employee, a word of correction may be all that is required.
H. Attempt to distinguish between unintentional error and deliberate misbehavior. An error due to ignorance requires training and not censure.
I. Administer criticism in a controlled, even tone of voice, never in anger. Make it clear that you are acting as an agent of the department. In general, criticism should refer to the job or the employee's actions and not to the person. Criticism of the employee's work is not an attack on the individual.
J. Be sure the interview does not destroy the employee's self-confidence. Mention his good qualities and assure him that you feel confident that he can improve his performance.
K. Wherever possible, before the employee leaves the interview, satisfy him that the incident is closed, that nothing more will be said on the subject unless the offense is repeated.

www.ingramcontent.com/pod-product-compliance
Lightning Source LLC
Chambersburg PA
CBHW081806300426
44116CB00014B/2251
9781799348900